THE AGE OF
RICHARD II

THE AGE OF RICHARD II

EDITED BY
JAMES L. GILLESPIE

SUTTON PUBLISHING, STROUD
ST. MARTIN'S PRESS, NEW YORK

First published in the United Kingdom in 1997 by
Sutton Publishing Limited · Phoenix Mill
Thrupp · Stroud · Gloucestershire · GL5 2BU

First published in the United States by St. Martin's Press
Scholarly and Reference Division
175 Fifth Avenue · New York · N.Y. 10010

British Library Cataloguing in Publication Data
A catalogue record for this book is available from the British Library

ISBN 0-7509-1452-1 (hardback)
ISBN 0-7509-1453-X (paperback)

Library of Congress Cataloging-in-Publication Data

The Age of Richard II / edited by James L. Gillespie.
    p.   cm.
    Includes bibliographical references and index.
    ISBN 0-312-17584-1
    1. Great Britain–History–Richard II. 1377–1399. 2. Richard II,
King of England, 1367–1400. 3. Civilization, Medieval–14th
century. I. Gillespie, James L. II. Title: Age of Richard 2.
III. Title: Age of Richard the Second.
DA235.A37 1997
942.03'8–DC21   97–8878
                                                                 CIP

Cover illustration: Richard II, c. 1395 (by courtesy of the Dean and Chapter of Westminster)

 ALAN SUTTON™ and SUTTON™ are the trade
marks of Sutton Publishing Limited

Typeset in 10/15 pt Baskerville.
Typesetting and origination by
Sutton Publishing Limited.
Printed in Great Britain by
Hartnolls, Bodmin, Cornwall.

CONTENTS

LIST OF CONTRIBUTORS

Frank L. Wiswall III is Instructor of History at St Mary's Hall, San Antonio, Texas, USA. He holds a M.Litt. in Mediaeval History from the University of St Andrews, Scotland. He has presented several papers on aspects of English medieval history. This is his first publication.

Wendy R. Childs is Senior Lecturer in Medieval History at the University of Leeds, England. Her research interests lie mainly in the field of medieval international trade. She has written a monograph on *Anglo-Castilian Trade in the Later Middle Ages*. She has edited a volume of *The Customs Accounts of Hull, 1463–1490* and she has written numerous articles on England's overseas trade. She has recently contributed a chapter on European trade to the *New Cambridge Medieval History*, vol. VII.

G.H. Martin CBE is Research Professor of History at the University of Essex, England. He has served as Keeper of the Public Records. He is the author of several articles on medieval diplomatic, urban history, and bibliography, and he is the editor of *The Chronicle of Henry Knighton*.

Nigel Saul is Reader in Medieval History at Royal Holloway College, University of London, England. He is the author of *Knights and Esquires: the Gloucestershire Gentry in the Fourteenth Century*, and he is the editor of and a contributor to *The Age of Chivalry*. His *Richard II* will be published in 1997 by Yale University Press.

A.K. McHardy is Senior Lecturer in Medieval History at the University of Nottingham, England. She is the author of *The Church in London, 1375–92* and *Clerical Poll-Taxes of the Diocese of Lincoln, 1377–1381*, as well as many articles on the English Church in the later Middle Ages.

James L. Gillespie is a Senior Research Fellow at the American Center of Oriental Research in Amman, Jordan. He is presently working on the Hashemite monarchy. He has served as president of the Society of the White Hart, and has published numerous studies on the reign of Richard II. He has worked with Professor Anthony Goodman on *Richard II: Power and Prerogative*.

John L. Leland is Associate Professor of Humanities and Social Science at Salem-Teikyo University, USA. His current research involves the creation of a database recording all pardons listed in the *Calendar of Patent Rolls* for the reign of Richard II. He has just published an article on the general pardon of 1388 in *Medieval Prosopography*.

Doris Fletcher is an independent scholar affiliated with the Institute of Historical Research, University of London, England. Her research interests are focused in the Italian Renaissance. She is interested in questions of art at the service of diplomacy and the state, and she has published an article on 'Why Castiglione went to England'.

J.M. Theilmann is Associate Professor of History and Politics at Converse College, USA. His present research includes an examination of royal-baronial conflict in the reign on Richard II from the perspective of the new institutionalism. He is the author of a book and several articles on late medieval history and politics.

David K. Maxfield is a retired university librarian. He last served at the University of Michigan, USA. He studies medieval history with William E. Lunt. He has published numerous articles on bibliographical topics as well as on late medieval history. His medieval articles have appeared in *Journal of Ecclesiastical History*, *Chaucer Review*, and *Cheshire History*.

INTRODUCTION

Humpty Dumpty sat on a wall,
Humpty Dumpty had a great fall.
All the king's horses,
And all the king's men
Couldn't put Humpty together again.

This rhyme, which has often been associated with Richard III, is equally appropriate to efforts to understand the late Middle Ages in England. Ironically, modern scholarship has shattered and scattered still further the pieces that once made up the *tableau vivant* of late medieval life. The epoch has been viewed through a kaleidoscope rather than *A Distant Mirror*. Scholars have beautifully and richly coloured the broken pieces of the *tableau vivant*, but they have been even less successful than all the king's men in the production of a portrait – even an impressionist portrait. This book acknowledges the kaleidoscopic nature of modern historiography. A team of scholars has been assembled, each asked to produce a mosaic tile to be fit into a larger portrait. Such an approach to scholarship has become increasingly common as specialization has produced a generation of scholars lacking the rash self-confidence of the historical synthesizers who once popularized the discipline. A perusal of the *Annual Bibliography of British and Irish History* for the years 1981 and 1990 reveals that volumes of collected essays accounted for 13 of 2,594 entries in 1981; a decade later such collections had increased over ten-fold (150 out of 4,169 total entries). How did we reach this point?

The historical profession has broadened the scope of its purview, and this has made the task of the synthesizer all the more daunting. The push to expand the domain of historical studies into the concerns of daily life has been both necessary and salutary. It has, however, led to a dangerous tendency to 'throw the baby out with the bath water'. Political and diplomatic history is condemned as 'old-fashioned'. I do not wish to challenge the importance of learning more about Norfolk haywards, or even Gloucestershire gentry, but that does not mean that the political milieu in which these 'real people' functioned was irrelevant to them – or to us. The events of the past decade in Eastern Europe, the former Soviet Union and the Middle East should make this clear. Politics remains a lens through which we can bring the late medieval kaleidoscope into focus without unduly narrowing our range of vision.

It must be conceded that such a focus has never been clear. While 'old-fashioned' scholars scanned the political and diplomatic horizon and theorists searched the clouds of the arts and intellect, social and economic historians explored the morass of everyday life. The results have been important. Much has been learned about *The Turbulent London of Richard II* as well as the turbulence of other urban centres, and great insights have been offered into the socio-economic causes and consequences of profiteering in the Hundred Years' War and the Peasants' Revolt of 1381. Sadly, however, these historians have had their gaze fixed too firmly on the ground and their perspective was often too limited to offer a real understanding of the character and concerns of the age.

In spite of the prejudice against politics, the present generation of scholars has done some admirable work in illuminating the nooks and crannies of the political world. Prosopographers have looked at the Lords Appellants as well as the Ricardian Appellants of 1397. The idiosyncrasies of the Cheshire archers have been reported in great detail. Anthony Tuck has undertaken the very useful analysis of Richard II's relationships with the nobility, and Chris Given-Wilson has shed much light on the royal household and the king's affinity. Antonia Gransden, John Taylor and George Stow have combined to provide a much clearer understanding of the narrative sources for the period. Mark Ormrod has produced a fine biography of Edward III, and Nigel Saul is about to give us a similar volume on Richard II. The period, however, remains obscure. The mosaic has too often been lost in the tesserae.

Although the present volume scatters several more tesserae, it is founded upon the efforts of the Society of the White Hart to bring scholars of the period together. The Society was created to ensure that the political and diplomatic history of late medieval Britain could find a forum at the annual rite of spring, The International Congress on Medieval Studies, the largest gathering of medievalists in the world. Increasingly, the sessions at the International

Congress had been directed away from the areas of interest of the Society's founders. The Society was also founded in an effort to bridge the gap of mistrust between historians working in the United Kingdom and those scholars who labour far from the Public Record Office and the British Library. Since a number of the Society's founders – George Stow, Anthony Goodman, Nigel Saul, and myself – concentrated on the reign of Richard II, the Society's name and much of its scholarship reflect that emphasis. The Society – and this volume – are not, however, the exclusive preserve of Ricardians. The current president of the Society, Jeffrey S. Hamilton, is the biographer of Piers Gaveston. None the less, some may wonder that the volume contains eleven essays rather than the more usual ten or twelve. The answer, of course, is that there are eleven Ricardian angels depicted in the Wilton Diptych.

Frank Wiswall begins our survey by raising the question of why the precedents of the previous century were ignored at the accession of the young Edward III in 1327. The failure to elaborate a coherent structure for political life during royal minorities would plague the realm in the reigns of Richard II, Henry VI, Edward V, and Edward VI. Edward III's own subsequent efforts to paper over the cracks in fourteenth-century kingship through martial exploits in France have caused historians to neglect the investigation of England's other diplomatic and economic interests. Wendy Childs provides one missing piece of the mosaic in her essay on 'Anglo-Portuguese Relations in the Fourteenth Century'.

One of the most basic questions is what can we hope to know of the character of medieval men? Closely related to this is the utility of biographical studies of the key figures of the age. No character was more enigmatic than Richard II himself. We are, none the less, left with a dilemma. Are we trying to picture Richard of Bordeaux, or are we looking to a broader canvas of governance and government? Can these perspectives be separated? The character of Richard II was a vital, if not indeed central, issue for the king's contemporaries, and it has remained a focal point for scholarly and popular historians. Deconstructionalist criticism, however, has made us increasingly aware of our inabilities to see other men in other times and other societies with any degree of clarity. Yet, the reigns of Edward II and Henry VI – as well as that of Richard II – make it obvious that we cannot understand governance without a look at men as well as measures. Deconstructionalist caveats provide a salutary warning, but we also need the courage to extend our vision of the past. Geoffrey Martin has taken up this challenge as he returns to the narrative sources for Richard's reign. He demonstrates that these narrative sources, long scorned by 'scientific' historians, provide important perspectives to our view of both the reign and the man who exercised his kingship.

That kingship also requires a careful examination of the tactics employed to implement its ideals. Nigel Saul provides one dimension through such an examination of Richard II's involvement with York. The king was accused of attempting to establish a northern capital for himself at York in order to escape the interference of the Londoners. Dr Saul provides an assessment of the evidence rather than the allegations related to the king's travels to York. Thomas Haxey offered a direct challenge to Ricardian kingship in 1397 when he presented a petition to parliament questioning the king's control of his own household. Not surprisingly, Richard II reacted violently. Haxey's petition proved to be the catalyst for the king's attack on his enemies. But who exactly was Thomas Haxey, and what were his motives in offering his infamous petition? Alison McHardy provides an unconventional look at these questions in her contribution.

Conventionality, in fact, cuts both ways. Historians have also become bound to conventional outlooks. My two essays attempt to look at the military and chivalric components of Ricardian rule which have been dismissed by modern historians as unrelated to the real foundations of Richard's conception of kingship. These very conventional attributes of kingship were, however, essential to the survival of any medieval monarch. We have focused so much on the fall of Richard II that we have forgotten that he reigned for over twenty-two years. To survive that long, Richard had to make use of the conventional values and symbols of his own age.

One characteristic feature of late medieval society was the use of symbolism. Doris Fletcher provides a link between the symbolic and the practical implications of lordship in that society through her examination of the Lancastrian collar of 'esses'. She carries the tale forward into the Tudor age in an effort to understand changing perspectives on lordship and its symbols. John Leland provides yet another form of linkage in his essay on 'The Oxford Trial of 1400: Royal Politics and the County Gentry'. Leland spans the gap between politics and society which scholars have dug for themselves, a gap unknown to the people of the late Middle Ages.

This same artificial chasm is leapt in the studies of public health and charitable foundations which conclude this volume. John Theilmann provides a fine piece of modern interdisciplinary scholarship which highlights the relationship between government and health issues in 'The Regulation of Public Health in Late Medieval England'. Finally, David Maxfield ties politics and diplomacy to the daily affairs of a London hospital, a hospital closely associated with the Ricardian courtier, John de Macclesfield.

The pieces of the mosaic still await their synthesizer. We are still looking at an abstract, kaleidoscopic view. Yet, perhaps such a disjointed perspective was characteristic of the late Middle Ages; it is certainly characteristic of our time. Both ages have been times of upheaval when people, ideas – and politics – jostle for attention. In this volume, we of the Society of the White Hart can but hope to realign the focus on some of the tesseræ of the mosaic.

> For you have but mistook me all this while.
> *Richard II*, Act III, Scene 2.

It remains to offer thanks to the members of the Society of the White Hart for their scholarship and fellowship and to the contributors to this volume for their patience and support. Thanks are due to Karen Zoller and the staff of the Clara Fritzsche Library, and to Susan Cannavino, Christine Greeney, and Colleen Elligott for their help in the production of this volume. Professors George Stow and Anthony Goodman have provided sound advice. Finally, I must give thanks to Professor Joel Rosenthal and especially to Professor Ralph Griffiths for shouldering the responsibilities of seeing this volume to press in the face of my exile from American academia as penance for my own misdoings in failing to genuflect before the icons of political correctness.

J.L. Gillespie
Amman

POLITICS, PROCEDURE AND THE 'NON-MINORITY' OF EDWARD III: SOME COMPARISONS

Frank L. Wiswall III

Woe to thee, O land, when thy king is a child,
and thy princes eat in the morning!

Ecclesiastes, 10:16

This biblical text was familiar to English politicians in the later Middle Ages, and aptly described an inevitable consequence of hereditary monarchy. Between 1216 and 1547 no fewer than six kings succeeded to the English throne as minors; one of them, Henry VI, later lost his mental capacity to rule as an adult, which proved to be a major precipitant of the Wars of the Roses.[1] While each minority was different from the others in important respects and arose from immediate and unique circumstances, certain basic issues usually defined the way in which politics and government were conducted. Who should exercise royal authority on behalf of a minor king? How should such a disposition of power be arrived at, and by whom? On what basis could the royal authority, theoretically absolute, be removed from the person of the king and placed in another for a temporary period, particularly without the king's consent? Such issues were explicitly addressed only rarely, most notably in 1422 upon the death of Henry V and the succession of his son at the age of nine months;[2] but they were avoided almost completely during the early years of the reign of Edward III, from late 1326 to November 1330.[3]

Despite the numerous extant accounts of the history of these years in England, the story is worth re-examining. I have chosen to call this period a 'non-minority' because, regardless of any formal arrangements for a regency, it was quite dissimilar to any likely precedent such as the early reign of Henry III.

This dissimilarity manifested itself in two ways: first, the official forms of government established for the minority were blatantly overridden by the overt self-interest of a partisan political clique surrounding the household of the queen mother; and second, the age of the king at the time of his accession – fourteen years – allowed him to take a more active role in political affairs, both public and private, than his thirteenth-century predecessor had done.[4] Indeed, the brevity of the minority period itself made a strict observance of any formal arrangements for an alternative government less likely than it otherwise might have been. While Henry III had been nine years old on his accession in England in 1216, his minority resulted from somewhat more natural circumstances than those of 1326, and allowed experienced adults to make, and keep to, the formal organization of a regency in the interest of political stability.[5] Such was not the case in 1326 and 1327; the accession of Edward III resulted from the first successful removal of an English king by force since 1066, an event probably more likely to engender the pursuit of ulterior motives, rivalries, and covert political agendas than the death of a king by natural causes. Moreover, in many ways Edward III's early reign was different from the minority of his successor, Richard II, from 1377 to 1389; yet important, and destabilizing, political similarities arose in the latter case as well, and points of comparison between the minorities will be drawn throughout this essay.[6]

The active involvement of the king in political procedure was the *sine qua non* of medieval government, and the most basic issue underlying all three instances of minority rule was the extent to which the king himself, despite his youth, should take any active role in the political decision-making process. This question underlay all others, and raised numerous potential difficulties in the administration of day-to-day government. Such matters included the use (or lack thereof) of the various royal seals, for purposes either practical or symbolic; the control and alienation of royal property and lands; and the dispensation of patronage. In each case, the way in which these issues were settled, or glossed over, had enormous ramifications for the political atmosphere of the realm.

The accession of Henry III in 1216 at the age of nine inaugurated administrative difficulties which were for all practical purposes unprecedented. Although there had been more recent royal minorities in France and the Holy Roman Empire, England had not witnessed one since the succession of

Aethelred the Unready in 978, an event too remote to be of any use in providing useful administrative examples.[7] The reliance upon the great and privy seals, and the essential role of a competent adult king to authorize their use, demanded that rapid alternatives be found in order to prevent the government, in the midst of civil war, from coming to a standstill. Accordingly, there was no real attempt in October 1216 to maintain the fiction that Henry III was competent to govern the realm, and authority was given outright to William the Marshal as *rector regis et regni*, a title which essentially constituted an office of regent and which the Marshal held until his death in 1219.[8] The Marshal's authority was granted to him apparently by the consensus of the magnates who remained loyal to the Plantagenet cause, including Ranulf of Chester, Peter des Roches, bishop of Winchester (who served as guardian of the king's person), and the papal legate.[9] The Marshal was able to authorize charters with his own seal, and Henry III had no great seal of his own until November 1218; even then, he was not allowed the use of it at his own discretion until 1223, at the direction of Pope Honorius III.[10] The great seal issued for Henry bore the usual depiction of the king as fully grown, a fact which is interesting if not significant.[11] Moreover, Henry III was denied the use of a privy seal, a device which King John had used widely, until December 1230 (probably by his justiciar, Hubert de Burgh), by which time the king was twenty-three years old.[12] The lack of seals meant also that the normal order of government business had to be suspended, and as a consequence the alienation of royal properties in perpetuity was explicitly prohibited until the king's coming of age.[13] Indeed, the first letters patent under the great seal issued in 1218 confirmed the inalienability of such properties, and the measure was perhaps reinforced by a formal destruction of the charter roll being kept at the time. No new charter roll appeared until 1227.[14]

Although the nature of the political settlement of 1216 necessitated a genuine regency, the events and circumstances of Edward III's accession in 1326 and 1327 enabled those in power to bypass the need for such an arrangement. Part of the reason lay in the new king's greater age at his accession. Much concern had been expressed by those around Henry III regarding the significance, if any, which should attach to his fourteenth year; in Roman law, fourteen was the age at which tutelage of young men ceased.[15] In September 1326, when Isabella of

France and Roger Mortimer landed in Suffolk to depose Edward II, the prince was already fourteen, and this obviated the need for any special arrangements in his regard. Indeed, it perhaps contributed to the prince's ability to assume an important symbolic role in the downfall of his father's régime. On 26 October 1326 an impromptu assembly of Isabella's supporters (in an obvious attempt to appear 'parliamentary') claimed to speak for the 'community of the realm' by appointing Prince Edward to serve as *custos* or 'keeper' of the kingdom in the fictional absence of the king, as Edward II had abandoned London to his adversaries and fled into Wales along with his chancellor, Robert Baldock, and his great seal.[16] Strictly speaking, Edward II's flight should probably have made no difference on an administrative level, as Wales was not the sort of foreign territory which would normally have necessitated the arrangement of a regency of absence; it was enough, however, for the queen's party to try to exploit when there was precious little available to legitimize their actions in law.[17] For the next month, until the capture of both Edward II and his great seal, business and necessary orders were issued in the name of the prince in his capacity as duke of Aquitaine, using his own privy seal ostensibly on his father's behalf.[18] There is evidence that Prince Edward's status as *custos* was quickly recognized: a letter from a Rouen merchant, dated some time in October or November of 1326, was addressed to Edward in that capacity and requested that he authorize the release of a ship and cargo impounded at sea.[19] The use of the prince's privy seal in this manner illustrates the extent to which the device had become a fundamental part of the machinery of government in the century since the minority of Henry III. Although it was probably unimportant from the standpoint of Edward holding any real political power in 1326, it is interesting insofar as it indicates the importance which Isabella's adherents placed on promoting the appearance of leadership on the prince's part.

After the coronation of Edward III on 1 February 1327,[20] the king was granted both a new great seal and a new privy seal, although the latter was apparently under the control primarily of the bishop of Lincoln, Henry Burghersh, during his tenure as treasurer from March 1327 to July 1328.[21] While the policy of allowing Edward III to possess both seals at the time of his accession was therefore a definite break with the arrangements of the early thirteenth century, several things are clear. First, Edward did not necessarily have any personal initiative, at least before 1329 or so, in determining how the seals were used; in this his minority displayed an explicit contrast with that of Richard II after 1383. Second, the existence of the seals did not constitute any open recognition of Edward's competence to rule in his own right, but was more a mechanism of maintaining the fiction that he was competent. In cases in which such a fiction had to be abandoned, however, it was readily set aside, as in the situation surrounding a proposed revision of the Charter of the Forest. At the request of the Commons in the first parliament of the reign, any such revision was postponed until the king should come of age.[22]

Regardless of the implications suggested by the seals' existence, they were used profusely from the commencement of Edward III's reign. For example, Dr Given-Wilson's recent examination of the witness lists for royal charters from 1327 to 1399 provides much valuable information on the use of the great seal, and on those behind it, in this period.[23] The average number of charters issued per year from 1327 to 1330 was almost 87, or nearly four times greater than the yearly average (between 23 and 24) for the entire period of Edward III's majority rule thereafter.[24] Certainly there are many reasons for the comparatively high number of charters issued at the outset of the reign, and by itself this statistic may seem meaningless, but this information at least reveals that those in control in the period 1327–30 (especially Roger Mortimer, who naturally witnessed more charters than anyone else) felt perfectly comfortable conducting government business in a normal manner, in contrast to the difficult arrangements for the minority of Henry III.

In the case of Richard II, the use of the seals underwent further changes during the king's minority, particularly from 1383 to October 1386. It was in this period that Richard undertook to assume a more direct role in government than he had been afforded hitherto, by expediting administrative procedures – or bypassing them altogether – through the use of the signet seal.[25] Like his grandfather, Richard had been provided with the major seals from the outset of his reign, and no formal means had been established by which to bypass the king's ostensibly personal authority for their use;[26] but after 1383 a pattern began to develop which witnessed a decline in the use of the privy seal to authenticate chancery warrants. In its place the signet was increasingly used to move the great seal, and as Richard, for a time at least, made use of a personal signet ring it is apparent that a prime mover of this change in policy was the king himself, despite both his youth and the existence of a king's secretary.[27] Under John Bacon, secretary from May 1381 to March 1385, the signet gradually began to appear on public as well as private documents, and even was used to authorize the writs of summons for the parliament held in May 1382.[28] After 1384 the use of the signet in this manner, and the consequent decline in the observance of normal procedure, accelerated, particularly during the tenure of Richard Medford, Bacon's successor. According to Dr Tuck:

> During Medford's secretaryship, the signet became the most potent instrument of Richard's personal power. From January 1385 to January 1386 there survive nearly three hundred signet letters sent direct to the chancellor; by the autumn of 1385 as many grants are warranted by the signet as by all other authorities combined; and by the summer of 1386 the signet had become the most common means of moving the great seal.[29]

There is evidence, moreover, that Richard II used the signet in this period to arrange financial matters: in April 1385, for instance, the treasurer was ordered by signet letter to transfer 1,000 marks from the exchequer into the king's chamber, disregarding the contrary procedures outlined in the Walton Ordinances of 1338.[30] The king's use of the signet in such a public manner stopped abruptly in October 1386, however, when the royal administration was reorganized by the initiative of parliament. Bishop Arundel of Ely, who replaced Michael de la Pole as chancellor, refused to recognize the authority of the signet as sufficient to move the great seal, and the signet's use for this purpose ceased.[31]

A second area in which the involvement of a minor king might have important consequences for the politics of the realm was the control of royal property, lands, and entitlements. In the early years of Henry III, the nature of the problem was relatively straightforward: under both the regency of the Marshal to 1219, and the collective government largely under the justiciar thereafter, the need for resumption of the king's property (much of it in the form of castles) was widely recognized.[32] As noted above, part of the procedure involved the preventative measure of stopping the financial haemorrhaging by banning permanent alienations from the royal demesne until the king came of age. This policy, though, had several disadvantages. First, it created difficulties for the Marshal in his attempts to reward Henry III's adherents in the king's nonage; second, it opened to question the right of the government to reverse the grants made to minor officials, such as sheriffs and castellans, by King John;[33] and third, it required Henry III to reconfirm all charters and grants made on his behalf, including Magna Carta and the Forest Charter, after he declared his majority in 1227.[34] In a sense, this lent some additional stability to Henry III's early government, since many magnates argued that appointments to office under John remained valid until his successor's majority, a principle which Hubert de Burgh, as justiciar, probably would not have disputed.[35] The pope also took a role in encouraging the resumption of royal property through letters to the papal legate as early as April 1219,[36] and in 1220 and 1221 Honorius III demanded such resumptions outright, disbelieving the explanations of the barons that they were protecting the king's castles on his behalf.[37] By letters of April 1223, however, the pope commanded Burgh to allow Henry III the initiative in the use of the great seal, and again to undertake a resumption of royal castles and properties.[38] In a separate letter, he ordered the barons, on pain of excommunication, to surrender such properties as they had hitherto usurped.[39]

The widespread recognition on the part of both Henry III's government and the papacy of the need to preserve royal financial assets contrasts sharply with the profligate dissipation of the remnants of Edward II's treasury by Mortimer and Isabella by the end of 1328. According to Dr Natalie Fryde, the total traceable financial assets left to the new régime from the treasuries of Westminster and the Tower of London amounted to £61,921 4s 9½d; an accounting taken as of 27 March 1327, when Bishop Burghersh of Lincoln succeeded Bishop Orleton of Hereford as treasurer, revealed only £12,031 2s 8d remaining, a loss of nearly £50,000 in only four months.[40] This included the removal of several lump sums totalling £31,000 in February 1327 alone.[41] Much of the money undoubtedly went to various useful purposes such as rewarding supporters of the régime, but it cannot be accounted for with any precision. Aside from such apparently disposable funds, Isabella arranged for numerous grants of lands and properties to be made to her directly from royal holdings, as well as from lands confiscated from Edward II's former favourites. She began by gaining the largest share of the holdings of the younger Despenser.[42] She also absorbed, on 10 January 1327, the county of Cornwall, along with castles, manors, and towns which Edward III had granted to her for life in dower.[43] On 1 February of that year, however – the date of her son's coronation – she took over what amounted to an enormous 'block grant' of manors, farms, and other lands, roughly 130 properties in all, in thirty different counties and north Wales, to a value of £8,722 4s 4d *per annum*.[44] Along with other grants, this contributed to an increase in her annual endowment from 6,750 marks (prior to 1325) to about 20,000 marks.[45] According to Dr Wolffe: '[T]his endowment . . . in effect constituted the whole of the permanent royal patrimony in lands, rents, and feefarms. The purpose of this parliamentary appropriation was probably not so much to provide her with a cash income as to place the whole royal patronage at the disposal of a *de facto* queen regnant.'[46]

Dr Wolffe's estimation of the queen mother's motives is sound: the evidence certainly indicates that Isabella viewed herself in this way, even as early as the closing weeks of 1326. On 21 November, for example, a letter from her and the prince (as duke of Aquitaine) requested Richard Damory to release lands of the former chamberlain of Earl Thomas of Lancaster, a sign of the Mortimer faction's early interest in officially rehabilitating the deceased earl.[47] Similarly, she sent a letter from Woodstock on 12 December to Bishop Airmyn of Norwich, who had temporary custody of the great seal, requesting the issue of a writ of *liberate*, a sign that she also exercised some control over financial affairs.[48] Such intrusive political activity continued after her son's accession: for instance, she withheld the castle and honour of Pontefract from the earl of Lancaster, and was known to have hosted a royal council there on at least one occasion.[49] She also personally supervised, several times, changes in the custody of the great seal.[50] Her authority even extended to issues such as patronage of offices: on 2 February 1328 she ordered the chancellor, Bishop Hotham of Ely, to appoint a new sheriff of Norfolk and Suffolk,[51] and many petitions for royal favour were addressed directly to her rather than to her son.[52]

Although she was deprived of most of her ill-gotten wealth after Edward III's assumption of personal authority,[53] Isabella's position ensured that Mortimer had an opportunity to share the spoils of power. Despite his opposition to the

Despenser faction in the middle of Edward II's reign, Mortimer had succeeded in creating a power base for himself by 1318 or so: in that year he received from the king the wardship of the lands and heir of the Beauchamp earldom of Warwick, which had been taken away from the elder Despenser.[54] In the following year, he increased his retinue by gaining the loyalty of Thomas, Lord Berkeley and his son, who had abandoned their role as retainers of Aymer de Valence, earl of Pembroke.[55] Not long after Edward III's coronation, though, Mortimer began the procurement of lands and wealth which would contribute heavily to his downfall. On 13 September 1327, at Lincoln, Edward III confirmed by privy seal a charter granting Mortimer lands in Wales and the western Marches, worth £1,000 *per annum*, which had formerly belonged to the younger Despenser.[56] The following year witnessed many more seizures of property by Mortimer, significant amounts of which were at the expense of the followers of Edward II and the Despensers. By the end of 1328 Mortimer had added to his considerable holdings the offices of justice of north and south Wales and justice of Ireland, as well as the wholly unprecedented title of earl of the March of Wales.[57] Mortimer was honoured with this title at the Salisbury parliament of 16–31 October 1328; one chronicler claimed that the simultaneous grant of the earldom of Cornwall to John of Eltham, the king's younger brother, was mainly an attempt to mitigate the shock caused to the peers by this move, which essentially gave Mortimer palatine powers in Wales and western England.[58] Nor did Mortimer possess any misgivings about displaying his new wealth in the most ostentatious manner possible; in 1328 he organized public celebrations in imitation of an Arthurian 'Round Table' at Bedford and Wigmore, and succeeded in marrying two of his daughters into the Norfolk and Pembroke inheritances.[59]

The matter of Mortimer's title and its effects on his relations with the nobility merits some discussion, since it raises interesting comparisons – and contrasts – with the enrichment of Richard II's favourites in the period before the 'Merciless Parliament' of 1388. In two cases, those of Michael de la Pole and Robert de Vere, earl of Oxford, Richard II awarded titles and properties which went well beyond anything the higher nobility deemed appropriate. Pole was in Richard II's service as chancellor from March 1383 to October 1386; he was created earl of Suffolk on 6 August 1385, following the death in 1382 of William Ufford, the previous holder of the title.[60] As of 12 September 1385 the new earl received much of the Ufford lands and estates, in addition to other endowments, up to the value of £500 *per annum*.[61] It is important to note here that, in this and other instances, Richard II granted titles before granting lands with which to support them; he made it clear that, in his view, much of the dignity of the peerage rested on royal favour alone, and served only to enhance the prestige of the Crown. This contrasts (particularly in Pole's case) with practices during the reign of Edward III, when 'it was commonly assumed that an income in land of £1,000 a year was necessary to maintain the estate of earl',[62] and in the later fifteenth century, for in 1478 Edward IV deprived George Neville of the title of duke of Bedford specifically because of the insufficiency of his lands.[63] Even at a value of only £500, however, many of Pole's peers felt that he had received more than he was entitled to, particularly since he served as chancellor; at the time of his impeachment in October 1386, parliament declared Pole's acceptance of these grants as incompatible with his duty as chancellor to protect the property of the Crown.[64]

Robert de Vere is perhaps even more closely comparable to Mortimer than is Pole, at least with regard to the advantage he took of the king's minority in order to secure lands and titles. Vere's family had received the earldom of Oxford from the Empress Matilda in 1141, and as the 9th earl, he was the holder of the longest-standing noble title in fourteenth-century England.[65] By that time, however, he was also the poorest among the English earls, holding only one major estate (Castle Hedingham in north Essex), although his family still held the hereditary chamberlainship.[66] Such relative poverty made his rapid rise in standing all the more galling among the peerage. He was an early favourite at Richard II's court, and was close to the king in age; as early as 1383 the king hinted to Vere in letters patent that he might receive promotion, as the family holdings were insufficient to uphold his dignity as earl.[67] His aggrandizement began early in 1385, with an unusual grant of the custody of Queenborough Castle in tail male upon the death of the king;[68] but on 1 December of that year he went much further when Richard II granted him the new title of marquess of Dublin, instantly raising his status above that of all the earls of the realm.[69] While the king made this move ostensibly in response to a request from his administration in Dublin that he replace his lieutenant there, Richard went far beyond, appointing Vere (who lacked any military experience) to the lieutenantship. He was authorized to bear the arms of Ireland, and writs were to run in his own name rather than in the king's.[70] When Richard added to Vere's titles by creating him duke of Ireland and giving him ostensibly palatine authority there in October 1386 – the same month as the impeachment of Pole – he took advantage of the absence of John of Gaunt, who had sailed for Spain the previous July, to create the first English duke in living memory who was not a member of the royal family.[71] However, the new title did not substantially increase Vere's authority in Ireland, but was intended only 'to give him equality in status and palatine powers with John of Gaunt . . . and the grant of the title was a shrewd means of conferring on Vere the shadow and trappings of power without its substance'.[72] Indeed, as a reflection of their illusory status about the king, both Pole and Vere appear in real positions of influence during relatively brief periods. As a witness on the charter rolls, Pole appeared only *ex officio* during his tenure as chancellor; and despite his lavish endowments, Vere witnessed only in 1385–6 (31.6 per cent of the time) and 1386–7 (81.8 per cent). Neither witnessed charters after 1387, and throughout Richard's minority the most frequent witnesses remained the king's three uncles.[73]

The issue of Richard's view of power is an important one, for it reflects the fact that he, unlike his grandfather, wielded a measure of real political power during his minority, at least through his use of patronage and favouritism. He used his position to grant posts of some authority to his chamber knights, such as the custody of royal castles, as early as 1378.[74] It must be pointed out that all these grants were for life only, and not in perpetuity; moreover, they were usually carried out by letters patent. This procedure marked a crucial difference between Richard's minority and that of either Henry III or Edward III, as it allowed Richard more freedom of action than his predecessors had enjoyed. However, the parliaments of 1386 and 1388 had to deal directly with the results of the king's profligacy, whether it took the form of perpetual grants or not; the king's actions served to lessen his income from his own properties and to increase his dependence on those who were in a position to lend him money, such as Gaunt, the earl of Warwick, or John, Lord Nevill.[75] Dr Given-Wilson has stated that:

The chamber knight whose service to the king opened up a route to permanent landed wealth, let alone a peerage, was a rare creature. This was because, firstly, for much of the reign there was little to give, and considerable pressure from both the commons and the lords to keep what there was in the king's hands, and secondly, because by rewarding men with such temporary sources of wealth Richard ensured that they remained bound to the king.[76]

Neither Edward III nor Henry III enjoyed such freedom of action during their minorities. In the latter's case the centre of power was, at least until 1223, in the control of the great officers of state such as the justiciar (albeit under some guidance from the pope), and in the former's it was in the hands of Mortimer. The clearest proof of this is that by 1386 opposition to the régime was directed largely against the king himself, despite protests to the contrary, while in 1328 and 1329, during Henry of Lancaster's rebellion, it was directed mainly at Mortimer. Edward III, indeed, remained deliberately aloof from what he saw as a purely baronial conflict, probably because he did not feel powerful enough to take sides and because he felt it would serve no useful purpose simply to displace one *de facto* regent with another.[77] Mortimer's reaction against Lancaster, and his subsequent destruction of the earl of Kent in 1330, may have contributed to Edward's eventual determination to depose his unwanted guardian.[78]

Mortimer's basis for wielding power from 1327 to 1330 was based not on any legal authority but largely upon his association with Isabella, although measures were taken in February 1327 to appoint an official council of sorts for the duration of the minority. The leadership of this council was granted to Henry of Lancaster, who had also been awarded custody of the deposed Edward II in Kenilworth Castle and the right to dub Edward III a knight.[79] The rest of the council was to be composed of four bishops, three other earls (among them the king's uncles, Edmund of Kent and Thomas of Norfolk) and four barons; it was later claimed that 'nothing should be done' without the council's approval, and certainly not without the oversight of a *quorum* composed of a bishop, an earl and two barons, who may have been expected to remain with the king at all times.[80] The appointment of the council came, nominally at least, at the request of the Commons in parliament, but Henry of Lancaster gained in other ways as well; the first act of the first parliament of Edward III restored to him his late brother's title of earl and most of his lands.[81] The membership of the council was chosen largely from known opponents of Edward II and the Despensers, and although Mortimer himself was not a member, his interests were certainly represented: Bishop Orleton had accompanied Isabella in France, Oliver Ingham was an adherent of Mortimer, and John de Ros served only until early March 1327, when he was displaced by John Maltravers, a friend of Mortimer's and one of the alleged murderers of Edward II.[82] Despite careful descriptions of the council's duties in the parliament rolls, only one minor act – the gift of a covered gold cup to the mayor of London – is traceable to its direct initiative.[83] Mortimer not only blocked the council's action after the dismissal of parliament in early March, but made frequent changes in office-holders. The custody of the great seal alone changed seven times, and the office of treasurer five times, prior to Edward III's overthrow of Mortimer on 19 October 1330.[84]

The attempt to assemble a conciliar government in Richard II's minority was likewise a dismal failure, but for a different reason. Both the so-called 'continual councils', which were appointed annually from 1377 to 1380, and the commission council of 1386–7, were ineffective in establishing control over the royal household and its finances, leaving the need for armed force to be exercised by the Lords Appellant in 1387 and 1388.[85] Yet the failures of both Richard and Mortimer cannot be blamed solely on the collapse of conciliar experiments. Opposition was aroused by sharp changes in foreign policy as well, in Richard's case by the hugely unpopular peace initiative to Charles VI of France in 1387,[86] and in Mortimer's case largely by the humiliating settlement with Scotland in 1328 and the confused English response to the succession of the Valois dynasty in France in the same year. Mortimer's disastrous reaction to the encroachments of Robert Bruce in 1327 resulted in an English defeat, for which Edward III was forced to pawn the crown jewels in order to pay for the costs of the campaign.[87] By the terms of the subsequent treaty of Northampton of March 1328, Edward III renounced all English claims to overlordship of Scotland and agreed to recognize the Anglo-Scottish border as it had been in the time of Alexander III. Robert Bruce was also recognized as king of an independent Scotland in exchange for an indemnity of £20,000, much of which was embezzled by Isabella.[88] Relations with France proved equally uncertain. The death of Charles IV in 1328, and the succession of Philip VI of Valois in

May of that year, did not go unnoticed by Edward III in spite of his youth; on 16 May 1328 he authorized the bishops of Worcester and Chester to journey to France to demand on his behalf his right to be considered as a legitimate heir to the French throne.[89] Regardless of Isabella's position, this does not appear to have been a high priority issue for Mortimer's régime, and Edward was compelled in June 1329 to travel to France and to perform homage to Philip VI for Aquitaine, effectively recognizing Philip's accession as king of France.[90] Even more humiliating from Edward's standpoint was his admission in March 1331, under pressure from Philip VI, that his homage to the French king should be considered liege. While this admission apparently caused diplomatic problems during later stages of the Hundred Years' War, it did not stop Edward from publicly pursuing his claim to the French throne after 1337, regardless of whether he took it seriously or not.[91] It is reasonable to assume that he was aware of the fortunes of the Bruce family during the 'Great Cause' of the 1290s, and the fact that the willingness of Robert I's grandfather to recognize Edward I as feudal overlord of Scotland in exchange for the Scottish throne in 1290 did not prevent his grandson from becoming king of an independent Scotland – and recognized as such by the English – thirty-eight years later.[92]

This essay has attempted to examine the minority of Edward III in relation to those which preceded and followed it, by focusing on the position of the king in each instance and by drawing comparisons between the placement of authority and the exercise of power in each case. Henry III was gradually weaned from the tutelage of Hubert de Burgh and the oversight of the pope, a process which was not complete until the 1230s, while Richard II, in contrast, was able to exercise far more political influence during his youth than was good either for him or for the country as a whole. Edward III, however, was better prepared to exercise personal power as king than either of the others, largely because of his greater age at the time of his coronation. The subsequent failures of both Henry III and Richard II as adult rulers, moreover, were arguably the result both of their excessive youth at their accession and of the poorly managed political events of their minorities. The manipulation Edward endured under Mortimer and Isabella necessitated his use of both cunning and force to gain power in 1330, and following his arrest Mortimer was denied any right to respond to the numerous accusations against him in parliament, being convicted simply by notoriety. He was hanged, drawn and quartered as a traitor on 29 November 1330; these actions against Mortimer are ample evidence of Edward's feelings toward his earlier subordination.[93] The overriding factor which determined the course of political events during the 'non-minority' of Edward III was the flagrant separation between political power and legitimate authority under Mortimer's leadership. As Professor Wood has aptly put it, 'If woe came to a land when its king was a child, that was the inevitable consequence of the infighting that was sure to arise between and among those who ruled in his name'.[94]

Notes

[1] For a basic discussion of the problems of royal minorities, see C.T. Wood, 'The Child who Would be King', in *Joan of Arc and Richard III* (Oxford, 1988), pp. 29–44; see also F.L. Wiswall III, 'Royal Minorities and Protectorates in England, 1216–1549' (unpublished M.Litt. dissertation, University of St Andrews, 1989), esp. pp. 1–8. An earlier version of this essay was presented at the 28th International Congress on Medieval Studies, Western Michigan University, Kalamazoo, on 7 May 1993. I am grateful for the kind assistance of Professor James Gillespie, Dr Chris Given-Wilson, Professor Ralph Griffiths, and Dr Mark Ormrod; I have benefited greatly from discussions with them, and Dr Ormrod graciously read the original version of this essay and suggested numerous themes and revisions, as well as the phrase 'non-minority' to describe Edward III's early reign.

[2] The most complete recent examination of this matter may be found in R.A. Griffiths, *The Reign of King Henry VI* (London, 1981), pp. 11–24.

[3] W.M. Ormrod, *The Reign of Edward III* (New Haven, 1990), pp. 3–6; M.H. Keen, *England in the Later Middle Ages* (London, 1973), p. 105; *Adae Murimuth Continuatio Chronicarum*, ed. E.M. Thompson (Rolls Series, 1889), pp. 61–2. For general accounts of the period from 1326 to 1330, see M. McKisack, *The Fourteenth Century* (Oxford, 1959), pp. 83–104; T.F. Tout, *Chapters [in the Administrative History of Medieval England]* (6 vols, Manchester, 1920–33), III, pp. 1–30.

[4] For Henry III, see D.A. Carpenter, *The Minority of Henry III* (London, 1990); F.M. Powicke, *King Henry III and the Lord Edward* (2 vols, Oxford, 1947); K. Norgate, *The Minority of Henry the Third* (London, 1912). As will be seen below, much significance was attached to the age of fourteen as that of adulthood for certain limited purposes.

[5] *English Historical Documents (EHD)*, III, 1189–1327, ed. H. Rothwell (London, 1975), no. 3, pp. 83–4.

[6] For Richard II, see A. Tuck, *Richard II and the English Nobility* (London, 1973), an extremely useful work; also A. Goodman, *The Loyal Conspiracy* (London, 1971), and *John of Gaunt* (London, 1992). Richard II declared his own majority at a great council in May 1389, at the age of nearly twenty-two (Keen, p. 285).

[7] *Anglo-Saxon Chronicle* in *EHD*, c. 500–1042, ed. D. Whitelock (2nd edn, London, 1979), no. 1, p. 230; F.M. Stenton, *Anglo-Saxon England* (3rd edn, Oxford, 1971), pp. 372–4.

8 The most recent interpretations of the Marshal's regency are found in Carpenter, pp. 13–128; D. Crouch, *William Marshal: Court, Career and Chivalry in the Angevin Empire, 1147–1219* (London, 1990), pp. 117–30; R.C. Stacey, *Politics, Policy and Finance under Henry III, 1216–1245* (Oxford, 1987), pp. 1–13.

9 *EHD*, III, no. 3, pp. 82–4.

10 J.E. Sayers, *Papal Government and England during the Pontificate of Honorius III* (Cambridge, 1984), p. 169.

11 Carpenter, p. 94. This was apparently a standard practice in England and France; a striking exception is the miniature 'seal of minority' which was granted to Alexander III of Scotland in 1250. A.A.M. Duncan, *Scotland: The Making of the Kingdom* (Edinburgh, 1975), p. 556.

12 Tout, *Chapters,* I, pp. 206–9.

13 The inalienability of royal property was in fact confirmed on 6 November 1218, the same day as the introduction of the new great seal: *Calendar of Patent Rolls (CPR), 1216–25*, p. 177.

14 *Foedera [conventiones, litterae, et cujuscunque generis acta publica]*, ed. T. Rymer (London: Record Commission edn, 1816–69), I, i, p. 163; Carpenter, p. 95.

15 Carpenter, pp. 240–3; Peter des Roches was removed as the king's personal guardian in October 1221, about the time of Henry III's fourteenth birthday.

16 *Foedera*, II, i, p. 646, printed in *Select Documents of English Constitutional History, 1307–1485*, eds S.B. Chrimes and A.L. Brown (London, 1961), no. 18, p. 33.

17 Wales was (especially after the conquest of Edward I) part of the royal patrimony, and ought not to have required the appointment of a government official of special status in the king's absence there. See John Le Patourel, 'The Plantagenet Dominions' in *Feudal Empires: Norman and Plantagenet* (London, 1984), pp. 289–308; also W.M. Ormrod, 'Edward II at Neath Abbey, 1326' in *Neath Antiquarian Society Transactions, 1988–9*, ed. G. Eaton (Neath, 1988), pp. 107–12. I owe this point to the kind assistance of Dr Mark Ormrod.

18 *Calendar of Close Rolls (CCR), 1323–7*, p. 655; J.F. Baldwin, 'The King's Council', in *The English Government at Work (EGW), 1327–36*, vol. I, eds J.F. Willard and W.A. Morris (Cambridge, Mass., 1940), pp. 129–30. For privy seal grants of the prince during this period, see *CPR, 1327–30*, pp. 18–19, 241. A typical formula for a grant might read like that dated at Hereford, 20 November 1326: *teste Edwardo, filio nostro primogenito, custode regni,* warranted *per ipsum custodem et reginam* (Public Record Office (PRO), E159/103/23, cited in Tout, *Chapters*, III, p. 1 n. 2).

19 PRO, SC1/37/19.

20 *Foedera*, II, ii, p. 684.

21 Tout, *Chapters,* V, pp. 3–5; *Rotuli Parliamentorum (Rot. Parl.)*, II, pp. 45–6; *Handbook of British Chronology (HBC)*, (3rd edn, London, 1985), p. 105.

22 *Rot. Parl.,* II, pp. 7, 11; Ormrod, *Edward III*, p. 42; N. Neilson, 'The Forests', *EGW,* I, p. 396.

23 C. Given-Wilson, 'Royal Charter Witness Lists, 1327–1399', *Medieval Prosopography,* XII, 2 (Autumn, 1991), pp. 35–93. I owe the reference to this article to its author.

24 Ibid., pp. 61–71.

25 On Richard II's use of the signet, see Tout, *Chapters,* V, pp. 195–227; Tuck, *Richard II,* pp. 65–70.

26 Tout, *Chapters,* III, p. 323.

27 S.B. Chrimes, *An Introduction to the Administrative History of Mediaeval England* (3rd edn, Oxford, 1966), pp. 214–15. A list of secretaries of Richard II's reign is found in Tout, *Chapters*, VI, pp. 57–8.

28 Ibid.; PRO, C81/1339/42.

29 Tuck, *Richard II*, p. 67.

30 PRO, E404/14/91, no. 21; *EHD*, IV, *1327–1485*, ed. A.R. Myers (London, 1969), no. 309, pp. 497–8.

31 Tuck, *Richard II*, p. 70; Chrimes, p. 215.

32 On the resumption programme during Henry III's minority, see Carpenter, pp. 95–7, 325–9.

33 Ibid., pp. 126–7.

34 F. Pollock and F.W. Maitland, *History of English Law* (2nd edn, 2 vols, Cambridge, 1898), I, p. 523.

35 Crouch, p. 119.

36 *Calendar of Papal Registers Relating to Great Britain and Ireland, 1198–1304*, p. 65.

37 *Royal and other Historical Letters illustrative of the Reign of Henry III*, ed. W.W. Shirley (2 vols, Rolls Series, 1862–6), I, pp. 535–6; *Foedera*, I, i, p. 167.

38 Carpenter, pp. 301–2.

39 *Foedera*, I, i, p. 190.

40 N. Fryde, *The Tyranny and Fall of Edward II, 1321–1326* (Cambridge, 1979), p. 209; PRO, E101/332/21, E101/332/26.

41 Fryde, p. 209, n. 17.

42 Ibid., p. 208. Part of this increase consisted of a grant, in the first year of Edward III's reign, of the city of Winchester in feefarm to Isabella for life, resulting in an income of 100 marks per year to be rendered at the exchequer: see *Calendar of Charter Rolls (CChR), 1327–41*, pp. 11–12.

43 *CPR, 1324–7*, p. 346, cited in B.P. Wolffe, *The Royal Demesne in English History: The Crown Estate in the Governance of the Realm from the Conquest to 1509* (London, 1971), p. 232.

44 *CPR, 1327–30*, p. 177, cited in Wolffe, pp. 232–5.

45 Fryde, p. 208.

46 Wolffe, p. 55.

47 PRO, SC1/37/46.

48 PRO, SC1/36/86.

49 Baldwin, 'King's Council', *EGW*, I, p. 134; PRO, SC1/36/90.

50 *CCR, 1323–7*, p. 655; *CCR, 1327–30*, p. 547.

51 PRO, SC1/35/182.

52 Baldwin, 'King's Council', *EGW*, I, p. 135.

53 On 1 December 1330 Isabella surrendered all her dower lands to the Crown in exchange for an annual grant of £3,000 rendered at the exchequer (*CPR, 1327–30*, p. 48).

54 K.B. McFarlane, *The Nobility of Later Medieval England* (Oxford, 1973), p. 189.

55 J.M.W. Bean, *From Lord to Patron: Lordship in Late Medieval England* (Philadelphia, 1989), pp. 185–7.

56 *CChR, 1327–41*, p. 55.

57 Baldwin, 'King's Council', *EGW*, I, p. 136; Fryde, p. 208. He may have possessed the title of earl of March by early September, as he is referred to as such in a privy seal confirmation of a charter of Edward III from Wallingford on the 9th day of that month, allowing him an annual rent of £10 from lands in Staffordshire and Shropshire (*CChR, 1327–41*, p. 94).

[58] *Chronicon Henrici Knighton*, ed. J.R. Lumby (2 vols, Rolls Series, 1889), I, pp. 449–50; Baldwin, 'King's Council', *EGW*, I, p. 136.

[59] J. Barker, *The Tournament in England, 1100–1400* (Woodbridge, 1986), p. 67; *Knighton*, I, p. 449; *Murimuth*, p. 57; Fryde, p. 207. Barker demonstrates that such 'round tables' were a Mortimer family tradition dating back at least to the reign of Edward I. See also Ormrod, *Edward III*, p. 4.

[60] *HBC*, p. 87; J.S. Roskell, *The Impeachment of Michael de la Pole* (Manchester, 1984), p. 151, n. 66. Ufford had held the title in tail male, and Pole may have received it upon similar condition (Tuck, *Richard II*, pp. 76–7).

[61] Roskell, p. 140.

[62] Tuck, *Richard II*, pp. 83–4. Edward III was in fact careful to ensure that such grants of nobility were accompanied by commensurate endowments of wealth: when he rewarded four knights who had assisted him in removing Mortimer from power with earldoms on 16 March 1337, he supplied each of them with at least 1,000 marks *per annum* in lands and/or money (McFarlane, pp. 158–60).

[63] *Rot. Parl.*, VI, p. 173, trans. in *EHD*, IV, no. 289, pp. 477–8. Richard II's practice may, however, have been followed by Henry V, who apparently alienated Richard, earl of Cambridge, by denying him a sufficient endowment to support his noble title, granted to him in parliament in May 1414. This perhaps contributed to Cambridge's participation in the conspiracy of the following year to assassinate the king (C. Allmand, *Henry V* (London, 1993), p. 76).

[64] Roskell, pp. 138–9.

[65] M. Chibnall, *The Empress Matilda* (Oxford, 1991), pp. 107–12.

[66] Tuck, *Richard II*, pp. 77–8.

[67] *CPR, 1381–5*, p. 177.

[68] *CPR, 1381–5*, p. 442; see Tuck, *Richard II*, p. 79, for details of the terms of this grant.

[69] *Rot. Parl.*, III, pp. 209–11. The uncomfortable scene created when Vere pushed past the earls in order to take a higher seat in the parliament hall after receiving his grant is detailed in *EHD*, IV, no. 262, p. 451, and in *Thomae Walsingham Historia Anglicana*, ed. H.T. Riley (2 vols, Rolls Series, 1863–4), II, p. 140.

[70] *CPR, 1385–9*, p. 78; Tuck, *Richard II*, p. 81.

[71] Keen, p. 276; Goodman, *John of Gaunt*, pp. 102, 104.

[72] Tuck, *Richard II*, p. 82.

[73] Except for Gaunt's absence in Spain after July 1386: Given-Wilson, 'Witness Lists', pp. 74–6.

[74] Sir William Morers received the office of constable of Northampton Castle in October of this year (*CPR, 1377–81*, p. 277).

[75] C. Given-Wilson, 'Wealth and Credit, Public and Private: The Earls of Arundel 1306–1397', *English Historical Review (EHR)*, CCCCXVIII (January 1991), p. 16, n. 2.

[76] C. Given-Wilson, *The Royal Household and the King's Affinity* (New Haven, 1986), p. 167.

[77] A. Tuck, *Crown and Nobility, 1272–1461* (London, 1985), p. 101. Isabella's and Mortimer's ability to alienate many potentially valuable allies was demonstrated by the support of the Londoners for Lancaster's uprising: Ormrod, *Edward III*, p. 173.

[78] PRO, C49/6/13; G.A. Holmes, 'The Rebellion of the Earl of Lancaster, 1328–9', *Bulletin of the Institute of Historical Research (BIHR)*, XXVIII (1955), pp. 84–9.

[79] Lancaster's role as leader of this council was apparent to a contemporary London chronicler, who referred to him as 'the chief guardian of the king, by common assent of all the realm, from the time of the coronation' [*Croniques de London*, ed. G.J. Aungier (Camden Society, Original Series, XXVIII, 1844), p. 62, cited in A. Gransden, *Historical Writing in England II* (London, 1982), p. 72].

[80] R.M. Haines, *The Church and Politics in Fourteenth-Century England: The Career of Adam Orleton, c. 1275–1345* (Cambridge, 1978), p. 177. Haines observes that the failure of Mortimer to allow this council to operate in the prescribed fashion served as 'the initial article of accusation' against him in 1330 (*Knighton*, I, p. 454; *Rot. Parl.*, II, p. 52). The members of the council were Archbishops Reynolds of Canterbury and Melton of York; Bishops Orleton of Hereford and Stratford of Winchester; the earls of Lancaster, Kent, Norfolk, and Warenne; and Sir Thomas Wake, Sir Henry Percy, Sir Oliver Ingham, and John de Ros (Baldwin, 'King's Council', *EGW*, I, p. 132, citing Corpus Christi College, Cambridge, MS. 174, chap. 216).

[81] *Rot. Parl.*, II, p. 12; Tuck, *Crown and Nobility*, p. 95.

[82] Baldwin, 'King's Council', *EGW*, I, pp. 130–2, 133, n. 1.

[83] *Rot. Parl.*, II, p. 96.

[84] Tout, *Chapters*, VI, pp. 11, 21; *Murimuth*, pp. 61–2; Keen, p. 105.

[85] *Rot. Parl.*, III, pp. 5–6, 221; see also N.B. Lewis, 'The "Continual Council" in the Early Years of Richard II', *EHR*, XLI (1926), pp. 246–51.

[86] For Richard's attempted peace settlement, see J.J.N. Palmer, *England, France and Christendom, 1377–99* (London, 1972), chap. 6 *passim*.

[87] For the campaign, see Jean Froissart, *Chronicles*, ed. and trans. J. Jolliffe (New York, 1968), pp. 31–43; Edward's order to Treasurer Burghersh to sell the jewels (York, 20 August 1327) is found in *CCR, 1327–30*, p. 160.

[88] *Foedera*, II, ii, p. 730; Keen, pp. 77–8; McKisack, p. 99, n. 2.

[89] *Foedera*, II, ii, p. 743; M. Vale, *The Angevin Legacy and the Hundred Years War, 1250–1340* (Oxford, 1990), p. 249.

[90] *Foedera*, II, ii, p. 765; *EHD*, IV, no. 4, pp. 51–2; Keen, p. 114.

[91] Vale, p. 252.

[92] W.C. Dickinson, *Scotland from the Earliest Times to 1603*, 3rd edn, rev. A.A.M. Duncan (Oxford, 1977), p. 145; G.W.S. Barrow, *Robert Bruce* (3rd edn, Edinburgh, 1988), pp. 39–48.

[93] C.G. Crump, 'The Arrest of Roger Mortimer and Queen Isabel', *EHR*, XXVI (1911), pp. 331–2; Ormrod, *Edward III*, p. 6; *Select Documents*, no. 31, pp. 41–2; *Rot. Parl.*, II, p. 52.

[94] Wood, p. 39.

2

ANGLO-PORTUGUESE RELATIONS IN THE FOURTEENTH CENTURY

Wendy R. Childs

They bene oure frendes with their commodities.[1]

T‌hese words from the well-known and much used *Libelle of Englyshe Polycye*, a political poem written *c.* 1436 to encourage better keeping of the seas, illustrates excellently the attitude to Portugal bequeathed to the men of the fifteenth century by those of the fourteenth, and especially those of the reign of Richard II. The poem viewed few foreigners with favour, but the Portuguese were friends commercially and politically. Contacts between the two countries went back to the reconquest period when English crusaders helped the counts of Portugal in 1147 and 1189. They had been promoted commercially in the thirteenth century by the increase of Portuguese territory which made more southern Iberian goods available to northern markets, and by northern Europe's own expanding economy which increased the demand for southern goods. North and south were further linked by Catalans and Italians who opened the regular sea route round Iberia at the end of the thirteenth century. Such ease of access and complementary commodities drew Portugal and England together commercially; the possibility for the Portuguese of combining trade voyages to England and Flanders and for the English of combining voyages to Lisbon and Andalusia strengthened the attraction. Thus by the beginning of the fourteenth century, commercial relations were long-standing; they developed further to culminate in a mini-boom and the position was consolidated by close political alliances in the reign of Richard II.

Access between England and Portugal was straightforward, apart from the recognized dangers of storm and piracy. The sea routes were becoming well known. The surviving fifteenth-century *Directions for the Circumnavigation of England* allows the construction of a chart of the most frequented directions, which shows that direct crossings of the Bay of Biscay from Cape Clear in Ireland, the Scilly Islands, Ushant, and Belle Isle to Cape Ortegal and Finisterre were usual. Further directions to Cadiz and Seville used the Burlings Rocks, Cape Cintra, and Cape St Vincent as navigation points.[2] English merchants were familiar with the crossings from Ireland and from the Breton coasts. Already by the end of the fourteenth century some made the voyage regularly, and a round trip to Lisbon probably took three months, allowing for four or five weeks turn-round time, and waiting for good winds.

Goods were attractive although it is commonly said that Portugal's commercial products were limited. Salt, cork, fish and olive oil are mentioned as the main contributions until colonial sugar and slaves made strong appearances in the later fifteenth century; but Portugal had more to offer as well. A late thirteenth- or early fourteenth-century Flemish list of goods and their provenances indicates that Portugal produced honey, skins, wax, leather, scarlet grain to dye cloth, tallow (*oint*), olive oil, figs, raisins, and whale meat (*balai*).[3] In 1283 special brokers were set up in London to deal with the various leathers and cumin said to be coming from Portugal as well as Spain.[4] Cargoes brought to England in the fourteenth century were usually of oil, Lisbon and Algarve wines, some salt and very often dried figs and raisins for the winter. The cargoes of three ships in Bristol in March 1309 were overwhelmingly of figs and raisins worth £264 19s 7d, while small amounts of oil, honey, coneyskins and pomegranates were worth less than £8.[5] In return Portugal received predominantly English cloth – broadcloths, Welsh straits, and some as bed-hangings, together with hose, a little lead and tin, corn, occasionally lances and wainscots. In the fifteenth century the variety of manufactured and re-exported goods grew.[6]

Ease of access, attractive goods, and a climate of general friendship promoted commercial relations in the thirteenth and early fourteenth centuries, but the scale of trade was limited. The smaller size of Portugal, and its merchants' apparent preference for the greater entrepôts in Flanders, kept its trade to England modest, while throughout the Middle Ages Castile was the main focus of English interest. Its size and closeness to Gascony inevitably made it so, and Anglo-Portuguese trade was generally overshadowed by the larger Anglo-Spanish trade.

It is necessary to survey the early trade to evaluate more accurately the expansion in Richard II's reign. There seems to have been no English

commercial activity in Portugal in the thirteenth century, despite the earlier
crusading voyages, and Portuguese activity in England also seems to have been
low early in the century. King John's two general safe-conducts in 1202 and
1204[7] for Portuguese merchants suggest regular trade by that time, but other
references for the period are scarce. A Joscelin de Portugal received a personal
safe-conduct to trade in 1208, and a Bartholomew of Portugal was active with
three London merchants in 1220.[8] The two sets of safe-conducts, granted in
June and November 1226, for some 75 to 100 named Portuguese, several of
them men from Guimarãis (near Braga), Oporto, and Coimbra, to come to
England,[9] suggest considerable trade, but may include sailors as well as
merchants.[10] Indeed, the first safe-conducts, granted in June, recorded the
names in four groups of 13, 10, 9, and 10, perhaps representing four ships.
These numbers would be quite reasonable for groups of shippers including
some crew members in that period. Shippers on the three Portuguese vessels at
Bristol in 1309 were, respectively, 3 merchants and 7 crew, 7 merchants and
10 crew, and 5 merchants and 16 crew.[11] The second set of safe-conducts for
61 men (some 26 of whom appear also on the first set), granted in November,
might thus represent from three to six trading vessels.

By mid-century a number of Portuguese merchants were dealing in Bordeaux
and London. In 1243 nine Portuguese merchants supplied wax and coneyskins
worth £805 4s 6d to the king in Bordeaux, and one lent the king £300 there. In
March that year he and three others in Bordeaux received royal protection.[12] In
London in the summer of 1251 Lourenço Martini of Portugal struggled to gain
repayment for debt from the lands and chattels of Henry le Feyte; again
Portuguese appear as suppliers of wax to the queen (1253–4) and the king
(1258); and in that year seven Portuguese merchants received safe-conducts to
trade in England for as long as there was peace between England and
Portugal.[13] In return for their goods they probably took English cloth; English
scarlets and other London cloths appeared on a price-fixing list proclaimed in
Portugal in December 1253.[14]

From the 1260s to the 1290s trade seems to have languished, no doubt in the
face of Castilian competition, further boosted by Edward I's marriage to
Eleanor of Castile. Increasing English references from the 1290s illustrate
Portuguese links with Gascony and Flanders as often as they do direct links with

England. Merchants of Bayonne such as William de Saltu and Bernard de Grisil complained from time to time of robberies when they were trading in Lisbon and had Portuguese ships arrested at Sandwich (1293) and Romney (1298 or 1299); and although in the last case the Portuguese merchants in London in 1299 took their case as far as parliament, they lost.[15] Merchants of Bayonne continued to work the Lisbon route and continued to seek support and justice from the English king when plundered or attacked en route by Flemings (1304), Spaniards (1309), and Bretons (1330).[16]

The *Bolsa* set up in Portugal in 1293 was for those sailing to England as well as Flanders, but the latter seems to have been the more important centre. The fund was to be held in Bruges and Portuguese merchants complained to Edward I in 1295 of being forced to sell goods in England as they sailed to Flanders. They presumably saw Flanders as more profitable,[17] and the strong Flemish connection is confirmed by the letters from the count of Flanders in 1297 urging England and Portugal to give mutual safe-conducts, and so avoid the damaging reprisals still taking place over the Gascons' losses in Lisbon. The safe-conducts were duly given in 1297 and confirmed in 1299,[18] but they were not sufficient to protect the Portuguese at Romney, nor to stop locals plundering the ship of Francis Johannis of Portugal, which was wrecked between Shoreham and Portsmouth in 1299.[19] Peaceful trading relations between the two countries, however, continued to be promoted by their kings. Edward II duly responded in 1308 and 1309 to a request from King Diniz for safe-conducts for his merchants coming to England, and these would have protected the three Portuguese ships at Bristol in 1309. In 1325 and 1326 Edward also responded gracefully but negatively to suggestions for Portuguese marriages for his children.[20] As always, however, royal goodwill was not sufficient to stop local misdemeanours. A ship with a cargo of dried fruit belonging to Lisbon merchants was looted by locals when it was wrecked off Hove in the winter of 1309–10; in 1313 two Lisbon merchants returning from Flanders ran aground off Romney and arranged salvage with local men for one-quarter of the value, only to find the locals then demanded one-third and eventually took one-half; in 1318 João and Pero Dominges, taking a cargo of wine to Flanders, anchored off Padstow in contrary winds and found their cargo looted when the cables parted and the ship was driven ashore; and similarly in 1320 the *Jesus* of Oporto, bound for England

and driven ashore on the Isle of Wight, was looted. In 1321 the *Antonio* of Lisbon, also bound for England with salt and other goods worth £400, was boarded and robbed off Falmouth. Fewer problems then occur until in 1337 João Alfonso of Tavile was robbed of £90 worth of figs and raisins from a Spanish ship at Sandwich and forced, he claimed under pain of death, to give acquittance to the robbers and to pay the shipmaster (presumably in collusion with the English robbers) £30.[21]

In the early fourteenth century we have the first clear information that English ships and possibly merchants were joining the merchants of Bayonne in the voyage to Portugal. In 1311 Peter Barde, described as a king's mariner, was sent by the king with a royal ship to Spain and Portugal, and officials were instructed not to interfere with the merchants' goods on it. Then in 1338 the English ship *Juliane* of Southampton was hired by Portuguese merchants to pick up wine in Spain and Portugal.[22]

The Portuguese were thus visible enough to be included among the nations in the Carta Mercatoria of 1303 but their activity appears rather limited when compared with that of the Spaniards. In patent, close, and other chancery rolls, thirty Spanish merchants are repeatedly recorded in London between 1271 and 1287, but no Portuguese; Spanish merchants became denizens in the 1270s and again in the 1330s but no Portuguese did so; five references to Portuguese ships off the English coast between 1310 and 1340 are matched by twenty-four references to Spanish vessels. London municipal records confirm this picture. The London letter books and the recognizance rolls record 727 debts involving alien merchants between 1276 and 1326, but while 129 involved Spaniards, only one case clearly involved a Portuguese – Martim Garsye of Lisbon, who was owed 54 marks by Peter de Lyons of Southampton in 1299.[23] The butler's accounts of imported wines which survive for fourteen years between 1327 and 1340 show at least twenty-eight Spanish ships in various ports from Bristol to London, but only two Portuguese, both from Lisbon, one in 1327–8 and one in 1336–7.[24]

The earliest national customs accounts, which record the general trade of aliens from 1303, survive very patchily at this period, so estimates of total trade are impossible, but again comparison can be made with Spanish activity. In London there were no recorded Portuguese merchants or ships in 1303–40. The same is surprisingly also so in Southampton, though this was later to be a firm centre for them and was easily combined with sailings for Flanders; in this period, however, these records show 21 or 22 Spanish ships and about 70 Spanish merchants, with Spanish trade making up about 20 per cent of the port's alien import trade in 1310–11 and 1330–1. Sandwich is the only southern port to record Portuguese merchants and ships, and even there they were always overshadowed by Spanish activity. They were not attracted to the smaller south-western ports, but in Bristol in 1308–9 three Portuguese ships unloaded fruit valued at £265. Again the patchy survival of records must be emphasized and there may be Portuguese here outside the years of the surviving records, but comparison with the Spanish presence is none the less telling. Clearly it would be wrong at this time to write of a vigorous Portuguese trade with England. The surviving national accounts show at most 7 Portuguese ships and possibly 20 merchants in English ports in 1300–40, while they show 59 Spanish ships and at least 28 and possibly 50 further merchants from Spain.[25] Certainly the records are not exhaustive and provide only glimpses of ways in which alien merchants came in contact with English officialdom, but the near-unanimous picture from a variety of sources argues convincingly for a very modest but regular direct Anglo-Portuguese trade at this time.

The 1340s seem to be a watershed: the trade of Portuguese merchants was clearly already increasing, and English merchant interest was becoming more visible before the surge of activity in Richard's reign. From about 1340 until 1369 all records indicate an increase in Portuguese activity, although the few surviving customs accounts rarely show more than one or two ships in any port in a year.[26] However, the Spaniards were still dominant on Iberian routes. The various legal and administrative records which refer to 14 Portuguese ships in English ports, also refer to 58 Spanish ships in, or intending to come to, English ports and a further 18 robbed or wrecked on their way past English coasts. The surviving butler's accounts of alien-owned wine imports, which survive for twenty-four of the years between 1340 and 1370, record 18 Portuguese ships bringing 693 tuns of wine, but also show 96 Spanish ships to have brought 4,302 tuns,[27] and in Bordeaux in 1355–61 the five Portuguese ships loading 365 tuns were surpassed by 104 Basque ships loading 11,008 tuns.[28]

To consolidate their position, in 1352 the Portuguese began to negotiate a fifty-year commercial agreement, and during the negotiations on 20 October

1353 eleven shipmasters and a few merchants requested safe-conducts.[29] This is not as great a number as the twenty-three Spanish shipmasters caught at Sluys in 1345 who chose to throw in their lot with England rather than France and Flanders, but it is clear evidence of a conscious group identity. The Portuguese merchants trading in England, or passing its coasts, were a large enough and self-conscious enough group to negotiate cooperatively and to be accepted by Edward III as a distinct body.

The negotiations were probably stimulated by the similar commercial truce of 1351 arranged by the Spaniards in the anxious wake of the battle of Les-Espagnols-sur-Mer in 1350. The terms were similar but safe-guards were less detailed, possibly because there were fewer fears of open hostility, or because Spanish merchants were already deeply involved in Channel and English trade and saw the problems as real ones of past experience, while Portuguese negotiators were perhaps less vividly aware of potential problems.

The route between England and Portugal was now busier as the Portuguese were joined by the English merchants. The little information which we have on English activity shows some merchants to have become long-term dealers in the Portuguese market by this time. In 1352 John Worthy, the apprentice of John Wycombe of Bristol, had been in Portugal for three years when he died from plague. Wycombe complained that his goods had been seized by another English merchant, John Appelayne, 'now remaining' in Portugal, under Worthy's will, but Wycombe claimed that Worthy had nothing of his own to leave, and all his goods should have come to Wycombe. In 1366 the *Clement* belonging to Ellis Spelly and William Canynges of Bristol put in to Lisbon and was robbed and burnt by Spaniards there.[30] Both Spelly and Canynges are shown in later documents to be steady traders to Portugal, and this may well not be their first visit.

The great potential for Anglo-Portuguese trade, and especially for the Portuguese in England, came after 1369 as a result of the breakdown of Anglo-Castilian relations. The death of the English ally Pedro I of Castile, and the usurpation with French help of the Castilian throne by Enrique Trastamara, severed Anglo-Castilian relations and trade for nearly twenty years.[31] The rift deepened and Trastamara became even more closely tied to his French allies when Pedro's legitimate heiress Constanza, and her sister Isabella, married and settled in England with a court in exile. With Castilian ports now inaccessible to the English, Portugal could supply at least some of the typical Iberian goods wanted by the English – wines, olive oil, special leathers, figs and raisins in winter and kermes dye for the cloth industry – and could provide a continuing western market for cloth. Lancaster's persuasion of Richard II's government to adopt the military strategy of the 'way of Spain' by which he hoped to gain his wife's throne and remove Castile's strength from France led to new alliances and closer connections with Portugal. The policy was, of course, a total disaster. Two military expeditions left hundreds of English soldiers of all classes with less than fond memories of Portugal and the Portuguese, and left the Portuguese disgruntled at the English behaviour, but some shipmen and merchants profited from war, and became even more familiar with each other's harbours. They naturally provided transports and sent supplies to Lancaster's troops in Portugal and Spain, and those English ships which took soldiers and equipment to Lisbon in 1381 are recorded as carrying merchantable goods home from Portugal.[32] Moreover, the treaties, especially that of 1386, positively encouraged commerce, and the marriage of Lancaster's daughter Philippa to João I also ensured closer relations between the two courts for almost two generations from 1386.

Closer political relations were not, however, immediate, complete, or without problems. At first, the separation of Portugal and Castile was rarely clear cut, and periods of Castilian invasion and of civil war made life difficult for merchants. Production areas, particularly of wine, might be damaged, and Lisbon, the main trading port, was threatened by Castilian troops in 1372–3, by the Castilian fleet in the Tagus in 1382, and by a long blockade in 1384–5. After 1369, it was four years before an Anglo-Portuguese alliance was agreed in June 1373, and Fernão I was never free from Castilian pressure. In March 1373 he had already made a treaty with Castile to get Trastamara's invading forces, then camped near Lisbon, to leave Portugal. This treaty remained in force until Trastamara's death in 1379 and Fernão at least once fulfilled its naval clauses and sent galleys to help the Castilian raids on English coasts in 1377. Portuguese action as an ally of Castile caused Walter Cokkesdon, factor for John Polymond of Southampton, described as having 'long time abode in Portugal', to flee for his life leaving Polymond's goods behind; and caused the loss of goods worth £232 11s 8d for John Aubrey and William Baret of London.[33]

The ambiguous position with Portugal an ally of both England and Castile caused many problems for merchants. Edward's and Richard's governments alternately ordered arrests of Portuguese ships to provide justice for their own merchants, and proclaimed that the Portuguese were friends who might freely trade. In 1374 at least twelve Portuguese ships were arrested in various ports; and Polymond, Aubrey, and Baret made successful claims for compensation from the Portuguese goods; but in orders concerning these claims the king wrote at one time (February 1374) that the treaty should not be infringed, and at another (April 1374) that before Portuguese goods were returned there should be an inquiry into whether the English were well treated in Portugal or not.[34] A similar inquiry about how well the English were being treated there was made in Bristol in 1379, when Portuguese merchants requested a safe-conduct. Bristol men stated that they had been well treated for two years.[35] On the whole, the treaty 'won'. Fernão's allegiance to Castile was not deep. He brought his galleys home from Castile immediately Trastamara died, and the Anglo-Portuguese treaty was confirmed in 1380. The ambiguities and the Portuguese naval help to Castile in these years may explain why few Portuguese appear in the surviving customs accounts for Bristol in 1376–7 and 1377–8 and only rise thereafter. Even the firm treaty from 1380 did not make things easy. Shipping was disrupted when Cambridge's expedition to Portugal in 1381–2 occupied a fleet of 41 vessels (16 of them Portuguese) for six months. English support for João I's usurpation in Portugal in 1383 finally brought Portugal firmly to the English side, but civil war in 1383–4 again disrupted Lisbon and its hinterland. The treaty of Windsor, agreed on 9 May 1386, and the marriage of Lancaster's daughter Philippa to João consolidated their mutual interests, but still the path was not entirely smooth. The loans raised by João's ambassadors to England in 1385 were largely left unpaid, and aggrieved creditors had Portuguese ships and goods impounded from time to time well into the fifteenth century.[36] Then, after 1388, Portugal's competitive edge was lost when Lancaster's agreement with Castile and the later Anglo-French truces restored a measure of peace to the Channel and reopened the Anglo-Iberian trade to Spanish activity once more.

The Portuguese opportunity to move into English trade without Castilian competition was therefore neither very long nor untroubled, and the Portuguese surge was neither as dramatic nor as sustained as might have been expected.

None the less, some merchants took the opportunity offered and documents which show the Spaniards' withdrawal equally show the Portuguese advance.

The butler's accounts of alien-owned wine imports show no Spanish activity at all in the 1370s and early 1380s, while in 1372 two Portuguese ships brought wine to London and Bristol, and in the three years 1379–82 three, six, and two Portuguese wine ships appeared. However, in 1392–3 there were again only two, in 1393–4 none, and in 1394–5 again two, and in these years they were again surpassed by five, nine, and ten Spanish vessels respectively. Portuguese merchants owned very small proportions of the alien wines except for 1380–1, when their 330 tuns were 28 per cent of the total.[37] Their wine was almost certainly Portuguese as there is no evidence of their picking up cargoes in Bordeaux.

The general customs accounts show a similar pattern of increase then of fading. The Portuguese were mainly attracted to the three major ports of Southampton, London, and Bristol. Southampton was the regular port of call on the Channel coast, as Sandwich, beginning to silt seriously, lost its modest appeal to all Iberians. The Portuguese clearly took over from the Spaniards in Iberian trade up to 1388, sending up to five ships a year as in 1380–1 and 1383–4, but they dropped out as the Spaniards pushed back.[38] Some ships made repeated voyages, as did the *St Mary Grace* (master, Nicholas Yanus), which exported cloth for Portuguese and Italian merchants in June 1383, was back with 102 tuns of wine in October, and left once more with a large consignment of cloth worth £1,016 mainly for Italians in January 1384. As well as carrying for Italians, the Portuguese were involved in trade between the Low Countries and Southampton. In 1388 the *St Mary* of Oporto (master, Andres Peres), unloaded figs and raisins for Portuguese shippers and herring and garlic for another alien. This combination suggests the type of voyage that Italians also did: a first landfall in Flanders and a call at Southampton afterwards. At London the same pattern of increase and slackened interest may have happened, but accounts are fewer. Not surprisingly, no Portuguese ships exported wool; and none appeared in the short general account for July to September 1384, which was the summer in which Lisbon was closely besieged by Castilian troops.[39] The city was starving and in no position to take part in normal international trade. The other two surviving accounts are both after 1388. Already in 1389 four Spanish vessels were back in London, alongside one

Portuguese ship, but in 1390–1 there were still four Portuguese, although these were now matched by four Spanish ships, the import values on which (£422) were worth over twice those on the Portuguese ships (£200). The Spanish vessels also carried goods worth £569 for Italian shippers.[40] Bristol has a good series of export accounts surviving from 1376, with full details of shipping provenance and destinations, which give interesting information on the Portuguese activity.[41] Portuguese ships did not appear there in 1376–7 or 1377–8, either because they were slow to perceive any advantages in sailing off the Channel routes, or, perhaps more likely, because they had been put off by the breakdown of the 1373 treaty; 1377–8 was the year the Portuguese galleys helped Castile raid the south coast. Ships from Bruges and Sluys were used in Bristol to supplement English shipping on the Iberian route in the mid-1370s.[42] Then, between 1378 and 1383, there was heavy Portuguese activity. This reached ten ships in 1379–80 (six of Lisbon, three of Oporto, and one of Viaña) and seven in 1380–1 (three each of Lisbon and Oporto and the *Mary Oliver*). These are the encouraging years of Trastamara's death and the confirmation of the English treaty. Some shipmasters, such as Egidius Rotriges with the *Katherine* of Lisbon, João Andres with the *Grace Dieu* of Oporto, and Afonso Passe with the *George* of Lisbon, repeated journeys, but none seems to have come more than twice, and the quick rise equally quickly faded. Although four ships came in 1382–3, this steadily dropped to three in 1387, one in 1390–1, possibly one in 1391–2, and one in 1394–5. No Portuguese ships were recorded after 1395, although occasional merchants shipped aboard Bristol vessels.

By this time, however, English activity in Portugal was considerable. The Bristol men's role is well known: their factors and ships were already in Lisbon in the 1350s and 1360s and they were frequent traders. Ellis Spelly, whose ship the *Clement* was burnt in Lisbon in 1366, also owned the *Cogge John*, which carried wine, wax, fruit, and oil to Ireland from Lisbon in 1377 and was arrested at Kinsale as an enemy alien because the crew contained five Spanish seamen. He appeared often in the customs accounts. Thomas Daniel, a Bristol merchant who dealt with Portugal, was prominent enough to be used as an ambassador to England in 1383. This possibly shows João's lack of aristocratic support, but it was not unusual to use a foreign national as part of an embassy for help with language and practical travel arrangements.[43] The Bristol customs accounts are particularly important because their records of destinations show more clearly than any others the extent of English trade in Portugal. In the period 1376–1400 overall, two-thirds of the shipping leaving Bristol for Portugal was English. The English share dropped at the height of the Portuguese interest, to 30 per cent in 1378–9 and even lower to 8 per cent in 1379–80. Then there was only one English ship on the route alongside ten Portuguese and one ship from Bruges, but it was the English interest in Portugal which was more consistent in the long run. In 1390–1 a single Portuguese ship exported cloth, alongside seventeen English vessels (fourteen of Bristol itself). Regularly between ten and twenty English ships a year went to Iberia, and this pattern remained until late in the fifteenth century. Generally, somewhat under 1,000 broadcloths a year, but in peak years up to 1,800, were recorded as exported to Portugal, some 20 to 30 per cent of Bristol's total exports. Even in the four-year period 1378 to 1382, when Portuguese shipping movements were at their height, it was still English merchants who handled most of the cloth exports meant for Portugal. They owned between 70 and 86 per cent, and shipped mainly on English and Low Country ships. Between 1377 and 1402, 286 Bristol merchants (34 per cent of the total of 834 native shippers who appear in the Bristol accounts for the period) shipped goods to Spain or Portugal at some time. Of the 45 major Bristol merchants (defined as those with exports averaging 40 cloths a year), 80 per cent showed an interest in Iberia, and many shipped repeatedly. Men such as William Canynges, Thomas Colston, Ellis Spelly and their factors knew Portugal well. These records allow some estimate of the total Portuguese trade in Bristol. Over the period 1376–1400, Iberia as a whole took about 24 per cent of Bristol's cloth exports, and about 13 per cent was specifically recorded as exported to Portugal.[44] There is a problem in disentangling precisely the destinations of Bristol's Iberian trade at this time. Some of that recorded for Portugal may have been destined for Spain through Portugal, and sometimes the collectors during the crisis years seem to have used Portugal and Spain interchangeably. Most of the detected smuggling in 1386–8 was said to be to Spain and in English ships, but two ships of Lisbon were also involved at Chepstow in voyages said to be to Spain.[45] These offences were revealed in an enquiry of 1389 and prosecutions dragged on in the exchequer until 1393. Clearly the king believed a significant amount of trade was still going to Portugal in the 1390s, and it may have been partly in response to these smuggling cases from the west country and south Wales that Richard decided to place searchers at the Portuguese end with powers to check all ships, goods, and custom cockets in ports throughout Portugal.[46] It was certainly a sign of friendship that João allowed foreign officials to operate in Portuguese ports.

Some Southampton and London merchants also invested regularly and in substantial amounts in the Portuguese trade, but in the absence of the recording of destinations and last ports of call in these customs accounts, we cannot make clear estimates of the scale of English merchants' trade in different markets. Judging by cargoes imported to other ports, however, English shipping operating on the Portuguese route was rarely as high as at Bristol. Often only one English ship a year seems to have operated on the route from Southampton.[47] At Southampton John Polymond was probably the most dominant figure in Portuguese trade. He was seven times mayor, at one time a customs collector, and the man to whom Portuguese matters were referred in Southampton. In 1373 he enquired into the robbery of a Portuguese ship seized off Guernsey and brought into Southampton; in that year his yeoman, Walter Cokkesdon (mentioned above), who had 'long time abode there', was robbed of goods during the political disputes, and in 1374 Polymond successfully sued for compensation for this from Portuguese arrested in England. In 1380 he was one of those who kept in custody the goods of the *Jesus Christ* of Portugal; in 1382 he was to keep in honourable arrest all Portuguese ships in Southampton; in 1385 he arrested all Portuguese ships there and was appointed to sell the goods on behalf of the Portuguese ambassador, as part of the repayment of the ambassador's debts; in 1389 one of his ships was coming back from Portugal when it seized goods from an Italian ship sailing in its company.[48] On the whole, however, relatively few Southampton men went to Portugal. London merchants were more important, and also traded through Southampton and Sandwich.

Unfortunately, few London customs accounts survive, but traces of London's interest in Portuguese trade are found in a variety of other documents. For instance, the London letter books specifically list wax and oil of Lisbon in regulations of 1366 and 1371, and the *Black Book of the Admiralty*'s list of standard seamen's wages for common voyages in 1375 included London to Lisbon but nothing for voyages to Spain.[49] Among the Londoners, William Baret was repeatedly active. He and Henry Herbury of London shipped wine from Lisbon in 1370; and he and John Aubrey of London had goods worth £232 11s 8d stolen from them in Portugal at about the same time that Polymond's factor's goods were seized in 1373; merchants of London and Salisbury loaded goods in Lisbon for Waterford in 1374; and in 1387 Richard Neville, Richard Odiham, and other London merchants used a Plymouth ship which foundered off Sandwich while taking their goods from London to Lisbon.[50] Neville and Odiham also traded through Sandwich and Southampton, using them as London outports. Neville imported figs, raisins, soap, and 10 tuns of Algarve wine to Sandwich in November 1386, and in June 1387 at Southampton he exported the very high number of 174.5 broadcloths on the *Katherine* of Oporto. In the same month, Odiham sent 58 cloths from Southampton in a large cargo of 467 cloths of other London merchants on a ship of Greenwich. It was probably sailing westward, and if this was consigned to Portugal, it indicates significant English interest.[51] The London customs account for 1389 shows four English ships importing Iberian cargoes of fruit, oil, and wax worth £1,175 which may have come from Portugal.[52] It is, however, always difficult to distinguish Portuguese goods from Andalusian; and although the agreement with Castile was only very recent, in that year already four ships from Castile had arrived in London. Even in wartime, English merchants could prosper.

Not only were merchants of these three ports interested, but even some of York and Hull by the end of the century. Six merchants of York, who had brought wine, oil and dried fruit from Portugal to London, shipped it on to Hull and York in February 1388, and William Salley and Walter Benton of York were in Faro with John Brynneston, factor for Robert de Crosse of Hull, when they loaded figs and raisins on the *Peter* of Caen for trade in Harfleur.[53]

This last instance is a reminder that England and English merchants were part of an extensive Atlantic and Channel network which linked England and Portugal in various ways, through various markets and nationalities. English ports were often a staging post on the route to the Low Countries. Some ships sailing between Lisbon and Flanders or Middelburg came inadvertently to England through storm, arrest, or piracy,[54] but in other cases goods were deliberately trans-shipped in London to safer shipping, and some cloths were even sent from London to Bristol for trans-shipment.[55] Flemish ships were used between Bristol and Lisbon, sometimes by Italians, who dealt frequently in Lisbon.[56] Irish trade with Lisbon was also entwined with that of England: London and Salisbury merchants took goods from Lisbon to Waterford in the Portuguese ship *St Mary Oliver* in 1374; Ellis Spelly of Bristol used his ship to trade between Ireland and Lisbon; and in 1380, at the height of the Portuguese activity in Bristol and the west, they were important enough for the Irish to ask for confirmation that they should come freely to Ireland with their wine and that the Irish should go freely to Portugal.[57]

Within the international community trading in Lisbon, the English merchant group, like the Portuguese in England who negotiated the agreement in 1353, became distinct and cooperative enough to acquire group privileges. They received some of those well before the treaty of Windsor. In 1367 the judge of the customs house was ordered to provide them with swift justice, to avoid the delays of the normal courts. Swift justice was always sought in commercial circles, but this order may also imply that, despite evidence for some long-stay factors, many merchants were still non-resident in Lisbon in the 1360s. In the treaty period the English did better. They were, it is true, never exempt from the general obligation on foreign merchants to deal in avoirdupois goods only in Lisbon, but since Lisbon was an attractive market this was probably no hardship. Moreover the regulation may not have been well enforced; merchants of Hull and York were present in Faro in 1395. However, in 1383 they were exempted from the navigation act requiring use of Portuguese vessels, and in 1389 they were allowed the privileges already enjoyed by the Italians.[58] Probably the most appreciated of these was the exemption from lading supervision and the reduction of 25 per cent of the *sisa*. It is difficult to assess the exact importance of the last grant. It came in the aftermath of particularly close political cooperation and soon after the perpetual treaty of 1386. It may, therefore, be due as much to political sympathy as to economic might, and it certainly did not put the English in the position of most favoured nation above others such as the Italians. However, the grants altogether mark a considerable change in the English presence on this route from the early fourteenth century.

We must not overestimate the scale, but it is incontrovertible that Richard II's reign saw a transformation in Anglo-Portuguese trade. For a short time in the 1370s and early 1380s, the Portuguese themselves became particularly important commercially. At Bristol their interest was intense but fleeting; at Southampton their interest was more regular, part of a triangular trade with Flanders, and linked with carrying goods for Italians; at London their presence was also more regular, but less linked with Flanders; here, too, by 1389–90 they had become again overshadowed by Spanish activity. Elsewhere, they appeared only occasionally, except at Plymouth where, like many shipmen of all nationalities, they often anchored to wait for good winds to cross the Channel westwards, or made for the port as their first shelter as they sailed north. The picture of their 'normal' trade is blurred because of the lack of good detailed customs accounts for all ports, but the impression of general activity in each port suggests that, at the peak of their activity, it might have been possible to find anything from a dozen to eighteen Portuguese ships lying in English ports on major trading ventures, but by the 1390s this would have dropped to about six to eight a year, mainly at Southampton and London. Their own cargoes were usually modest. Their own imports of wine were rarely over 50 tuns a year, except in the 1380s when they passed 300 tuns. Their exports of English cloth were probably no more than 400 cloths a year. Their cargoes of fruit, oil, and other goods can rarely have been valued at more than £300 to £400 a year, except once more in the 1370s and 1380s when they reached 800.[59] But without doubt their presence was now much more familiar on English quays. Moreover, Anglo-Portuguese trade was much greater than this suggests, since the Portuguese had by now been joined for at least two generations by English merchants and shipowners who took the route seriously. Many years ago, a Miss Shillington concluded that English activity on the route had surpassed Portuguese some time between 1380 and 1400,[60] and this is undoubtedly true, both overall, and for Bristol and London. Elsewhere in individual ports, the picture is less clear. Englishmen were particularly familiar with Lisbon which became their centre, but they also visited the Algarve, and their ships passing to Huelva and Seville were familiar with all Portugal's coastline. Unfortunately, it is not always possible, even at Bristol, to distinguish in the customs accounts England's Portuguese and Andalusian trade, and thus the precise importance of each market. But it is clear that about ten to twenty English ships a year went to Iberia, and outside Bristol perhaps eight or more English ships a year went to Portugal and Andalusia. English merchants' interest is apparent in that they invested in larger cargoes than did Portuguese merchants, a pattern which continued throughout the fifteenth century. Miss Shillington also wrote of the great vigour of the trade in Richard II's reign and its continued growth in the fifteenth century. These broad conclusions stand, but her precise position needs some qualification. Certainly a trade involving seventeen or twenty-one ships a year, as happened in Bristol in 1380–1 and 1390–1, can be called vigorous, but these were exceptional years, and by taking these as a yardstick, and by not comparing the Portuguese with the Spanish trade over a longer period, the importance of the Anglo-Portuguese trade may be overestimated, and the basis from which the trade increased in the fifteenth century set too high.

What is without doubt none the less is that Richard II's reign saw a great change in Anglo-Portuguese trade. Whereas Spain had previously been the main focus of English commercial attention, now, for a short time, Portugal and the Portuguese became more important. Spain would regain its position in the later fifteenth century, but even when the Anglo-Portuguese trade peak had passed, the trade maintained the solid base in mutual activity which it had developed in Richard's reign, and continued to hold up well in the difficult commercial years of the early fifteenth century.[61]

The commercial contacts were obviously strengthened by the close political links of Richard II's reign, which lasted into the fifteenth century and kept Portuguese interests in the minds of the English kings. Richard's court was exceptionally cosmopolitan, with Spanish, Portuguese, and Bohemian marriages enriching the more usual French and Flemish influences. Italian cultural developments were also appreciated at court. But during this reign political events made the Portuguese connections particularly strong in many areas. Knowledge, and probably some understanding, of each other's country spread through a variety of social groups not only mercantile. The close political relations, culminating in the marriage of Philippa of Lancaster and João Aviz in 1386, had been dictated by particular Iberian circumstances, and as these changed, the need for mutual military and political support diminished, but at court Philippa and her brother, Henry IV, helped to keep contacts alive well into the fifteenth century.[62] When he came to the English throne, Henry IV was generous to his Portuguese nephews and nieces; in 1401 he sent a handsome gift of eight gold collars which cost him £250 to Philippa's eldest son.[63] Several of

Philippa's six surviving children maintained English contacts after her death in 1416. Duarte (named for Philippa's grandfather Edward III) succeeded as king in 1433 and kept formal contacts open. Pedro, duke of Coimbra, later regent for Duarte's young son, probably knew England best. He came to England in 1425,[64] in 1428 for his installation as Knight of the Garter,[65] and in 1429 for the coronation of Henry VI.[66] At this time he may have met, or narrowly missed, his sister Isabella, who was driven by storms to Plymouth at the end of November on her way to marry the Duke of Burgundy.[67] She became prominent in Anglo-Burgundian diplomacy in the 1430s, 1440s and 1450s, and hoped to help her Portuguese nephews, sons of Pedro, find openings in England.[68] The Order of the Garter was from time to time presented to foreign royalty, but never so frequently as to the Portuguese. It was held by Pedro of Coimbra (1428), King Duarte (elected 1436), Henry the Navigator (elected 1443), and their nephew Afonso V (elected 1447). Afonso's successor, João II, received the Garter in 1489.

Aristocratic connections also continued. Members of Philippa's English household retired to England or came home on visits. She further strengthened links by encouraging the marriage of the earl of Arundel to João's illegitimate daughter Beatriz. Beatriz brought with her a Portuguese household, which included the six-year-old Aliana who later married John Hill of Oxfordshire, and who was still here in *c.* 1440 when she sued for denization in order to enjoy her full dower.[69] At the turn of the century there were still hundreds of men through all classes of society in England who had spent time in England's armies in Portugal, or in Spain with Portuguese troops. Not many would have come back with warm memories; but they disseminated awareness and first-hand knowledge of Portugal more widely through England. In the fifteenth century these hundreds gradually decreased to scores, but military contacts were boosted by some Portuguese recruitment of English soldiers for their campaigns against Ceuta, and by some Portuguese men in English armies in France. A small number of Portuguese, apart from those in Beatriz's retinue, made careers in England. João Vasques de Almada was retained by Henry IV for life in 1400; Alvaro Vaz de Almada, friend and supporter of Pedro of Coimbra, took part in the siege of Rouen in 1417–19, and was given the title count of Avranches in 1445.[70]

Regular messengers in both directions maintained contacts at court level. Ambassadors frequently stayed for weeks and might be used repeatedly, thus becoming 'specialists' in each other's country, able to pick up news, life-style, literature, and ideas, if they were so inclined. A handful of religious and scholars also moved between the two countries probably quite independently of political events. The Dominican James of Almaida was ordained in England in 1390; four apparently Portuguese Franciscans appeared at Oxford and Cambridge between 1371 and 1389; and the Portuguese-born Franciscan John of Portugal, who had lived in the Exeter convent for three years by September 1373, was allowed to stay there despite orders to expel all alien friars.[71] Possibly more influence drifted from England to Portugal than *vice versa*. Philippa introduced the Use of Sarum in her own devotions; Robert Payn, once a member of her household, translated Gower's *Confessio Amantis*;[72] and the Portuguese earl of Avranches was much impressed with Henry's court, and asked the dean of his chapel to write an account of the royal chapel for Afonso V.[73] The romance *Torrent of Portugal* suggests a possible acquisition in the other direction, but there is no proof of a Portuguese origin, and Portugal may simply be chosen as a glamorous foreign setting.[74] There is no doubt that Portugal would have such glamour with its mixture of Moorish and Christian background, and the goods which came from Portugal brought the flavour of the Mediterranean and North Africa.

As shown above, in Richard II's reign the Portuguese connection in all its aspects became very strong. In his reign and in the early fifteenth century there was certainly much coming and going at the royal, ambassadorial and aristocratic level, but the merchants were another important regular channel of communication; Englishmen in ports as well as those at court were more conversant with things Portuguese than ever before, and merchants and seamen were a more immediate and potent source of information for most people in the English towns and coastal areas. Those who consumed figs, raisins, Algarve wine, and who used kermes dye far inland might also be prompted to think of Portugal. More significantly, while military experiences and court connections began to fade, mercantile links remained.

In this branch of trade as in others, it was commercial not political circumstances which promoted stable trade and ultimately dictated the level of trade, but the political events of the last thirty years of the fourteenth century profoundly influenced Anglo-Portuguese commercial relations. It was not, however, so much the specific treaties of 1373 and 1386 as the general political situation which boosted trade in the 1370s and 1380s. The treaty of Windsor was a useful confirmation and consolidation of the commercial position. Its clause allowing merchants and others to come and go freely, provided they paid due customs, offered a stable framework of protection to which merchants could appeal if necessary, and Portuguese merchants constantly cited it in their pursuit of justice if things went wrong for them then and in the fifteenth century. However, it was the totality of the political events in England, Portugal, and Spain from 1369 which opened further opportunities for trade by removing Castilian competition. These political events encouraged the growth of Anglo-Portuguese connections, and with them the combination of commercial profitability and political warmth, which led the author of 1436 to say with conviction of the Portuguese, 'they bene oure frendes'.

Notes

[1] *The Libelle of Englyshe Polycye*, ed. Sir George Warner (Oxford, 1923), l, 130.

[2] *Sailing Directions for the Circumnavigation of England and for a Voyage to the Straits of Gibraltar*, ed. J. Gairdner (Hakluyt Society, 1889), reprinted D. Waters, *The Rutters of the Sea* (New Haven and London, 1967), pp. 181–95.

[3] L. Gilliodts van Severen, *Cartulaire de l'Ancienne Etaple de Bruges* (2 vols, Bruges, 1903–6), I, no. 14.

[4] *Calendar of London Letter Books preserved among the Archives of the City of London, 1275–1498*, ed. R.R. Sharpe (11 vols, 1899–1912), *Letter Book 'B'*, p. 206; all the merchants dealing in the goods appear to be from northern Spain, not Portugal.

[5] PRO, E122/15/1.

[6] For fifteenth-century developments, see W.R. Childs, 'Anglo-Portuguese trade in the fifteenth century', *Transactions of the Royal Historical Society*, 6th series, vol. 2 (1992), 195–219.

[7] *Rotuli Litterarum Patentium (RLP), 1201–16*, ed. T.D. Hardy (1835), pp. 20b, 44a.

[8] Ibid., p. 87; *Rotuli Litterarum Clausarum (RLC), 1204–24*, ed. T.D. Hardy (1833), p. 419.

[9] *Patent Rolls, 1225–32*, pp. 42–3, 53. There are 103 names altogether, but some 25 appear on both lists. Whether they are the same men is unclear.

[10] The Portuguese ship, the *Cardinale*, which was seized by the English in 1225, had a complement of thirty merchants and crew (*RLC, 1224–7*, ed. T.D. Hardy, 1844, pp. 63, 66, 69, 84, 89, 92, 116, 119), but two safe-conducts for Galicians in 1296 were for smaller groups of fourteen and eighteen, including all the crews by name, *CPR, 1292–1301*, p. 203.

[11] PRO, E122/15/1.

[12] *CPR, 1232–47*, pp. 359, 360, 368, 369.

[13] *CR, 1247–51*, pp. 532, 552–5; *CPR, 1247–58*, pp. 613, 650; *CR, 1256–9*, p. 255; *CLibR, 1251–60*, pp. 168, 498.

14 V.M. Shillington and A.B. Wallis Chapman, *The Commercial Relations of England and Portugal* (1907), p. 30; A. Oliviera Marques, 'Notas para a história da feitoria portuguesa', *Studi in Onore di Armando Fanfani*, II (Milan, 1962), 449.

15 *CCR, 1288–96*, p. 283; *CPR, 1292–1301*, pp. 16, 34, 69, 519.

16 *CPR, 1301–7*, p. 210; ibid., *1307–13*, pp. 88, 186, 223–4, 274; *CCR, 1330–3*, pp. 153, 308.

17 A.H. Oliviera Marques, *Historia de Portugal* (2 vols, Lisbon, 1978), I, 133.

18 *Treaty Rolls, 1234–1325*, p. 447; *CPR, 1292–1301*, pp. 234, 482; *CCR, 1296–1302*, p. 139.

19 *CPR, 1292–1301*, p. 544.

20 *CPR, 1307–14*, pp. 106, 138; *CCR, 1323–7*, pp. 496, 556. By this time Edward had opened negotiations for a Spanish marriage for the future Edward III, but was in no position to do anything, since his son was with Queen Isabella in France and refusing to return to England while the Despensers remained at court.

21 *CPR, 1307–14*, p. 252; ibid., *1313–17*, pp. 67, 142; ibid., *1317–21*, pp. 169, 296, 403, 538, 546, 604, 609; *CCR, 1318–23*, p. 410; *CPR, 1334–8*, p. 403; *CCR, 1337–9*, p. 130. The case of the ship wrecked off Padstow dragged on until 1336, *CPR, 1321–4*, pp. 315, 380; *CPR, 1334–8*, p. 298.

22 *CPR, 1307–14*, p. 375; ibid., *1338–40*, p. 1.

23 *Letter Books 'A'–'D'*, *passim*; London Record Office, Recognizance Rolls I–X, *passim*. For Garcia, see Roll V, m. 2. For Spanish activity, see W.R. Childs, *Anglo-Castilian Trade in the later Middle Ages* (Manchester, 1978), pp. 11ff.

24 PRO, E101/78/3a, 4, 4a, 5, 8, 9, 10a, 11–14, 16, 18, 19; 79/1, 2, 3, 5, 6.

25 PRO, E122, for all dates between 1303–40, *passim*. No records were kept when the tax was suspended during the period of the Ordinances between 1311 and 1322.

26 Bristol saw at least three with wine in 1347–8: PRO, E101/79/19.

27 PRO, E101/79/3, 6, 8, 10, 12, 15, 19, 24; 80/1, 3–7, 9, 11–19.

28 PRO, E101/173/4, 182/2.

29 *CPR, 1350–4*, pp. 311, 487; *Foedera*, ed. T. Rymer (10 vols, The Hague, 1739–45), III, i, 264.

30 *CCR, 1349–54*, p. 491; ibid., *1364–8*, p. 255.

31 For the drop in trade, see Childs, *Anglo-Castilian Trade*, pp. 33, 40–3.

32 Carus-Wilson, *Overseas Trade of Bristol*, nos 23–6; F. Lopes, *The English in Portugal 1367–87*, eds D.W. Lomax and R.J. Oakley (Warminster, 1988), pp. 73, 81.

33 *CCR, 1374–7*, pp. 8, 41.

34 *CCR, 1374–7*, pp. 3, 8, 12, 27, 41; *CPR, 1370–4*, p. 430; Shillington, *Commercial Relations*, app. I, no. 6 (PRO, C76, 48 Ed. III m. 19).

35 *CCR, 1377–81*, p. 268.

36 P.E. Russell, *The English Intervention in Spain and Portugal in the time of Edward III and Richard II* (Oxford, 1955), pp. 370, 537 n. 3; for fifteenth-century arrests, see *CCR, 1399–1402*, p. 871; ibid., *1402–5*, pp. 196, 236, 242, 317; *CPR, 1408–13*, p. 234.

37 PRO, E101/80/20, 22, 23, 25.

38 PRO, E122/137/19; 138/3, 8, 10, 11, 16, 20, 21, 22, 24, 25. There were also at least five ships arrested in Southampton in 1374, see above note 34.

39 Russell, *Intervention*, pp. 367–8.

40 PRO, E122/71/4, 8, 9, 13, 16.

[41] Accounts survive for ten full years and two part-years, with destinations given: 1376–7, 1377–8, 1378–9, 1379–80, 1380–1, 1381–2, 1382–3, part 1386–7, 1390–1, part 1391–2, 1398–9, 1399–1400; two full years and three part-years without destinations: part 1393–4, 1394–5, 1395–6, part 1396–7, part 1398. PRO, E122/15/8; 16/2–6, 8–24, 26–35; 17/1; 40/12, 17; 181/23; 212/12.

[42] PRO, E122 *passim*; see also *CCR, 1377–81*, p. 22; E.M. Carus-Wilson, *The Overseas Trade of Bristol in the Later Middle Ages* (1933), nos 17, 18.

[43] *CCR, 1377–81*, p. 24; Lopes, *English in Portugal*, eds Lomax and Oakley, p. 169 and n. 1.

[44] For comment on the difficulty of separating Spanish and Portuguese trade at this time, see Childs, *Anglo-Castilian Trade*, p. 85.

[45] PRO, E159/166, Recorda, Hilary and Easter, Somerset.

[46] Shillington, *Commercial Relations*, app. I, no. 7.

[47] PRO, E122/137/19; 139/4.

[48] *CPR, 1370–4*, p. 393; *Cal. Misc. Inq., 1348–77*, no. 900; *CCR, 1374–7*, p. 8; *CCR, 1377–81*, pp. 296, 317, 396, 399; *CPR, 1381–5*, p. 564; *CCR, 1381–5*, pp. 63, 549, 552; *CPR, 1388–92*, p. 27.

[49] *Letter Book 'G'*, p. 209; *Letter Book 'H'*, p. 175; *Black Book of the Admiralty*, ed. Sir T. Twiss, I (Rolls Series, 1871), 139–43.

[50] *CPR, 1367–70*, p. 339; *CCR, 1374–7*, pp. 13, 41; *CCR, 1385–9*, p. 228.

[51] PRO, E122/126/17; 138/16.

[52] PRO, E122/71/13.

[53] *CCR, 1385–9*, p. 368; *CCR, 1392–6*, p. 324.

[54] *CCR, 1381–5*, pp. 354–5; *CCR, 1381–5*, pp. 358, 367; *CCR, 1385–9*, pp. 31, 204, 205; ibid., *1389–92*, pp. 424, 427.

[55] *CCR, 1381–5*, p. 167; *CCR, 1385–9*, pp. 28, 61–2, 166, 175.

[56] *CCR, 1377–81*, pp. 22, 411; *CPR, 1381–5*, p. 348; Carus-Wilson, *Overseas Trade of Bristol*, no. 17.

[57] *CCR, 1364–8*, pp. 322, 323, 368; *CCR, 1374–7*, p. 13; *Rot. Parl.*, III, 86a.

[58] H. Livermore, 'The "Privileges of an Englishman in the kingdoms and dominions of Portugal"', *Atlante*, II (1954), 65–6.

[59] PRO, E122 *passim*; E101 (butlers' accounts), *passim*.

[60] Shillington, *Commercial Relations*, pp. 53–4; her analyses of the accounts on p. 54 n. 1 need minor amendments.

[61] For further developments in the fifteenth century, see Childs, 'Anglo-Portuguese Trade', pp. 195–219.

[62] For an assessment of Philippa's role, see Russell, *Intervention*, pp. 541–8.

[63] F. Devon (ed.), *Issues of the Exchequer* (1837), p. 288.

[64] *Gregory's Chronicle*, p. 159; Sir N.H. Nicolas (ed.), *Proceedings and Ordinances of the Privy Council of England, 10 Richard II–33 Henry VIII* (3 vols, 1834–7), III, 178, 180.

[65] *Foedera*, IV, iv, 140.

[66] *Gregory's Chronicle*, p. 165.

[67] The English government helped provide for her expenses as she passed through; Nicolas, *Privy Council*, IV, 9.

[68] *Foedera*, V, ii, 30, 39.

[69] PRO, SC8/4227.

[70] *Gregory's Chronicle*, p. 122; *Foedera*, V, i, 146, 147. I am grateful to Professor A. Goodman for providing me with a copy of Carlos Guilherme Riley, 'Da origem inglesa dos Almadas: genealogia de uma ficção linhagística', *Arquipélago, Revista da Universidade dos Açores*, Série História, XI (1989), pp. 153–69.

[71] A.B. Emden, *A Biographical Register of the University of Oxford to 1500, s.n.* (1957–9); idem, *A Biographical Register of the University of Cambridge to 1500, s.n.* (1963); idem, *A Survey of Dominicans in England* (Rome, 1967); *CCR, 1369–74*, p. 517.

[72] Russell, *Intervention*, p. 543; idem, 'Robert Payne and Juan de Cuenca, translators of Gower's *Confessio Amantis*', *Medium Aevum*, 30 (1961), pp. 26–32.

[73] W. Ullmann (ed.), *Liber Regie Capelle* (Henry Bradshaw Society, XCII, 1961), pp. 10ff.

[74] E. Adam (ed.), *Torrent of Portugal* (EETS, extra series, 5, 1887), pp. xxi–xxxi.

3

NARRATIVE SOURCES FOR THE REIGN OF RICHARD II

G.H. Martin

s G.O. Sayles remarked in 1979, 'One day the history of Richard II's reign will be written from the records.'[1] No doubt it will be, but there is still a good deal of material to assimilate. The very intensity of the work entails its own problems. We have only to think of Dr Given-Wilson's work on the royal household[2] to remind ourselves both of the richness and intricacy of the archives that have survived, and of the ingenuity with which they can be used.

There are also the narrative sources to consider. They have, in the nature of things, been under scrutiny for a much longer time than the records. Even in an uncertain world we can assume that the clerks of the medieval chancery and the exchequer, whatsoever their other apprehensions, wrote without thought of T.F. Tout at their shoulders. Chroniclers, on the other hand, even if they never communed with a colleague like Bishop Stubbs, wrote for a contemporary audience, and had intimations of posterity. Before the later nineteenth century, medieval English history was written almost exclusively from such works, and as Sayles ruefully attested, their influence is not yet spent. Nor should we wish things otherwise. Medieval chronicles may have their shortcomings, but it will be some time before we can be sure that our own work will wear as well. A century ago it may have seemed that there was little more to be extracted from them, and that the future lay in exploiting archival sources. It is true that no one has since surpassed the masterly knowledge of chronicles which Stubbs displayed in the *Constitutional History*.[3] It is also true that the calendars of the chancery rolls which Henry Maxwell Lyte began to publish from the Public Record Office in 1894, thus opening those records to systematic use in any library, transformed the study of the Middle Ages in England.[4]

However, all historical investigations are interconnected. The narrative sources of Richard II's reign still hold their place, and their interest has been

enlarged rather than diminished by the widening scope of archival work. The
past 100 years have, accordingly, seen some discoveries, some advances in
editorial techniques, and some new editions of major texts. As with the archival
sources, there is still much work to be done, and the best guide to that lies in the
lineaments of what has already been accomplished.

By the last decade of the nineteenth century, the editions of historical texts
commissioned for the Rolls Series extended to 100 titles and some 240
volumes.[5] The series, issued on the authority of the Master of the Rolls, the
senior chancery judge who was the titular keeper of the public records, had
replaced most of, though not all, the published editions of chronicles which had
supported the earlier phases of English medieval scholarship. Those displaced
were by no means a ragged army, but certainly a variegated and sometimes
motley force. So, for that matter, were the constituents of the Rolls Series itself.
After all, published editions of chronicles extended back to the earliest days of
printing in England, when they appealed to Caxton and his successors precisely
because they were, with romances, a well-established and popular kind of
literature, with an assured sale.[6]

In the intervening age, the development of critical techniques benefited the
editing of texts, although the energies of historians and antiquaries were
directed to some strange ends, particularly during the sixteenth century.[7]
However, the dissemination of printed texts was at the worst a safeguard against
the loss of manuscripts, and there are, though their defects are obvious enough,
also positive merits to be discerned in such editions as those undertaken by
Archbishop Parker and Sir Henry Savile.[8] In the seventeenth century, when the
study of both the county community and the monastic orders was transformed
by Dugdale and his associates, the editorial work of Sir Roger Twysden stands
out as a further reminder of the intellectual vigour and enterprise of the age.[9]
Historiæ Anglicanæ Scriptores Decem was a product of Twysden's political
disillusionment, and probably on every count a better use of his time and talents
than contending with his Roundhead neighbours in Kent.[10] He chose his
manuscripts, with the help of John Selden, from some nine repositories and
private collections, and produced coherent and well-considered texts.[11]

In the early eighteenth century, Thomas Hearne used some of the material
which Twysden had collected for a second volume of chronicles, and Hearne

was not an easy man to please. He has since been criticized himself, though mainly for the want of an historical sense that was not an accomplishment of his age. However, none of his editorial work was otiose, and his perception of the ways in which manuscripts were interrelated, and his care in constructing a coherent text, mark him out as an editor in his time.[12] After Hearne, historical studies turned for the rest of the century on the one hand to local antiquities and, on the other, to editing archival texts,[13] though the eccentric and tireless John Pinkerton entertained a scheme for a series of English Monkish Chronicles, of which Gibbon approved.[14]

Pinkerton's project was taken up in several forms during the nineteenth century. In 1799 Charles Abbot, later Speaker, proposed a parliamentary committee on the ancient records of the Crown. The committee reported in 1800,[15] and was followed by a series of six Royal Commissions on the Public Records (1800–37) to consider the safe-keeping and publication of what was recognized as an archive of the highest historical interest.[16] The commissioners' reports included experimental facsimiles of records, and they expanded their work to a wide view of historical evidence. In 1821 they were persuaded by Henry Petrie, who was then keeper of the records in the Tower of London, to support the compilation of an exhaustive *corpus historicum* of early English history. The scheme achieved only a single preliminary volume, which was left unfinished when Petrie died in 1842.[17] It was eventually published in 1848 by Thomas Duffus Hardy,[18] who like his brother William had been Petrie's pupil and apprentice in the Tower record office.

The most important outcome of the commissioners' long and much-criticized deliberations was not a programme of publication but the establishment of the Public Record Office in 1838.[19] There were, however, some significant publications in those same years, and from various hands. The most consistent were the work of the English Historical Society, an undertaking which produced an anonymous prospectus and plan in 1836,[20] and a creditable series of some fifteen titles, including Benjamin Williams's edition of the *Chronique de la Traïson et Mort de Richart Deux*,[21] between 1838 and 1856. The prospectus was probably the work of the redoubtable Joseph Stevenson, who became the society's general editor, and subsequently contributed four of its titles.[22]

The society's principles were irreproachable: its declared object was to 'print an accurate, uniform, and elegant edition of the most valuable English chronicles' from the earliest times to the Reformation, and 'a few additional volumes of lives of Saints, letters and state papers, historical poems, proceedings of councils and synods, papal bulls, and decretal epistles'.[23] In implementing that sweeping programme, it intended to limit the editors' introductory commentaries, and to deal by a system of cross-references with what was regarded as the chroniclers' plagiaristic and reprehensible habit of copying earlier chroniclers.[24] The prospectus was careful to disclaim any intention of slighting or encroaching upon Petrie's *corpus historicum*, which was then believed to be on the point of publication,[25] but the society's founders saw a gap in the historical literature of the day, and planned boldly to fill it. Their words suggest that their ambitions would soon have outrun their resources, but they too were overtaken by events.

When the Public Record Office was established in 1838, it was committed, to T.D. Hardy's deep and galling disappointment, to Sir Francis Palgrave.[26] The consequent assembly, ordering, and listing of the historic records in the repository in Chancery Lane was a decisive event in British historical studies, and Palgrave managed the early stages in a masterly way, proving himself a natural archivist of exceptional ability. When Hardy eventually succeeded him in 1861, he continued the main lines of Palgrave's work, but at the same time he sought as far as he could to dissociate himself from Palgrave's example. In particular, he devoted his energy to the publication of historical texts, a matter which Palgrave viewed as secondary to the care of the records.

Hardy had already played a substantial role in launching the Rolls Series,[27] and as though that were not enough he was also influential in establishing in 1869 the Royal Commission on Historical Manuscripts, of which he was one of the original commissioners. The commission, which has made a powerful contribution to historical studies, was confined by its warrant to records other than the public records. Hardy was a conscientious director of the Public Record Office, but Palgrave's shade never ceased to haunt him there, and it seems that he chose to see his role primarily as that of a scholar and editor.

The Rolls Series, officially styled *Chronicles and Memorials of Great Britain and Ireland during the Middle Ages*, represents a remarkable achievement. It was, as we have seen, not the only nor the first venture of its kind, but it was by far the largest and most imposing. Its constituents are principally but not exclusively chronicles, and they include almost every Latin narrative text of consequence for the history of England from the twelfth century onwards.

The enterprise was subject, however, to various influences and restrictions. The last word on the choice of editors and texts remained with Lord Romilly, the Master of the Rolls, though Hardy's well-informed opinions evidently weighed with him.[28] Both men were subject to the Treasury, which had accepted the original proposal quite readily, but thereafter was more concerned with means than with ends. It was agreed that the works chosen were to be edited critically, in the best text that could be established. The introductions were to assess the historical significance of the text, and to say what was known of the author's life, but the editorial apparatus was to be strictly confined to illustrating variant readings. A coloured facsimile of a specimen page, provided as a frontispiece, was an enterprising feature of the series.

Everything turned, as it was bound to do, upon the quality of the editors. William Stubbs, who was rejected three times as a presumptuous interloper before he was entrusted with the *Chronicles and Memorials of Richard I* in 1863, produced work that was a model of its kind. Others, recruited more readily and on a variety of recommendations, proved disappointing, and on occasions expensively incompetent.[29] The proportion of serious failures among the 100 volumes published in the first fifteen years was quite small, but the disappointments naturally bulked larger as the impetus of the work declined.

If, in retrospect, the series gives an impression of amateurishness it is because it was literally and unavoidably dependent on amateurs: the venture was beset by a simple want of scholarly resources. The financial provision was comparatively generous, and was certainly carefully managed. The problem was that there was as yet in England nowhere outside the Record Office and the major libraries where editors could be trained in historical as distinct from literary techniques. The great luminaries of the age – men such as Francis Madden and Stubbs – had supplemented the critical skills of classical scholarship with a wide experience of handling medieval manuscripts. In all the essentials of their business they were self-taught. The century was almost over before there were university courses which could supplement the light of nature in those of more ordinary talents and opportunities.[30] By that time, however, there was a new deputy keeper in the Public Record Office. Henry Maxwell Lyte, who brought the Rolls Series to an end, turned his own and his colleagues' editorial energies to publishing guides and calendars to the records. In doing so, he made the Office not merely a great repository, but also itself a notable centre of scholarship.[31]

It is often easier now to see the defects than the merits of the Rolls Series, but in its time it made an impressive body of medieval material available for study, and its influence has lasted well into our own time. Its principal strength has probably been that, as its promoters hoped and intended, it established a critical mass of scholarly material, a series of works broadly uniform and readily available to those who wished to study them. Its literal replacement would certainly be no light matter, and is now probably beyond us, despite our many advantages. In the meantime, we can acknowledge that while there have been substantial advances in the critical study of chronicles during our own century, they have been made as much with the aid of the Rolls Series as at its expense.

The major chronicles of the later fourteenth century were quite well served by the time that the Rolls Series came to an end. There have since been some significant revisions, but the only arresting addition to their number has been the Anonimalle chronicle.[32] The Rolls Series provided texts of the *Polychronicon* and its principal continuations, and of the various recensions of the St Albans chronicles. Edward Maunde Thompson, who contributed several competent titles to the Rolls Series, also edited Adam of Usk's chronicle for the Royal Society for Literature.[33]

The least satisfactory of the new texts was probably J.R. Lumby's edition of Knighton's chronicle, both volumes of which ran into raking fire in the *English Historical Review*,[34] and confirmed Maxwell Lyte's opinion that the Rolls Series had outlived its usefulness. Lumby, who had completed the text of the *Polychronicon* in succession to Churchill Babington, the naturalist, perpetuated W.S. Shirley's notion that the final part of Knighton was a continuation by another hand. It is not clear that he himself believed it, but his nerve had been broken by his unhappy experience with the first volume, and he was entirely out of sympathy with his author.[35]

Nevertheless, it was possible by the beginning of the twentieth century to consider the historical output of the later English Middle Ages as a whole. When Charles Gross published *The Sources and Literature of English History*,[36] he included a *catalogue raisonnée* of chronicles and royal lives which was itself a scholarly landmark, and which is still worth consulting.[37] The later chronicles were mainly a product of the monastic houses, and although there may have been some falling-off in quality in the fourteenth century, they make up a substantial part of Gross's list.[38] The survey showed that while the quality of individual editions varied a good deal, the manuscript traditions of the texts had generally been well established, and that at a time when the detailed evaluation of medieval codices was still in its infancy in England.[39]

There were, broadly, three things which remained to be done if twentieth-century historians were to match the exertions of the Victorians. We have made some progress with them, but they offer us some challenges still. The first was to raise the standard of all the published texts of chronicles to, and where possible above, the level of the best work in the Rolls Series. That work is in hand, and has produced some notable results in the accumulated volumes of Nelson's Medieval Texts and their successors, the Oxford Medieval Texts. In the process, new standards have naturally emerged, but there is a continuity in the work of which all editors are gratefully aware.

The second task, more obvious to the user, potentially more dramatically rewarding, but dependent to a large degree on chance, was to discover, or occasionally to rediscover, and publish other and previously unknown texts. The most remarkable example of that kind is the Anonimalle chronicle, a work of the highest interest, and perhaps the most reassuring dividend of scholarly vigilance in modern studies.[40] Nevertheless, the odds seem even longer against the existence of such prizes than they are against their discovery.

The third task, as exacting and open-ended as either of the others, is largely dependent on them. It is to consider the interrelationship of texts, and through them the nature of historical writing in the later Middle Ages. The nineteenth century was not altogether happy with chronicles. The tradition of classical letters distinguished them, as medieval writers themselves were apt to do, from history, which was elevated by a moral purpose and a flourish of literary style.[41] Chronicles could be seen as an intellectual advance upon mere annals, but that merit was vitiated in Victorian eyes by the established scribal practice of copying and incorporating other texts, which argued a weakness of will when it was acknowledged, and an insolent depravity when it was not.[42]

Nevertheless, the availability of printed texts revealed patterns. The Rolls Series, having established the useful convention of printing derived material in a smaller type, made the extent and nature of borrowings plain, and its editors struggled with more or less success to convey information in face of the prohibition of critical notes that were not exclusively concerned with establishing the text.[43] The outstanding feature of the fourteenth-century chronicles was the success of Ralph Higden's *Polychronicon* as an exemplar, and the proliferation of its continuations. At the same time, there appeared to be a continuous tradition of historical writing at St Albans, though it evidently entailed much copying, and some cautious emendation of texts for political reasons. With the idiosyncrasies of medieval Latin also in the scale, chronicle-writing might be regarded as a deplorable example to the young.

Subsequent reflection has softened those and other morose apprehensions. Medieval Latinity is entitled to be judged on its own terms, but those who scouted it in the nineteenth century would surely have regarded it more kindly if they had seen what can pass for literacy in the twentieth. The study of early printed books has underlined the difficulty of multiplying manuscript texts, and has encouraged us to think more productively of the attitudes and assumptions of those who read and wrote under those conditions.[44] Such considerations are important whether we study chronicles for their own sake or for the matter which they retail.

There is in fact no hard line between the work of nineteenth- and twentieth-century scholars in that regard. The revision of the older editions is work common to both, and James Tait's version of John of Reading and the anonymous Canterbury chronicle would have been a credit to either century.[45] Tait was a scholar with a singularly felicitous touch, whose interests ranged widely from Domesday Book through a variety of topographical and local studies and the critical edition of texts. In general, the Manchester school of history is associated with T.F. Tout, and the succession of administrative history to the constitutional interests of the nineteenth century, but it was a much-prized pupil of Tait's, V.H. Galbraith, who did most for the study of both chronicles and Domesday.

Galbraith's great contributions were to identify and edit the Anonimalle chronicle, a valuable addition to our *corpus* of texts, and to demonstrate the coherence of Thomas Walsingham's work at St Albans.[46] On the one hand, he effectively dismantled the St Albans school as a self-conscious succession of chroniclers writing in the house from generation to generation. On the other, he illustrated both the variety and interest of the sources which a single text might contain, and the importance in the fourteenth century of the *Brut*, the overwhelmingly popular version of Geoffrey of Monmouth's *Historia Regum Britannie*, as a vehicle for recent and contemporary history.[47]

By the time Galbraith turned his attention to Domesday Book, around the beginning of the Second World War, he had transformed the study of the later medieval chronicle in England. The intensive activity which he had revealed at St Albans, where Walsingham produced a whole new history of England to continue and complement the work of Matthew Paris, made it necessary to reconsider the entire range of texts from that source published in the Rolls Series. It was also clear that historical writing in the monasteries was closely attuned to contemporary politics, and by no means an isolated or other-worldly activity.

One other service of Galbraith's was, in partnership with R.A.B. Mynors, to persuade Thomas Nelson & Sons to undertake the series known as Nelson's Medieval Classics, which since 1965 has continued as Oxford Medieval Texts. There is now an exemplary edition of the Westminster chronicle, by the late L.C. Hector and Barbara Harvey, to replace Vol. VIII of the Rolls Series *Polychronicon*, and work is in progress on other Ricardian titles.[48] Subsequently, in 1956, Galbraith himself swooped on Knighton's chronicle, and in a model essay demonstrated the unity of its authorship and text.[49]

Two minor texts were made available by May McKisack's edition of Favent's *Historia* in 1926, and a translation by A.H. Davis of William Thorne's chronicle of St Augustine's Abbey, which is otherwise only to be found in Twysden's *Decem Scriptores*.[50] Favent's work is an interesting polemical essay, carefully edited from the single late manuscript, but as a product of the brief period of the Appellants' ascendancy it is still in need of detailed examination to determine its sources. Thorne is closely focused on the affairs of St Augustine's, but the importance of the house, its enjoyment of royal patronage, and its concern with the looming figure of the archbishop, all give the narrative a wider interest. It is also distinguished by a view of Simon Burley as embittered as the animadversions of any other of his enemies.[51]

The principal constituents of the fourteenth-century chronicles have been discussed in a learned series of studies by John Taylor. The first, following upon his edition of the chronicles of Kirkstall Abbey,[52] was his monograph, *The Universal Chronicle of Ranulf Higden* (Oxford, 1966). The book examines the content and form of the *Polychronicon*, in the context of Higden's other writings and of fourteenth-century literary scholarship at large, together with an account of its influence on historical writing. The brief elucidation of the continuations which bear on Richard II's reign is a work of reference in itself.[53]

John Taylor's other studies, arising in part from his work on the *Polychronicon* and in part from a continuing interest in the Anonimalle chronicle,[54] have mainly been concerned with the French *Brut*. The tradition of the text is considerably more complicated than that of the *Polychronicon*, and has not as yet been determined in any detail, but the very substantial numbers of manuscripts surviving, and the regular appearance of echoes of the *Brut* in the chronicles of the later century, show that it is fundamentally important to any further consideration of the topic.[55]

The most striking single study of medieval English historiography now available ranges over the whole expanse of the Middle Ages. Dr Antonia Gransden's *Historical Writing in England*, which appeared in two volumes between 1974 and 1982,[56] has put in her debt all who work in that field. The work is characterized by its lucid discussion of interdependent texts, and a wide-ranging apparatus of reference. Its extensive commentary is well-sustained, and makes it a natural and rewarding starting-point for any future investigation of chronicles and chroniclers.

It is unlikely now that even the most minute research will uncover any major additional accounts of Richard II's reign. Indeed, it would be ungrateful to expect them: the Anonimalle chronicle was a remarkable bonus, and we have not yet unravelled its constituents. On the other hand, minute research is not only its own reward, but produces cumulative benefits. The patient investigation of surviving manuscripts, and particularly the reconstruction of medieval libraries, has produced some notable results, and we can look to learn much from it.[57] Such material, in its bearing upon the affiliation of texts and the hands and practices of scribes, can at any time throw new light on familiar sources.

The chronicles of Richard's reign can be variously ordered, but in particular they can be divided between those which were written before, and those which were written or revised after, his final catastrophe. The first category contains Knighton, Favent, and the Westminster and Anonimalle chronicles, together with the earlier part of the *Vita Ricardi*.[58] The second, in addition to the narratives of the deposition,[59] includes Walsingham's works, the continuation of the *Eulogium Historiarum*, and the interesting cluster of chronicles from Cistercian houses.[60] Adam of Usk's chronicle, one of the latest of the *Polychronicon* continuations, falls in both groups, for Usk seems to have begun his work in the midst of the crisis. He may have envisaged a substantial history of the new house of Lancaster, but although he continued to write in his last years, he ended his life remote from the places of power, and probably a disillusioned man. What he says is nevertheless interesting, and can be quite closely dated. He certainly produced a work with the stamp of some personal authority about it.[61]

Adam of Usk was a secular clerk, a more substantial figure than Favent, but like him a member of a professional class, the growth of which is a commonplace of the period. If we add to the tale the name of John Gower, esquire and citizen of London, whose *Confessio amantis* lies between political commentary, literature, and history,[62] the contribution of the laity is quite strong. It is, nevertheless, also remarkable to see how many products of religious houses there are, in both groups. The day of the monastic chronicler may have been far advanced by the end of the fourteenth century, but there was still a good deal of light in the sky.

The distinction between the two groups of sources is fundamentally important. Richard's deposition and death decisively affect the historic perspective of the reign. Even without the poignant contrast between the child who melted hearts at his coronation and the man left to die in prison because no one could trust his word, we are ourselves constantly mindful of the impending disaster, and look for its signs and portents. It is therefore particularly valuable to be able to see Richard as he appeared to his contemporaries while they were unaware of his ultimate fate.

Of the two chief sources in the first group, the Westminster chronicle, though not uncritical of the king's friends, comes from a house closely associated with the court, and an assured recipient of royal patronage. Both of its authors, before and after the year 1383, dwell upon Richard's generosity, his reverence for St Edward, and his devotions at the saint's shrine and other altars in the abbey church at times of perplexity and danger.[63] The king emerges as a model of orthodoxy, and essentially as a man of innate dignity, impetuous by nature but impressively patient in adversity.[64]

To Henry Knighton the king was a more remote, though not an entirely unfamiliar, figure. As a centre of Lancastrian power, Leicester normally saw the court through that medium and, with the daily comings and goings of the duke's officers, enjoyed a regular flow of news and intelligence, both mundane and alarming. We owe to Knighton a glimpse of one of the most piquant episodes in the drama of 1381, when the abbot of Leicester refused shelter to John of Gaunt's effects from Leicester castle. The keeper of the duke's wardrobe was anxious to save what he could from such destruction as had fallen upon the Savoy, and the abbot feared that to admit the carts would bring disaster upon his house. Knighton says much of Gaunt's mildness of temper, which was not a quality which everyone perceived in him. It must have been keenly tested upon his next visit to St Mary's of the Meadows.[65]

There is no doubt that for Knighton, Gaunt's splendour moderated that of the king, as in his time Henry of Grosmont, the first duke of Lancaster, had at least rivalled Edward III as an object of admiration in Leicester.[66] At the same time, the presence of the king on any occasion outweighed all else: Knighton like other chroniclers was proud to write 'as I heard him say'.[67] He described the crisis of 1386–8 and the proceedings of the Merciless Parliament as an apologist of the Appellants, but his strictures upon the king's friends, Richard's *auriculares* and *seductores*, were abated in his account of the court's passage through Leicester, when the light of the king's countenance evidently outshone the sins of his counsellors.[68]

Knighton describes Richard's resumption, or assertion, of power in 1389 in positive terms, and there is no trace of sympathy for the Londoners in his account of the king's dealings with the city in 1392.[69] Whilst the Westminster chronicler speaks of ministers and counsellors nursing resentment against the citizens, and Richard himself offended by their coolness over a loan,[70] Knighton simply sees the city in default, and the king displaying first firmness and then, at a price, clemency, in bringing them to book.

The picture of Richard that Knighton presents throughout is unambiguously one of a king, resolute and resourceful in 1381, eloquent, intelligent, and redoubtable as he grows into maturity. It was a representation probably convincing to most people down to 1396. Knighton apparently did not live to see respect growing into apprehension and alarm from that time.

Over the whole range of the chronicles, setting the *Brut* aside, the chief matter still to be determined is the precise sequence of Thomas Walsingham's revision of his work. Galbraith perceived that the St Albans school of historians was at the most a manifestation of Walsingham's editorship, and that Walsingham's major and minor chronicles represented many second thoughts as well as much primary exertion. Galbraith's hypothesis is still, and seems likely to remain, the best general array that the facts allow, but it is undoubtedly open to refinement, as George Stow has recently suggested.[71]

The detail of such editing in the scriptorium, the business of amending words and phrases, cancelling passages, and transposing quires, is minute but by no means trivial. Walsingham appears to have been influenced by at least three considerations. His own observation of Richard seems to have moved him from a sympathetic to a critical view of the young king. After 1394 the developing crisis would have had its own effect, but there may also have been then some shift of sympathy towards the house of Lancaster that preceded a more urgent desire to avoid giving offence to Gaunt and Bolingbroke.[72] A further complication is that St Albans was in dispute with Westminster during those years and perceived the king as Westminster's champion.[73] After the revolution, there was no doubt but that the chronicles should reflect the glories of the new dynasty. Sensibility may have gone so far as to reflect Henry V's compassion for Richard: it would not have been unnatural if it did.

Beyond the question of Walsingham's motives and opinions, and of those of the convent, so far as they might be distinguished, is that of the nature of chronicles themselves. *Hic labor*. History's moral purpose is (or should be) signalled by literary elegance. Annals are in the nature of memoranda, characteristically associated with chronological devices of a utilitarian kind.[74]

Chronicles are commonly regarded as annals which have struggled more or less successfully towards the status of history, and howsoever the authors regarded them, we are apt to judge them, and on the whole to accept them, as monographs on the then recent and recoverable past.

They were not, however, simply or even primarily academic monographs, and any prolonged consideration of them suggests that their political and journalistic content was high. The broad chronology of Walsingham's work speaks for itself: it would have been very remarkable if there had been no changes of allegiance and direction over so raucous a period. Yet both the Westminster chronicler and Knighton used extraneous texts which were derived from official documents, and Knighton seems, in particular, to have been in close touch with, and to have received documents from, the Appellants, no doubt through Derby.[75]

When such material is taken in conjunction with the newsletters which many chroniclers used,[76] the chronicle can be seen to be as much a means of informing and even diverting contemporaries as one of instructing posterity. Indeed, a chronicler might well seek and expect to do both. Chronicles were read in the houses which produced them, and no doubt in the presence of patrons and other distinguished visitors.[77] They must often have been read in drafts which were subsequently altered for one reason or another; what is unusual about Walsingham's work, apart from the size of the undertaking, is that we can watch it in progress.

To regard our narrative sources in that way is not to disparage them; indeed, if anything it increases their historical interest. We might, however, as a consequence, be encouraged to scrutinize other material in the same fashion, to the advantage of our critical techniques. One relatively neglected text from Richard's reign is the *Chronique de la Traïson et Mort*, which is now perceived, quite correctly, as a work of the imagination, derived in part from Creton, and therefore of no value as a corroborative source.[78] Creton himself, who wrote with a propagandist fervour in Richard's cause, is esteemed as a witness who had authentic material of his own, and can therefore take his place with the historians – or chroniclers. Yet the author of the *Traïson* also wrote to convince, and we can at least assume that he intended his material to carry conviction, and in so assuming, find a means of enlarging our perceptions of the time.

To recruit the *Traïson* to that end is to concern ourselves with what people thought and supposed as well as with what they did. That path has its dangers, though the views that it affords may be rewarding. It leads us back ultimately to the writings of Geoffrey of Monmouth, but there at least we shall also find our chroniclers, and in a receptive mood. The fact is that the history of the reign of Richard II, like others, will eventually have to be written not so much from the records, nor yet from the narrative sources, nor from some simple amalgam of the two, but from all the evidence that the times and time have afforded us.

Notes

[1] See G.O. Sayles, 'Richard II in 1381 and 1399', *EHR*, XCIV (1979), pp. 820–9, at p. 820. Sayles had an Hegelian history in mind. In the sublunary world we are now fortunate to have Dr Nigel Saul's *Richard II* (New Haven and London, 1997).

[2] C. Given-Wilson, *The Royal Household and the King's Affinity: Service, Politics, and Finance in England, 1360–1413* (New Haven and London, 1986).

[3] W. Stubbs, *Constitutional History of England* (3 vols, Oxford, 1873–8). There is, as it happens, a remarkable display of expertise in the life of Richard II which James Tait contributed to the *Dictionary of National Biography* in 1896, a study which has lost none of its lucidity over a century.

[4] On Maxwell Lyte's publishing policy, see further J.B. Post, 'Public Record Office publication: past performance and future prospects', in *The Records of the Nation: The Public Record Office 1838–1988, The British Record Society, 1888–1988*, eds G.H. Martin and P. Spufford (Woodbridge, 1990), pp. 89–99, at p. 93. Beyond the competence with which the contents of the rolls were summarized, it was particularly the indexes which put the series into the forefront of English historical studies.

[5] For a brief account of the undertaking, see M.D. Knowles, 'Great historical enterprises: IV. The Rolls Series', *TRHS*, 5th series, XI (1961), pp. 137–59.

[6] See, for example, *STC* 13438–9 (Trevisa/Higden), and 9991–6 (St Albans). See further H.S. Bennett, *English Books and Readers, being a History of the Book Trade, 1475–1557* (2nd edn, Cambridge, 1969).

[7] The best account of the post-medieval life of 'The British History', with much other learning lightly worn, is in T.D. Kendrick's *British Antiquity* (London, 1950).

[8] See, for example, the remarks of May McKisack in *Medieval History in the Tudor Age* (Oxford, 1971), pp. 41–2 (on the *Historia Anglorum*, 1574), and 64–5 (on Savile's *Scriptores post Bedam*, 1596). Parker's *Asser* may fall short of critical perfection, but it is literally better than nothing, which is what we might well have had. In the same way, Savile preserved the text of Æthelweard, and an additional text of Ingulph, from MSS. now lost.

[9] On historical scholarship in the early modern period, see D.C. Douglas, *English Scholars, 1660–1730* (2nd edn, London, 1951).

[10] *Historiae Anglicanae Scriptores Decem*, ed. R. Twysden (London, 1652). See further J.R. Twysden and C.H.D. Ward, *The Family of Twysden and Twisden* (London, 1939), pp. 196–200; and F.W. Jessup, *Sir Roger Twysden, 1597–1672* (London, 1965), pp. 44–68.

[11] Selden contributed a preface to the book, and William Somner a glossary (*Scriptores Decem*, pp. i–xlviii, and 'Glossarium', ibid., pp. 1–82). Twysden acknowledges his debt to his amanuensis, Ralph Jennynge, but he transcribed several texts himself, and he certainly handled the manuscripts. He relied on Jennynge particularly to work in Cambridge, and as a copyist as much as an editor. See also D.C. Douglas, *English Scholars*, p. 167.

[12] On Hearne's complex character and wide learning, see D.C. Douglas, *English Scholars*, pp. 178–94. All other considerations aside, we owe our knowledge of the *Vita Edwardi II* to Hearne's transcript and edition of 1730: see *Chronicles of the reigns of Edward I and Edward II*, ed. W. Stubbs, II (1883), pp. xxxi–xxxix.

[13] There is a valuable review of English record-editing in M.M. Condon and E.M. Hallam, 'Government printing of the public records in the eighteenth century', *Journal of the Society of Archivists*, VII (1982–5), pp. 348–88.

[14] See *DNB, s.n.* Pinkerton.

[15] *Reports from the Select Committee appointed to inquire into the state of the Public Records of the Kingdom, etc.* (Reports from Committees of the House of Commons, XV, 1803).

[16] The commissions produced two reports with appendices published and republished between 1807 and 1819 (Parliamentary Papers, 1819, XX). Their proceedings were not published between 1819 and 1831. For what followed, see *Proceedings of His Majesty's Commissioners on the Public Records of the Kingdom*, ed. C.P. Cooper (London, 1833); *General Report to the King in Council from the Commissioners on the Public Records (1831–7)* (Parliamentary Papers, 1837, XXXIV); and *Return of all the Record Publications relating to England and Wales published by the late Record and State-Paper Commissioners, or under the Master of the Rolls, up to 1866* (Parliamentary Papers, 1867–8, LV).

[17] In 1835 the commissioners had ordered work on the project to cease, as a result of a misunderstanding with Petrie: *DNB, s.n.* Petrie.

[18] *Monumenta Historica Britannica, or Materials for the History of Great Britain from the Earliest Period to the Norman Conquest*, eds H. Petrie and J. Sharpe (London, 1848).

[19] See further J.D. Cantwell, *The Public Record Office, 1838–1958* (London, 1991), pp. 1–12.

[20] The prospectus is entitled *Plan of the English Historical Society* (London, 1836, 20pp.). It seems simultaneously or subsequently to have been issued in a shortened version under the title *General Introduction* (London, 1836, xxi pp.), which may have been intended to preface all volumes, though I have not yet come across an instance of it being so used. The *Plan* refers to Joseph Stevenson's appointment as general editor, but has nothing to say about the constitution of the society. There is a list of 116 members, including H.O. Coxe and Anthony Panizzi, together with the names of the officers and council of the society, prefixed to Thomas Hog's *Triveti Annales* of 1845.

[21] *Chronique de la Traïson et Mort de Richart Deux Roy Dengleterre* (London, 1846). See also below, pp. 64–5.

[22] On Stevenson, see further *DNB*; and M.D. Knowles, 'The Rolls Series', pp. 140–1.

[23] *Plan*, p. 2.

[24] The Rolls Series subsequently used a smaller type to distinguish such interpolated material. It is interesting that the society's prospectus refers (p. 5) to the fact that Knighton, whose work was not

proposed as one of the first titles, 'incorporates a large share of Hemingford [*sc.* Guisborough]', an observation which would have saved J.R. Lumby much grief if he had ever come upon it. See below, p. 56, n. 35.

25 Its publication had just been abandoned: see above, n. 17.

26 See J.D. Cantwell, *The Public Record Office*, pp. 13–22.

27 See M.D. Knowles, 'The Rolls Series', pp. 141–3.

28 Hardy's own principal and most striking contribution to the Rolls Series was *The Descriptive Catalogue of Materials relating to the History of Great Britain and Ireland (to 1327)* (3 vols in 4 parts, RS, XXVI, London, 1862–71), which was eventually seen through the press by William Hardy and C.T. Martin. The materials for the last volume, to 1485, are in the Public Record Office (PRO, 37/75–8).

29 Compare the several misadventures of Sir Henry Ellis, the Revd F.C. Hingeston, and Benjamin Thorpe, as sketched in Knowles, 'The Rolls Series', pp. 145–7.

30 Much of the same applies to the work of the Early English Text Society, with a more formidable output than the Rolls Series, mainly driven by the wayward energies of F.J. Furnivall, and with an even wider range of abilities among its editors. For an illuminating sketch of Furnivall, see K.M.E. Murray, *Caught in a Web of Words: James A.H. Murray and the Oxford English Dictionary* (New Haven and London, 1977), pp. 87–99.

31 See further G.H. Martin, 'The Public Records in 1988', in *The Records of the Nation*, eds G.H. Martin and P. Spufford (London, 1990), pp. 17–22, at pp. 20–1. The closure of the Rolls Series was accelerated by the misfortunes of J.R. Lumby's edition of Knighton's chronicle: see below, nn. 54, 55.

32 See below, p. 57.

33 See below, p. 61, n. 61.

34 *Chronicon Henrici Knighton uel Cnitthon, Monachi Leycestrensis*, ed. J.R. Lumby (RS, XCII, London, 1889–95). The two volumes were denounced one after the other in reviews by R.L. Poole (*EHR*, VI, 1891, pp. 172–3) and James Tait (ibid., XI, 1896, pp. 568–9) respectively. See also below, n. 48.

35 Lumby was familiar with the *Polychronicon*, but did not discover that Knighton was also drawing on a copy of Guisborough's chronicle which he referred to as Leycestrensis (see above, n. 24). When R.L. Poole pointed out the error, Lumby turned to blame Knighton, whom he came to regard as a shifty and thoroughly unsatisfactory character. For a new edition, see below, n. 48.

36 C. Gross, *The Sources and Literature of English History from the Earliest Times to about 1485* (London, 1900).

37 The work, which provided a pattern for subsequent historical bibliographies in England, has been revised and augmented by Professor E.B. Graves as part of the Royal Historical Society's current programme: *A Bibliography of English History to 1485, based on The Sources and Literature of English History by Charles Gross* (Oxford, 1975).

38 See below, p. 61.

39 See, for example, R. Pfaff, *Montague Rhodes James* (London, 1980), pp. 172–208.

40 *The Anonimalle Chronicle, 1333–81*, ed. V.H. Galbraith (Manchester, 1927). The MS., now University of Leeds, Brotherton MS. 29, came in October 1920, at Sotheby's, under the eye of Robin Flower, who then described it to Galbraith as they sat in one of the Aerated Bread Company's tea-shops, 'near the British Museum'. An earlier section of the MS. is now in print as *The Anonimalle Chronicle, 1307–34*, eds W.R. Childs and J. Taylor (Yorkshire Archaeological Society Record Series, CXLVII, 1991).

[41] See below, n. 74.

[42] The English Historical Society's *Plan* (above, p. 53) refers to the industrious Walsingham as a plagiarist whose 'own' compositions would amount to only a handful of printed pages (op. cit., p. 8).

[43] See above, p. 55. The difference between E.M. Thompson's competent but austere *Chronica Adae Murimuth et Roberti de Avesbury* (RS, XCIII, London, 1889), and his richly informative annotation in the same year of *Chronicon Galfridi le Baker de Swynebroke* (Oxford, 1889) suggests that the Treasury could usefully have drawn a more flexible rule.

[44] There are some valuable observations on the concept of authorship in E.P. Goldschmidt's *Medieval Texts and their first appearance in print* (London, 1943), especially on pp. 89–99, but the most cogent study of its kind even now is H.J. Chaytor's *From Script to Print: an Introduction to Medieval Literature* (Cambridge, 1945).

[45] *Chronica Johannis de Reading et Anonymi Cantuariensis, 1346–67*, ed. J. Tait (Manchester, 1914).

[46] See above, n. 38; and *The St Albans Chronicle, 1406–20*, ed. V.H. Galbraith (Oxford, 1937). See also below, p. 63.

[47] For the *Brut*, see above, n. 7; F.W.D. Brie, *Geschichte und Quellen der mittelenglischen Prosachronik, The Brut of England' oder 'The Chronicles of England'* (Marburg, 1905); the revised list of MSS. in L.M. Matheson, 'The Middle English prose *Brut*', *Analytical and Enumerative Bibliography*, III (1979–80), pp. 254–66; and p. 60, below.

[48] *The Westminster Chronicle, 1381–94*, ed. L.C. Hector and B.F. Harvey (Oxford, 1982). *Knighton's Chronicle, 1337–96*, ed. G.H. Martin, was published in 1995. See also below, nn. 60, 61.

[49] V.H. Galbraith, 'The chronicle of Henry Knighton', in *Fritz Saxl, 1890–1948: A Volume of Memorial Essays from his Friends in England*, ed. D. Gordon (Edinburgh, 1957), pp. 136–48.

[50] *Historia . . . Mirabilis Parliamenti apud Westmonasterium AD Millesimo CCCLXXXVI . . . per Thomam Fauent clericum indictata*, ed. M. McKisack (Camden Miscellany, XIV, 1926); *William Thorne's Chronicle of St Augustine's Abbey, Canterbury*, ed. A.H. Davis (Oxford, 1934).

[51] *William Thorne's Chronicle*, pp. 650–4.

[52] *The Kirkstall Abbey Chronicles*, ed. J. Taylor (Thoresby Society, XLII, 1952).

[53] J. Taylor, *The Universal Chronicle*, pp. 124–33.

[54] See above, n. 40.

[55] See J. Taylor, 'The French prose *Brut*: popular history in fourteenth-century England', *England in the Fourteenth Century*, ed. W.M. Ormrod (Woodbridge, 1986), pp. 247–54; and J. Taylor, *English Historical Literature in the Fourteenth Century* (Oxford, 1987), pp. 110–32.

[56] A.G. Gransden, *Historical Writing in England*, I. *c. 550–c. 1307* (London, 1974); *Historical Writing in England*, II. *c. 1307 to the Early Sixteenth Century* (London, 1982).

[57] *Medieval Libraries of Great Britain: A List of Surviving Books*, ed. N.R. Ker; and *Medieval Libraries . . . Supplement to the Second Edition*, ed. A.G. Watson (Royal Historical Society Guides and Handbooks, III and XV, London, 1964–87). See further the Corpus of British Medieval Library Catalogues (5 vols, London, British Library/British Academy, 1990–, in progress).

[58] Thomas Hearne's *Historia Vitæ et Regni Ricardi Secundi Angliæ Regis* (Oxford, 1729) has now been superseded by G.B. Stow's *Historia Vitae et Regni Ricardi Secundi* (Philadelphia, 1977).

[59] That is to say, Jean Creton's 'Metrical history of the deposition of Richard II', ed. J. Webb, *Archaeologia*, XX (1824), 1–423, and *Chronique de la Traïson et Mort de Richart Deux Roy Dengleterre*, ed.

B. Williams (English Historical Society, London, 1846). See further J.J.N. Palmer, 'The authorship, date, and historical value of the French chronicles of the Lancastrian revolution', *BJRULM*, LXI (1978–9), pp. 145–81, 398–421. The whole crisis is now documented and reviewed in *Chronicles of the Revolution, 1397–1400: the Reign of Richard II*, ed. C. Given-Wilson (Manchester, 1993).

[60] See above, p. 60, n. 52. The continuation of the Eulogium is in vol. III of *Eulogium Historiarum sive Temporis*, ed. F.S. Haydon (RS, IX, London, 1858–63). A new edition is now in preparation for Oxford Medieval Texts.

[61] *Chronicon Adæ de Usk, 1377–1421*, ed. E.M. Thompson (Royal Society of Literature, 2nd edn, London, 1904). See further C. Given-Wilson, 'The dating and structure of the Chronicle of Adam of Usk', *Welsh Historical Review*, XVII, no. 4 (1995), pp. 520–33; and *The Chronicle of Adam of Usk, 1377–1421*, ed. C. Given-Wilson (Oxford Medieval Texts, 1997).

[62] *The English Works of John Gower*, ed. G.C. Macaulay (2 vols, Early English Text Society, Extra Series, LXXXI and LXXXII, I, 1–456; II, 1–480.

[63] See, for example, *Westminster Chronicle*, pp. 8–10 (1381); 206–8 (1387).

[64] *Westminster Chronicle*, p. 232.

[65] *Knighton's Chronicle*, pp. 228–30.

[66] It is an odd feature of Knighton's work that there is no detailed obituary of Duke Henry to match the threnody on Edward III (*Knighton's Chronicle*, p. 196), but the narrative is full of admiring references to his prowess, sang-froid, and nobility of spirit. See, for example, ibid., pp. 52, 114–18.

[67] Of Edward III: *Knighton's Chronicle*, pp. 188–90.

[68] Ibid., p. 400.

[69] Ibid., pp. 544–8.

[70] *Westminster Chronicle*, pp. 493–6, 499–500, 502–8. The Westminster account is, as might be expected, fuller and more circumstantial than Knighton's.

[71] G.B. Stow, 'Richard II in Thomas Walsingham's chronicles', *Speculum*, LIX (1984), pp. 68–102.

[72] See V.H. Galbraith, *The St Albans Chronicle*, pp. li, lxix.

[73] See G.B. Stow, 'Richard II in Thomas Walsingham's chronicles', pp. 83–4, 88.

[74] The literature is very extensive. There are succinct notes on the various genres in R.L. Poole, *Chronicles and Annals: a brief outline of their origin and growth* (Oxford, 1926), pp. 7–8; and D. Hay, *Annalists and Historians: Western Historiography from the VIIIth to the XVIIIth century* (London, 1977), pp. 3–7.

[75] See, for example, *Westminster Chronicle*, pp. xlvi–liv, and *Knighton's Chronicle*, pp. lxix–lxxii, 402–4.

[76] See further J. Taylor, *English Historical Literature in the Fourteenth Century* (Oxford, 1987), pp. 229–30.

[77] Henry III's interest in the work of Matthew Paris is well known, and Matthew wrote works explicitly for other members of the court: see, for example, A. Gransden, *Historical Writing*, I, pp. 357–60. See also *Knighton's Chronicle*, p. 238.

[78] See the analysis in J.J.N. Palmer, 'The French chronicles of the Lancastrian revolution', pp. 398–405.

4

RICHARD II, YORK, AND THE EVIDENCE OF THE KING'S ITINERARY[1]

Nigel Saul

Reconstructing the itinerary of a medieval king is no easy task for the historian. The sources for undertaking the exercise are relatively few, and those which there are raise difficult problems of interpretation. As Sir Henry Maxwell-Lyte pointed out, even as late as the mid-fourteenth century it is far from easy to gain a clear view of the king's movements.[2]

As yet there exists no complete itinerary for King Richard II for the whole of his reign, although a number of scholars have reconstructed the king's movements for certain relatively short periods. Tout, in his *Chapters in the Administrative History of Medieval England*, compiled an outline itinerary for Richard's movements in 1395–6 and for the period following the end of the Shrewsbury parliament in 1398.[3] More recently, Professor Tuck has charted the king's movements around the midlands in his 'gyration' of 1387.[4] Additionally, a little work has been done on the king's itinerary by scholars who have looked at particular aspects of the reign. In an influential paper on 'Richard II and York', John Harvey has pointed to the number of visits that Richard made to York in the 1390s. He has claimed that at the time of the transference of the courts to York in 1392 Richard 'stayed in that city for weeks on end – from early June to late November, with only occasional absences'; and he has gone on to argue that Richard 'revisited York for part of August 1393, and was there again in December 1395, when he kept Christmas at York'.[5] On the basis of the amount of time that the king spent at York, Harvey has argued that he saw the city as a possible alternative capital to London. Harvey's claim is one of considerable importance for a wider appreciation of Richard's kingship, and it needs to be more properly tested than it has been. The purpose of the present paper is to examine the evidence for the king's movements in the three or four years after 1392 to see if Richard's attachment to York was as deep as John Harvey believes that it was.

The source to which historians have most commonly resorted to compile royal itineraries is the dating clause in letters issued under the great seal. By the late fourteenth century, this clause generally followed the formula *Teste me ipso apud—, die—, anno regni nostri—*. The place and date recorded on the great seal letters were generally those in the equivalent clause in the originating warrant: that is to say, in the 1390s usually a ministerial or chamberlain's bill or a letter under the privy seal.[6] Thus, if letters patent under the great seal were place-dated at Westminster on 20 October 1392, it can be concluded that the bill or letter authorizing the issue of those letters was given at Westminster on 20 October 1392. For occasions when the keeper of the privy seal was in the king's company, the place-date clause offers a fairly secure way of tracing the king's itinerary, but by the late fourteenth century those times were relatively few. The privy seal office had moved out of court and was settling down in a secure home at Westminster. It was acquiring its own body of staff, and the keeper, now a great officer of state, was not always – indeed, perhaps, not often – with the king. It was for this reason that Richard II in the 1380s felt the need to adopt another seal, one that would be kept by a clerk who would always be in his company. This seal was known as the signet, and it was in active use in the first nine years of the reign.[7] During the three years from 1383, when it was regularly employed to move the great seal directly, it is possible to chart the king's movements in some detail. From 1386, however, when as a result of an order of Chancellor Arundel's the earlier procedures were reasserted, this is no longer the case.[8] A far higher proportion of letters was now place-dated at Westminster, where the privy seal office had settled; and at times when they are dated elsewhere it is often difficult to distinguish the king's movements from those of his officers. If an accurate picture of the king's itinerary is to be obtained, it is necessary to draw on evidence from other sources. Undoubtedly the most useful of these sources is the series of wardrobe books of the king's household. The *Dieta* sections of these – the summaries of daily living expenses – afford a precise day-by-day record of the movements of the kitchen departments of the household. It is fortunate, in view of the obvious importance of the source, that the best run of accounts for the reign comes from the three years from 1392, the period of greatest relevance to Harvey's argument. Secondly, and only slightly less valuable, is the evidence of the chronicle writers, who not uncommonly give information about the king's whereabouts at the major festivals of the year. Occasionally, as in the case of the Westminster writer, this information is supplemented by details of the king's whereabouts and movements at other times too. When the narrative evidence and the evidence of the wardrobe books is combined with that of the dating clauses it is possible to compile a fairly complete, and not altogether inaccurate, itinerary for the king. In the present paper, the main concern will be with the king's movements in the early to mid-1390s. It is appropriate to start with a review of the year 1392, the year when Richard's interest in York first manifested itself.

Richard's movements in the early part of 1392 are not well documented relative to the years which followed, but it is clear that his itinerary was confined entirely to southern England. There is evidence of his presence at the castles or manor houses of King's Langley, Leeds, Eltham and Windsor, and it is known that he attended a council at Westminster in February.[9] In the summer and autumn months, however, if the dating clause evidence is to be believed, he undertook two, perhaps as many as three, visits to the north. The first of these began in the spring. On 19 May his presence is attested at Stamford, where a week later a council was held which was widely reported in the chronicles.[10] From Stamford it is possible to trace his progress through Rockingham and Nottingham to York, where he stayed for ten days in mid-June.[11] On or around 15 June, it seems that he began to make a slow journey back to the south. He stayed for nearly a month at Nottingham, where another council was held, again reported by the chroniclers;[12] on 11 July his or his clerks' presence is recorded at Northampton, and a week later he is found at Windsor again.[13] From this time onwards there is only intermittent evidence of his movements in the narrative sources. If the evidence of the dating clauses is to be believed, however, he spent little more than a week at Windsor before setting out on another northern itinerary. Letters patent or close were dated at Stamford again on 29 and 30 July, at Nottingham for over a week from 2 August, and at either York or Beverley for the greater part of August and early September.[14] The journey back to the south of England began, according to the dating clause evidence, in the second week of September. On 11 September letters were dated at Doncaster, on the following day at Blyth and on the day after that at Nottingham.[15] At Nottingham there was a break in the journey for three or four days, but on the 17th the southward progress was resumed and on the 19th letters patent were attested at Woodstock.[16] At Woodstock, it appears, the king (or the clerks in his service) stayed for three weeks. In October, however, if the evidence of the dating clauses is again to be believed, there was a progress to the north for the third time in the year. The stages of the progress cannot on this occasion be traced in any detail, but on 22 October letters patent were dated at York, and it was from that city that they were dated until 25 November.[17] For the final six weeks of the year there is little evidence of the king's movements, but on 8 and 9 December letters were attested at King's Langley, and from the Westminster chronicle it is known that the king spent Christmas at Eltham.[18]

The impression of constant movement to which the evidence of the great seal instruments bear witness lends a touch of verisimilitude to this outline itinerary. However, it is hard to regard it other than sceptically when alongside it is set the evidence from other sources: for at least from July this evidence gives an entirely different picture. The differences begin in August. On 21 and 22 August, when the chancery enrolments say that the king was in Yorkshire, the Westminster chronicler says that he was in the south, at either Kennington or London.[19] There can be no questioning the Westminster writer's accuracy, for it was on these two days that the king attended the lavish festivities in the capital marking his reconciliation with the Londoners, of which the same writer and a number of his contemporaries offer detailed descriptions.[20] Two weeks later, on 5 September, a signet letter to the doge of Venice attests the king's presence at Woodstock, while the chancery enrolments have him at Beverley. There can be no doubting the accuracy of this source either, because the king would have taken the signet with him on his travels.[21] For late September and early October the few signet letters that survive concur with the dating clauses in attesting the king's presence at Woodstock. But from roughly the middle of October, the different classes of evidence begin to tell contrasting stories again. On 11 October, when according to the chancery enrolments Richard was either still at Woodstock or beginning his progress north, the Westminster chronicler has him performing the first of a series of pious observances at Westminster culminating in his attendance at mass on the feast day of St Edward the Confessor (13 October).[22] A week or so later it is clear that he was still moving in the environs of the capital, for on the 20th a signet letter records his presence at Sheen, and two days after that he is said by an anonymous correspondent to have entered London with his uncles and to have subsequently journeyed by water to Westminster.[23] From roughly October until Christmas, an approximate guide to his movements is provided by the entries in the *Dieta* section of the royal wardrobe book, which record his (or his establishment's) presence at King's Langley from 5 November to 9 December, at Windsor from 10 to 16 December, at Sheen for a week in mid-December and finally at Eltham for Christmas and the New Year.[24] The king's presence at King's Langley in November and early December is confirmed by the enrolment of letters patent issued there on 21 November and 9 December – on the latter occasion nearly a fortnight after the king's supposed 'return' from the north.[25]

A similarly conflicting story emerges from a consideration of the evidence for the king's movements in the latter half of 1393. Until roughly midsummer, there are no problems. All the sources agree that Richard spent the entire time in southern England, first at Winchester, where a parliament was held, and later at Sheen, Eltham and, in June, Canterbury.[26] From early July, however, two separate itineraries can be constructed on the evidence of the dating clauses alone. According to one, the king went off to northern England again. This itinerary is suggested by letters patent issued at Leicester on 24 July, Nottingham on the 25th, and then York, Ripon or Beverley from 2 August for a little over a month.[27] According to the second set of dates, the king stayed in southern England for the whole time. This itinerary is suggested by letters dated at Reading on 22 July, Salisbury on 16 and 22 August, and Beaulieu abbey intermittently between 27 August and 4 September.[28] Fortunately, the conflict between the two itineraries can be resolved by reference to the royal wardrobe book which survives for this year. From the record of daily expenses in this volume, there can be no doubt that the king was indeed making a perambulation across southern England. His (or his establishment's) presence is recorded at Henley-on-the-Heath, near Guildford, from 12 July, Romsey from 26 July, Downton, Cranborne and Wimborne in quick succession from 28 July,

Corfe from 31 July, Salisbury from 14 August, Beaulieu from 21 August, Winchester on 16 September, Farnham on 18 September and, finally, Windsor from 19 to 30 September, when the account closes.[29] In the light of this evidence, any suggestion that the king went to the north of England can be firmly dismissed.

Over two further periods in the 1390s conflicting patterns are to be observed in the evidence of the dating clauses. The first of these comes in the summer and early autumn of 1395 after Richard had returned from Ireland. According to one set of dates, Richard confined his itinerary to southern England, making his way to Westminster after disembarking at Bristol, and then spending a couple of months in Kent before returning to Windsor. According to another sequence of dates, however, he went to the north yet again and divided his time in that area between Worksop, Southwell, Hull and Beverley.[30] For these months there is not a great deal of parallel evidence that illuminates the king's movements, but there can be little doubt that the first itinerary was the one that the king actually followed. It is known that Richard returned from Ireland to the south-west of England, almost certainly to Bristol, and his presence in Kent is attested later in the year by a few signet letters surviving from that period.[31] The second and more serious period of difficulty with the itinerary comes four months later, in the closing weeks of 1395 and early ones of 1396. According to one set of letters under the great seal, Richard was again in the north, at York and Beverley, while according to another he was still in the south, in or around the Thames valley.[32] The conclusion that Harvey reached, drawing largely on York sources, was that Richard was in the north. Richard, he argued, had gone to York for Christmas and the New Year, and it was at this time that he 'gave to the Minster a relic of the Holy Innocents, which the chapter then had enclosed in a silver and gilt shrine and borne into the church in full procession . . . on the feast of the Innocents, evidently 28 December, while the king was still in York'.[33] The evidence on which Harvey based his argument was a chamberlain's account roll recording donations by the king to the minster, but it is far from clear that the document justifies the interpretation that he placed on it. According to the relevant entry in the account Richard gave *lvis. vd. de oblationibus factis Innocenti datis*.[34] Harvey took this to mean that the king made the offerings 'on the day of the Innocents' (28 December), but the sense could equally be that he made the gift 'to the Innocents' (and to have done so at any time within the accounting period). As Harvey himself later admits, the minster chronicler states unequivocally that Richard handed over the relic when he visited the city in March or April 1396, and the evidence of the king's itinerary suggests that the writer should be taken at his word.[35] Richard can be shown to have been in the north of England in the spring of 1396;[36] but at the previous Christmas season it is clear that he was in the south. The author of the *Historia Vitae et Regni*, generally a well-informed writer, maintains that he and his entourage spent Christmas and the New Year at the manor of Kennington.[37] The entries in the *Dieta* section of the wardrobe book, perhaps mirroring the movements of the household rather than the king, suggest that they were at King's Langley in the Chilterns.[38] Perhaps the king moved between the two. Whichever of the sources happens to be the more accurate, however, one thing is clear – that the king was never seen in York that winter at all.

When the evidence of the dating clauses is compared with that from other sources, notably the chronicles and the wardrobe books, it becomes clear how fragile are the foundations of the view that Richard spent long periods of time at York. What is recorded in the dating clauses is not the itinerary of the king but that of one or other of his officers of state. This is a point which can be demonstrated clearly by reference to the recorded movements of the chancellor, Thomas Arundel, archbishop of York. Arundel's presence in the north is attested over all of the periods when letters under the great seal were dated there. According to his register, in 1392 he was at Beverley for at least the first two weeks of September, and at York for the greater part of October and November.[39] As has already been shown, it was at Beverley that letters were dated from 17 August to 11 September, and at York that they were dated from 22 October to 26 November.[40] When the archbishop returned south, as it is recorded that he did in the last week of November, his letters begin to be dated in the south once again.[41] A similar story can be told for 1393. In the summer of that year, between approximately July and September, Arundel again visited his diocese, staying mainly at York and Beverley, and it is in the period of his residence in these two centres that the evidence is afforded of letters under the great seal being dated there.[42] Exactly the same pattern is to be seen in 1395. Twice in that year the archbishop went north, once in the spring and once more, this time for a longer spell, in the winter. In each period a crop of letters on the chancery rolls is place-dated at York.[43] In the light of this evidence, it is difficult to avoid the conclusion that the impression of the king's constant journeying to the north is one artificially created by the peregrinations of his chancellor.

Bearing in mind what is known of the dating procedures employed by chancery clerks in the late fourteenth century, this may appear a somewhat surprising conclusion. As Maxwell-Lyte showed, it was the clerks' practice, when dating great seal letters, generally to follow the place and date of the originating warrant. In other words, the movements reflected in the dating clauses of the letters should be those of the warranting authorities and not those of the chancellor and his clerks.[44] The fact that this was not so in the 1390s suggests that dating procedures were a good deal more complex than has been supposed. Any attempt to shed light on their working must begin by making a distinction between practice in the dating of documents in the summer and early autumn of 1392 and practice at the time of Arundel's other visits to the north. In 1392, as is well known, the entire apparatus of government was moved to York. Chancery, privy seal, exchequer and king's bench – all were uprooted and taken north, as they had been in the 1330s.[45] On the later occasions, however, this was not the case. The apparatus of government remained in the south, and the visits which Archbishop Arundel made were all either personal ones or ones made in connection with archiepiscopal business.[46] The distinction between the first and the later visits has a significant bearing on the nature of business transacted and the means by which it was warranted. In 1392, because all the organs of government went north together, there was no disturbance to the usual administrative rhythms; it was just that they were functioning in the north instead of at Westminster. In 1393 and 1395, however, the position was very different. In these years, when the chancery, council and privy seal were at Westminster while the chancellor was in the north, the normal rhythms were upset and different methods of warranty had to be employed. Generally, when he was away, the chancellor communicated with his staff by informal warrants. Largely for this reason, the range of business that he initiated was fairly limited. Sometimes it took the form of appointments to minor offices, sometimes the issue of commissions for the arrest of wanted felons, but most commonly the presentation of clerks to benefices in his gift as chancellor (that is, benefices worth 20 marks or less).[47] For business of this sort no note of warranty was entered on the great seal letter, and the only hint of the chancellor's responsibility for authorization is the place-date of York, Beverley or somewhere else in the north. The remaining government business – the greater part of it, that is – was initiated in these periods by the usual methods of ministerial bill or privy seal letter and is invariably place-dated in the south. It is the fact that in periods of the chancellor's absence, government business was initiated by these different methods which accounts for the apparent inconsistencies in the place-date evidence and for the impression that the king could be in two places at once. Peculiarities of this sort are a characteristic not only of the later years of Richard II's reign but of every other period when the chancellor was a prelate. The latter's vacation-time visits to his diocese left a trail of warrants on the rolls bearing witness to his, and not his master's journeyings.

Where do these findings leave Harvey's argument that Richard took a special interest in York and saw the city as an 'alternative' centre of government? Clearly Richard's visits to York were both fewer and shorter than Harvey supposed. It seems that they numbered four, or at the most five, in the course of the king's twenty-two-year reign. In the summer of 1383 Richard stayed at the archiepiscopal palace in the course of a wider itinerary of the north.[48] Two years later he passed through the city on the way to, and on the way back from, Scotland.[49] In 1392 he stayed for a period of ten days, from 5 to 15 June, when he brought the offices of government with him.[50] Then finally, in 1396, he stayed for nearly a fortnight, while making another wider progress of the north.[51] There is no evidence that he went to the city in the autumn of 1392; nor is there any evidence that he went there, or anywhere else in the north, in 1393 or 1395. After 1396 he appears never to have visited the city again.

The most important, and probably the most ceremonious, of the visits that Richard made to York was the one in 1392. This visit was the product of a wholly exceptional set of circumstances. In May 1392 a serious quarrel had broken out between the king and the rulers and citizens of London. According to two well-informed writers, Walsingham and the Monk of Westminster, the king had approached the Londoners for a loan, but his request had somewhat unwisely been refused.[52] As an act of spite, and to deprive the Londoners of business, on 30 May the king ordered the removal of the courts to York.[53] Shortly afterwards he gave orders to the exchequer, chancery and other organs of government to move too, and by the summer virtually the whole of the administration was operating from the north. As soon as the quarrel had been patched up, however, as it had been by August, orders were given for the offices to move back. Most of them had established themselves at Westminster again by Christmas, and by January they were reopening for business.[54] Richard himself, as we have seen, had returned south long before then. He had left York for Nottingham on about 15 June and was at Windsor by mid-July. Somewhat conspicuously, he had stayed in the north no longer than was necessary for the discharge of his business.

Richard's transference of the government to York was an episode that made a deep and lasting impression on contemporaries. It was widely reported in the chronicles, and the memory of it lingered in the minds of the Londoners. The main reason for this is to be found in the fact that the episode was without recent precedent: nothing like it had been seen for some fifty or sixty years. In the early part of the century, at the time of the Scottish wars, it had been far from uncommon for the departments of government to be uprooted and taken north. In 1298 Edward I had moved chancery, exchequer and other main offices to York for nearly six-and-a-half years; in 1332 his grandson had done the same for nearly five-and-a-half years; in 1319 and 1322 Edward II had moved the exchequer to York for two rather shorter periods.[55] These early fourteenth-century migrations had been occasioned by the need to establish a forward base from which to organize the Scottish wars. When the wars gradually wound down, as they did from mid-century, the migrations quickly ended, and government re-established itself in the south. It was in the south – or, to be more precise, in and around Westminster – that it then remained, almost without interruption, for the rest of the Middle Ages. Exchequer and the two benches settled in Westminster Hall, chancery in the White Hall of the palace, and the privy seal at a house in the Strand. It is against the background of these moves towards a more settled government that Richard's decision in 1392 to uproot the administration all over again has to be seen. The decision was a wholly anachronistic one. By the final decades of the century, Westminster had all but consolidated its position as the administrative capital of the realm, and to most people it would have appeared inconceivable that York could ever again mount a challenge to its pre-eminence. The significance of the 1392 migration was thus strictly limited – as it was also largely symbolic. What the migration did was bring to a formal end an era in English administrative history: that period of nearly a hundred years when government could all of a sudden be uprooted and taken north in response to a ruler's whim or the demands of war.

To say this is not to suggest that the monarchy in Richard's reign was in every respect a southern English monarchy; obviously it was not. Richard, to a greater extent than most of his line, had a sense of exercising a 'kingship of the British Isles'. In 1385 he had led what was probably the largest late-medieval expedition against the Scots; and twice in the 1390s he had sponsored major attempts to pacify Ireland and to bring the Irish chieftains within the fold of the English polity. According to the chronicler Walsingham, Richard's aim in the final years of his reign was to create a base for himself in Ireland from which to tyrannize the rest of his realm.[56] It is doubtful if Walsingham had adequate grounds for his allegation; but all the same it is striking how anxious after 1397 Richard was to escape from the southern heartland of his realm. In the spring of 1398, after adjourning parliament from Westminster to Shrewsbury, he moved restlessly around the counties of the north midlands and Welsh borders before slowly making his way back to the south. Later in the same year, he went back to the midlands, staying at Stafford, Lichfield, Nottingham and Newcastle-under-Lyme; and finally, after returning to the south in October, he set out north a third time in December and spent Christmas at Lichfield.[57] A number of factors help to account for Richard's attachment to the midlands and the Welsh marches. In the first place, the area allowed him relatively easy access to the lordship of Ireland, a part of his realm with which he appears to have been deeply fascinated. And secondly, it had the advantage of offering him proximity to the earldom and county of Chester. The earldom of Chester, as R.R. Davies has shown, was the 'inner citadel' of Richard's kingdom in the final two years of his reign.[58] A wealthy demesne lordship of the Crown, it provided Richard with vital military resources and served as the recruiting ground for the king's notorious corps of archers. Richard's affection for Cheshire is evident from the favours that he bestowed on it in the closing years of his reign. In 1397 he raised the county to a principality, and in the following two years he showered on it privileges and immunities that gave it a unique position in the English polity.[59] Considering the king's obvious attachment to the county, it is a curiosity of his itinerary that his visits there in the 1390s were actually few and far between. In the nine years between 1388 and 1397 he never went there at all; after 1397 he made only a couple of brief visits, staying at, or passing through, Macclesfield and Holywell.[60] The town of Chester itself he seems to have visited only once between 1387 and August 1399 when he came there as a prisoner.[61] For all his obvious affection for the county, his attitude to it was a curiously detached one. Chester was no more a 'substitute' or 'alternative' capital for him than York was.

Was there, in that case, anywhere at all away from Westminster that he did regard in some sense as a 'capital' in the final years of the reign? If the evidence of his itinerary is any guide, it is possible that he might have regarded either Nottingham or Lichfield (both of them significantly still in the midlands) in these terms. Richard spent nearly a month at Nottingham after leaving York in June 1392, and he returned there for several quite lengthy stays in 1395, 1396 and 1398;[62] throughout the middle and later years of his reign, Nottingham was the place that he favoured most after Westminster for the holding of councils and great councils.[63] Lichfield was a city which he came increasingly to grace with his favour in and after 1397. He spent the Christmas of 1397 there with his friend, Bishop Scrope, while journeying north to Shrewsbury for the adjourned session of parliament, and he returned there several times in the following year. In May 1398 he concluded a treaty of alliance with the duke of Brittany there. In September of the same year he attended the enthronement of his former confessor, Bishop Burghill, in the cathedral, and in December he spent Christmas there again. So frequent had his visits to the city become by 1398 that a special banqueting hall had to be built for his use, immediately next to the great hall of the episcopal palace.[64]

Richard's attachment to Lichfield and Nottingham is a striking characteristic of the middle and later years of his reign, but it should not be allowed to obscure what is undoubtedly the main point to emerge from a study of his itinerary – namely, that before 1396 his rule was based, as his predecessors' had been, largely in southern and south-central England. The manor houses and hunting lodges he frequented most often were all located in the Thames valley and its environs. He seems to have had a particular liking, at least until 1394, for the manor house of Sheen in Surrey; he was also drawn many times to King's Langley, a manor house much frequented by his grandfather, and to Kennington, a manor of the Black Prince's where he had spent much of his youth.[65] The summers he often spent hunting at Woodstock and Beckley.[66] In most years, either in spring or in summer, he undertook a more extended itinerary; but interestingly, when he did so, he still largely confined himself to the southern half of his realm. In 1382, after his wedding in Westminster abbey, he took his new queen on a progress west to Bristol, a part of her dower estate, and back.[67] In the following year, again in the company of his queen, he made a tour of East Anglia, taking in all the important shrines of that region, including Bury St Edmunds, Ely and Walsingham.[68] In 1384, after the meeting of parliament at Salisbury, he visited Corfe, Beaulieu, the hunting lodges of the New Forest and Arundel.[69] In 1386 he went to Bristol again, this time (so he supposed) to see Vere off to Ireland.[70] In the following decade he made at least three more westward itineraries. In 1390 he went to Marlborough, Devizes and probably Gloucester, in the following year to Bristol and again Gloucester, and in 1396 to Woodstock, Gloucester and Worcester, before heading northwards into the midlands.[71] At Worcester he stayed at the cathedral priory with his former confessor, Tideman of Winchcombe, whose enthronement in the cathedral he attended.[72] Richard's partiality for visiting towns in which cathedrals or great abbeys were located is a characteristic of his itinerary. Critics of his, like Walsingham, said that he was only interested in such places for the cheap lodgings they provided, but it would be wrong to place so cynical an interpretation on his motives.[73] Richard was a man passionately interested in the cult of saints, particularly English saints, and it seems that he arranged his itineraries so as to accommodate visits to churches with notable relics. It is striking, for example, that whenever he travelled into eastern Kent, he invariably fitted in a visit to Becket's shrine at Canterbury.[74] He made a particular point of visiting Becket's shrine before setting off for Ireland in 1399.[75]

It would be a misrepresentation of Dr Harvey's article, of course, to suggest that the argument he presents for Richard's interest in York rests solely on the evidence of the number or length of his visits there; manifestly this is not the case. His remarks on the king's visits formed no more than a brief prelude to a discussion of Richard's interest in the rebuilding programme then being undertaken at the minster. Unusually – not to say uniquely – among English kings, Richard actually contributed to the fabric fund established at the minster. In July 1395 he made a donation of 100 marks which was acknowledged by the carving of a white hart on a capital above the entry to the south choir aisle;[76] then in the following year he gave a valuable relic of one of the Holy Innocents, which the chapter had enclosed in a silver and gilt shrine.[77] Dr Harvey has suggested that it may have been to mark Richard's visit, and his favour to their church more generally, that the chapter commissioned the programme of painted decoration in the chapter house vestibule which alluded to the king in its heraldry (the shields of the Three Kings of the Epiphany were included).[78] It cannot be denied that Richard was, by the modest standards of English royalty, an exceptionally generous benefactor to the minster. But equally it cannot be denied that he was a still more generous benefactor to other great churches of the realm. To the fabric fund of Canterbury he made a quite exceptionally lavish donation. According to the cathedral's Kalendar of Obits, he gave a sum of over £1,000 sterling 'for the fabric of the high altar and the nave of the church'; and at the same time, according to the exchequer memoranda rolls, he remitted debts of £160 owed by the prior and chapter in satisfaction of a sum that he had promised to them on account of their expenditure on the works.[79] Still more striking is the evidence of Richard's favour to Westminster abbey. Westminster had a special place in the king's affections, partly because it was the royal coronation church but also because it housed the shrine of his patron and forebear, St Edward the Confessor. Richard gave many valuable gifts to St Edward's shrine, among them a silver portable altar enamelled with the story of the Confessor and the Pilgrim and a gold ring worth 1,000 marks. He also gave several magnificent sets of vestments to the monks, the most notable being a chasuble or cope (it is not clear which) worth 1,000 marks and a set consisting of a gold chasuble, three copes, three albs and three maniples, which it is said that he handed over 'at the shrine of St Edward the Confessor'. Besides offering these marks of favour to the convent, he provided the *novum opus* fund (the fund for the rebuilding of the nave) with a permanent endowment in the form of two alien priories, those of Folkestone and Stoke-by-Clare, together worth about £120 a year.[80] These were gifts more numerous and more valuable than those which Richard bestowed on either York minster or Canterbury. It is hardly surprising that this should have been so, because Westminster abbey was a royal *eigenkloster*: by its history, by its long association with the Crown, and by the presence in its midst of the royal tombs, the abbey bore witness to the theocratic basis of Richard's kingship. Neither York minster nor Canterbury could compete with it in this respect. Westminster's position in royal favour was unique and without challenge.

Alongside the abbey at Westminster stood another building which bore powerful witness to the aspirations of the English monarchy. This was the rambling assemblage of structures that made up Westminster palace. First called into being by Edward the Confessor, and greatly enlarged by William Rufus, the palace was both a seat of government and a place of residence for the king and his entourage. Successive rulers had left their mark on its fabric. Rufus, of course, had built the first great hall, which was in its time the largest in Europe; Henry III had rebuilt the great chamber, known from its decoration as the 'Painted Chamber'; and Edward I and his son and grandson had built the magnificent new chapel of St Stephen, to which was attached a college of canons.[81] It was Richard II, however, who was responsible for perhaps the most ambitious single undertaking at the palace in the later Middle Ages – the rebuilding of the great hall and the replacement of its Norman columns and roof with a single, vast hammer-beam roof. The decision to rebuild the hall appears to have been taken in the autumn of 1393, and work probably began early in the following year; by 1400 it appears to have been all but finished. Unfortunately, the total cost of the rebuilding cannot be established, but it can hardly have been less than the £8–£9,000 conservatively estimated by the editors of the *History of the King's Works*.[82] A roughly equivalent amount was probably spent over the same time on the rebuilding and embellishment of the abbey, though again it is impossible to be certain on the point.

The rebuilding of the abbey and the palace in the later fourteenth century bore witness to a growing appreciation by Richard of the importance of the concentration of government in and around Westminster. No longer was Westminster seen by the king and his advisers merely as an administrative headquarters or as one of a number of stopping places on the king's ceaseless itinerary of his realm; it was seen as something much more than that – as a ceremonial centre and a focus for the cult of monarchical authority. It was Westminster's emergence in this newer and grander role that marked its final arrival as the political and administrative capital of the realm.

To speak of Westminster's importance in these terms, however, raises important questions about Richard's conception of a 'capital'. Did he see a 'capital' as anything more than a centre of government? Did he see it as a place where he and his court could or would normally reside? Did he ever consider abandoning the itinerant life-style and settling down at Westminster? These are all questions on which a study of the king's itinerary can shed a little light – for an obvious way of assessing the value that Richard attached to Westminster is to consider in what proportions he divided his time between that township and the other parts of his realm. It is true that in some respects the evidence is unreliable: for example, it is difficult to be sure that Richard was at Westminster when the place-date clauses say that he was; but, even allowing for this, it is possible to suggest a few conclusions of significance. The first of these is that in the early to mid-1390s the king spent relatively little of his time at Westminster; and the second is that in the final years of the decade he spent hardly any at all. The evidence for a change in the nature of the king's movements in or around the year 1396 is too clear to be ignored. In the winter and spring of that year he went on the long itinerary that took him first to the west midlands and then to the north for three-and-a-half months. In the following year, he spent his time largely at Windsor and Eltham. In 1398, after leaving Shrewsbury, he went on an extensive itinerary of the west and north midlands. And finally, in 1399 he took himself off for a second time to Ireland. After the winter of 1396 he spent scarcely more than a few weeks of each year at Westminster. Paradoxically, at the very time when his programme of works at Westminster was reaching its climax he virtually deserted the place for the provinces.

To account for the sudden shift that occurred in the character of the king's movements in the final years of the reign would require a lengthier examination of his personality and political aims than can be attempted here: possible reasons can be found in his restlessness and his almost obsessive search for personal security. What is more relevant in the present context is the implications of that shift for his attitude towards his emergent 'capital'. There can be little doubt that he did not conceive of his 'capital' in the way that a princely ruler of the Renaissance would have done – that is, as a setting or backcloth for the ceremonies of the court. The great buildings which Richard commissioned at Westminster appear to have had no more than a symbolic significance for him. He saw the abbey principally as an affirmation of his personal devotion to St Edward, and the palace as an expression of the power and ambition of his monarchy. The fact that these buildings were a major adornment of the township of Westminster did not encourage him to spend more of his time there; he continued in the mid-1390s to itinerate around his kingdom just as he always had. There is a sense, then, in which it can be said that the 'capital' of England in Richard's reign was not Westminster, and certainly not York; it was wherever the king happened to be. The palaces, the hunting lodges and the manor houses that the king stayed in – these were the nerve-centres of Ricardian England, just as they had been of Henry II's England 200 years before.

Notes

All references to unpublished documents are to documents in the Public Record Office, London, unless otherwise stated.

[1] I am grateful to Dr W.M. Ormrod for commenting on an earlier draft of this paper.

[2] H. Maxwell-Lyte, *Historical Notes on the use of the Great Seal of England* (London, 1926), p. 251.

[3] T.F. Tout, *Chapters in the Administrative History of Medieval England* (6 vols, Manchester, 1920–33), IV, pp. 34, 222.

[4] A. Tuck, *Richard II and the English Nobility* (London, 1973), pp. 227–8.

[5] J. Harvey, 'Richard II and York', in *The Reign of Richard II*, eds F.R.H. Du Boulay and C.M. Barron (London, 1971), pp. 206–7.

[6] Maxwell-Lyte, *Historical Notes on the Great Seal*, pp. 242–56 *passim*; P. Chaplais, *English Royal Documents, King John–Henry VI, 1199–1461* (Oxford, 1971), pp. 18, 28, 41–2; A.L. Brown, 'The Authorisation of Letters under the Great Seal', *Bull. Inst. Hist. Res.*, XXXVII (1964), pp. 126, 131.

[7] Tout, *Chapters*, pp. 195–230; S.B. Chrimes, *An Introduction to the Administrative History of Medieval England* (Oxford, 1952), p. 203.

[8] Tuck, *Richard II and the English Nobility*, p. 70.

[9] *CPR, 1391–6*, pp. 12, 34, 38, 42, 45, 48, 57, 73, 286; J.F. Baldwin, *The King's Council in England during the Middle Ages* (Oxford, 1913), p. 493.

[10] *CPR, 1391–6*, p. 65; *Westminster Chronicle, 1381–1394*, ed. L.C. Hector and B.F. Harvey (Oxford, 1982), pp. 488–90, which gives the date; T. Walsingham, *Historia Anglicana* (2 vols, Rolls Series, 1863–4), II, p. 206.

[11] *CPR, 1391–6*, pp. 63, 65, 67.

12 *CPR, 1391–6*, pp. 64, 70, 96, 98, 103, 106, 123; *Westminster Chronicle*, p. 498, which again gives a date; *Historia Vitae et Regni Ricardi Secundi*, ed. G.B. Stow (Philadelphia, 1977), p. 133.

13 *CPR, 1391–6*, pp. 119, 123; *CCR, 1392–6*, p. 11.

14 *CPR, 1391–6*, pp. 132, 133, 135, 136, 141–6; *CCR, 1392–6*, pp. 13, 14, 17.

15 *CPR, 1391–6*, p. 150.

16 *CPR, 1391–6*, pp. 150–1, 155.

17 *CPR, 1391–6*, pp. 183, 196–7; *CCR, 1392–6*, pp. 24, 25, 27–32.

18 *CPR, 1391–6*, pp. 198–9; *Westminster Chronicle*, p. 510.

19 *Westminster Chronicle*, pp. 504–6.

20 Ibid.; H. Suggett, 'A letter describing Richard II's reconciliation with the city of London, 1392', *EHR*, LXII (1947), pp. 209–13. See also the Latin poem written by the Carmelite friar, Richard of Maidstone, to celebrate the occasion, *Political Poems and Songs*, ed. T. Wright (Rolls Series, 2 vols, 1859–61), I, pp. 282–300.

21 *The Diplomatic Correspondence of Richard II*, ed. É. Perroy (Camden Society, 3rd series, XLVIII, 1933), no. 152.

22 *Westminster Chronicle*, pp. 508–10.

23 *Diplomatic Correspondence*, no. 162; *Anglo-Norman Letters and Petitions*, ed. M.D. Legge (Anglo-Norman Text Society, III, 1941), p. 185.

24 E101/402/10, ff. 8^{v}–12^{v}.

25 *CPR, 1391–6*, pp. 198, 199.

26 *CPR, 1391–6*, pp. 214, 215, 247, 260, 269, 270, 276; 'Annales Ricardi Secundi', in J. de Trokelowe et Anon., *Chronica et Annales*, ed. H.T. Riley (Rolls Series, 1866), p. 155; Richard went to Canterbury in May in expectation of crossing the channel to meet the French king, Charles VI, but because of a recurrence of Charles's illness the proposed meeting never took place (J.J.N. Palmer, *England, France and Christendom, 1377–99* (London, 1972), pp. 148–9).

27 *CPR, 1391–6*, pp. 307, 308, 310, 312.

28 *CPR, 1391–6*, pp. 312, 318, 368; *Foedera*, ed. T. Rymer (20 vols, London, 1704–35), VII, p. 754.

29 E101/402/10, ff. 26^{r}–32^{r}. Beaulieu was a much favoured halt on Richard's itineraries of southern England (see, for example, C81/1342/2–6). This was partly because it was a royal foundation. An added attraction by 1391 was that the abbot was his friend and former physician, Tideman of Winchcombe [*CPR, 1391–6*, p. 325; *Victoria History of Hampshire and the Isle of Wight*, vol. 2 (London, 1903), p. 143].

30 *CPR, 1391–6*, pp. 566, 569, 575, 584, 593, 595, 604–15, 622; *CCR, 1392–6*, pp. 435, 438; *CFR, 1391–9*, pp. 160, 179–80.

31 Adam of Usk, writing several years later, says that Richard landed at Bristol (*Chronicon Adae de Usk*, ed. E.M. Thompson (London, 1904), p. 9). The other chroniclers are silent, but the accuracy of Adam's record is suggested by the fact that it was at Bristol that Nicholas Messager, who was sent to Wales with letters for the king, finally caught up with him (E403/551, *sub* 28 April). For Richard's movements in Kent between June and August, see *Foedera*, VII, pp. 805, 806, 808; *CPR, 1391–6*, pp. 593, 595, 606–9, 613, 615.

32 *CPR, 1391–6*, pp. 644, 646, 648, 649; *Foedera*, VII, pp. 812, 817.

[33] Harvey, 'Richard II and York', p. 209.

[34] York Minster Library, Dean and Chapter chamberlains' accounts, E1/23.

[35] Harvey, 'Richard II and York', p. 209, n. 30. Harvey then goes on to say, however, that the chronicler must have been wrong. The chronicler's narrative of 1396 is in *Historians of the Church of York*, ed. J. Raine (Rolls Series, 2 vols, 1886), II, p. 426.

[36] He was at York from 23 March to 5 April (E101/403/10, ff. 19ᵛ–20ᵛ).

[37] *Historia Vitae et Regni*, p. 136.

[38] E101/403/10, ff. 13ʳ–14ʳ; *CPR, 1391–6*, p. 646. The easiest way of reconciling the chronicler's statement with the evidence of the wardrobe book is to suppose that the king and his immediate entourage were at Kennington, while the kitchen departments of the household were at King's Langley. As Tout pointed out long ago, the wardrobe books can provide no more than an approximate guide to the king's itinerary because the king and his household were frequently separated – sometimes for periods of a week or more (*Chapters*, III, p. 469, n. 2). Counting against the possibility, however, is the time of year: it was Christmas, and Richard would have wanted the kitchen departments with him. It may be that the chronicler was quite simply mistaken in his statement. He had been wrong on a previous occasion – in 1393 he said that Richard spent Christmas at Windsor, when it is clear from the Westminster Chronicle that he was in fact at Westminster (*Historia Vitae et Regni*, p. 133; *Westminster Chronicle*, p. 516).

[39] For Archbishop Arundel's itinerary, see M. Aston, *Thomas Arundel* (Oxford, 1967), app. 2.

[40] *CPR, 1391–6*, pp. 150, 169, 183, 198.

[41] Arundel began heading south on or shortly before 28 November, when his presence is recorded at Scrooby, an archiepiscopal manor in Nottinghamshire (Aston, *Arundel*, app. 2). It was on 28 November that the last great seal letter was authorized at York (*CCR, 1392–6*, p. 30).

[42] Aston, *Thomas Arundel*, app. 2; *CPR, 1391–6*, pp. 307, 310, 312.

[43] Aston, *Thomas Arundel*, app. 2; *CPR, 1391–6*, pp. 644, 649.

[44] See above, p. 72.

[45] See below, pp. 79–81.

[46] Tout, *Chapters*, III, p. 493 and n. 2, supposed that the chancery went north with Arundel in the period December 1394–January 1395, while Richard was in Ireland. There is no reason to suppose that this was the case. The writs which Tout cites are informal ones which the chancellor sent to chancery for the issue of letters in the three fairly limited areas detailed below, pp. 78–9.

[47] *CPR, 1391–6*, pp. 312, 355–6. The chancellor's right to present to benefices in the royal gift worth 20 marks per annum or less is recognized and confirmed in the chancery ordinances of 1390 (B. Wilkinson, *The Chancery under Edward III* (Manchester, 1929), app. VI (which prints the ordinances) para. 21). It is interesting to note that no general attorneys were received at York in 1393 and 1395 in sharp contrast to the experience of 1392. It can be deduced from this that Arundel had gone north unaccompanied by any senior chancery staff: as Wilkinson shows (ibid., pp. 79–80), only clerks of the first grade could receive general attorneys.

[48] *CPR, 1381–5*, p. 311; C81/1340/8.

[49] *CCR, 1385–9*, p. 5; C81/1346/12, 13, 23.

[50] *CPR, 1391–6*, pp. 63, 65, 67.

51 E101/403/10, ff. 19ᵛ–20ᵛ. Harvey claimed that after leaving York in April Richard went back there in June for a special performance of the Corpus Christi plays ('Richard II and York', p. 211). The document that he cites is York Corporation Archives, C.1:1, a chamberlain's roll of account. The document, however, is undated, and it may not belong to this year. In any event, it refers only to the presence at the plays of the king's minstrels and not of the king himself. It is clear from the wardrobe book (E101/403/10, ff. 24ᵛ–25ᵛ) that Richard was in southern England at the time, moving between Windsor, Westminster and Havering.

52 Walsingham, *Historia Anglicana*, II, pp. 207–8; *Westminster Chronicle*, p. 496. For discussion, see C.M. Barron, 'The Quarrel of Richard II with London, 1392–7', in *The Reign of Richard II*, pp. 173–201.

53 *CCR, 1389–92*, p. 565.

54 Tout, *Chapters*, III, pp. 481–2.

55 Tout, *Chapters*, II, pp. 74–5; III, pp. 57–60; D.M. Broome, 'Exchequer Migrations to York in the Thirteenth and Fourteenth Centuries', *Essays in Medieval History presented to T.F. Tout*, eds A.G. Little and F.M. Powicke (Manchester, 1925), pp. 291–300.

56 'Annales Ricardi Secundi', in J. de Trokelowe et H. de Blaneforde, *Chronica et Annales*, ed. H.T. Riley (Rolls Series, 1866), pp. 239–40. A similar charge was made in the deposition articles (no. 24): *Rot. Parl.*, III, p. 420, reprinted in *Chronicles of the Revolution, 1397–1400*, ed. C. Given-Wilson (Manchester, 1993), p. 180.

57 Unfortunately, in the absence of a wardrobe book for the period, it is impossible to reconstruct Richard's itinerary in the final two years of his reign in any detail. A certain amount may be learned from the place-date evidence on the main chancery enrolments, and somewhat more from that on the supplementary patent roll (C67/30) which lists pardons granted between February and May 1398 to supporters of the former Appellants. For certain later periods, this evidence may be supplemented by the handful of signet letters in C81/1354. Richard's visit to Lichfield for Christmas 1398 is attested by *Historia Vitae et Regni*, p. 151. Tout offered an outline itinerary for February–April 1398 in *Chapters*, IV, p. 34.

58 R.R. Davies, 'Richard II and the Principality of Chester', in *The Reign of Richard II*, pp. 256–79.

59 Ibid., pp. 260–3.

60 C81/1354/28; E403/559, 24 July. Holywell technically was in Flint, a county under the administrative control of the palatine government in Chester and considered part and parcel of Richard's new principality of Chester.

61 *CCR, 1396–9*, p. 382.

62 *CPR, 1391–6*, pp. 614, 618; Tout, *Chapters*, IV, p. 222. Richard spent no less than forty-eight days at Nottingham in 1396, from 29 January to 15 March.

63 Significantly it was to Nottingham and not to York that in 1392 Richard summoned the Londoners to receive his judgement (*Westminster Chronicle*, p. 498). Five years before, in 1387, it had been at Nottingham that the king had convened the second of his two meetings with the judges. According to Walsingham, it was at Nottingham in 1397 that he had the indictments served against the duke of Gloucester and the earls of Warwick and Arundel (Walsingham, *Historia Anglicana*, II, p. 223).

64 *CPR, 1396–9*, pp. 376, 381; *Victoria History of the County of Stafford*, ed. M.W. Greenslade, vol. 14 (London, 1990), pp. 14, 59; Lichfield Joint Record Office, D30/2/1/1, f. 52ᵛ. According to *Historia*

Vitae et Regni, p. 151, Richard's guests at Christmas 1398 included a papal nuncio and an envoy of the eastern emperor. On at least one earlier occasion the king had been to Lichfield: in June 1387, in the course of his 'gyration' (A. Tuck, *Richard II and the English Nobility* (London, 1973), p. 227). It was probably then, and not in 1386, as maintained by H. Wharton, *Anglia Sacra*, I (London, 1691), p. 450, that he attended the enthronement of Bishop Scrope; there is no evidence in the signet warrants that he visited the midlands in 1386 (C81/1349–53). In addition to staying at Lichfield itself, Richard also periodically stayed at the episcopal manor of Great Haywood, near Rugeley (SC8/243/12148; *CPR, 1396–9*, pp. 280, 312, 317, 511). The manor is wrongly identified as Heywood-in-Cheswardine in the indexes to the *Calendars* of Close and Patent Rolls.

⁶⁵ The evidence for the king's residence in these places is scattered through the dating clauses of the royal correspondence and the *Dieta* sections of the wardrobe books of the reign. For King's Langley and Sheen, see also R.A. Brown, H.M. Colvin and A.J. Taylor (eds), *The History of the King's Works* (2 vols, London, 1963), II, pp. 975, 997–8, respectively. Richard ordered Sheen to be demolished after Queen Anne died there in June 1394.

⁶⁶ *CCR, 1377–81*, p. 149; *CPR, 1381–5*, pp. 156, 269; C81/1353/32–41; *Westminster Chronicle*, p. 342.

⁶⁷ *CPR, 1381–5*, pp. 92–3, 178; E403/490, 23 September.

⁶⁸ *Westminster Chronicle*, p. 42.

⁶⁹ The itinerary can be followed in the signet letters in C81/1341 and 1342.

⁷⁰ The signet letters again lay bare the itinerary: C81/1352 and 1353. Vere's proposed expedition to Ireland was cancelled, by July at the latest, because of the threat of invasion by the French.

⁷¹ For the 1390 itinerary, see the wardrobe book for the year, E101/402/5, ff. 21ᵛ–23ʳ, which, however, only takes the king (or, rather, the kitchen departments) as far west as Marlborough; his presence at Gloucester is attested by *Westminster Chronicle*, pp. 436–8. For the following year's itinerary, see *CPR, 1388–92*, pp. 386–90, and PSO/1/7, 8; and for that of 1396, *CPR, 1391–6*, pp. 661–9, and the record of daily expenses in the wardrobe book, E101/403/10, fos. 14ᵛ–16ʳ. In 1390, after concluding his western itinerary, Richard went north to Leicester, to join John of Gaunt's hunting party: *Westminster Chronicle*, p. 440.

⁷² *Historia Vitae et Regni*, pp. 135, 136.

⁷³ Walsingham, *Historia Anglicana*, II, pp. 96–7, 199.

⁷⁴ *CPR, 1391–6*, pp. 269–70, 276; *CCR, 1392–6*, pp. 473–4; *CPR, 1396–9*, p. 28; *CCR, 1396–9*, p. 9. For Richard's interest in Canterbury more generally, see below, p. 84.

⁷⁵ *Eulogium Historiarum sive Temporis*, ed. F.S. Haydon (3 vols, Rolls Series, 1858–63), III, pp. 379–80.

⁷⁶ E403/551, sub 12 July. The carving of the white hart is illustrated in Harvey, 'Richard II and York', plate 2b.

⁷⁷ Harvey, 'Richard II and York', pp. 207, 209; and see above, p. 76.

⁷⁸ Harvey, 'Richard II and York', pp. 211–13. Richard was born on the feast of the Epiphany, 6 January.

⁷⁹ *Inventories of Christ Church, Canterbury*, eds J. Wickham Legge and W. St John Hope (London, 1902), p. 109; E159/172, *Brevia directa*, Easter, *rot.* 9; E159/173, *Brevia directa*, Michaelmas, *rot.* 11. Harvey, 'Richard II and York', p. 209, n. 29, notes the last two references but not the first (crucial) one.

⁸⁰ J. Perkins, *Westminster Abbey. Its Worship and Ornaments* (Alcuin Club, XXXIV, 1930), p. 58; *Westminster Chronicle*, p. 372; Westminster Abbey Muniments 5262A; *Cal. Charter Rolls, 1341–1417*, p. 311; *CPR, 1385–9*, p. 188; 1388–92, p. 230; Westminster Abbey Muniments 6226. The evidence of Richard's favour to Westminster abbey is discussed in more detail in N.E. Saul, 'Richard II and Westminster Abbey', in *The Cloister and the World. Essays in Medieval History Presented to Barbara Harvey*, eds W.J. Blair and B. Golding (Oxford, 1994).

⁸¹ For the development of the palace, see *History of the King's Works. The Middle Ages*, I, pp. 491–526.

⁸² For the rebuilding of the hall and its cost, see ibid., pp. 527–33.

5

HAXEY'S CASE, 1397: THE PETITION AND ITS PRESENTER RECONSIDERED

A.K. McHardy

In January 1397 the political equilibrium was rocked by a petition to parliament which, among other matters, requested a curtailment of the expenses of the royal household.[1] In the resulting storm, the presenter of the petition was condemned to death for treason after the lords had enacted retrospective legislation. Historians have long been intrigued by this episode: did Haxey's petition reopen old scars in the king's psyche and lead him to plan the coup against the former Appellants which was carried out in the summer of that year? Or did the compliant demeanour of parliament encourage Richard to put into operation schemes for revenge which had been in his mind for some time? We may never know the answer. Yet a related series of questions may be more susceptible to enquiry: who was Thomas Haxey, the man who presented the petition? Did the petition arise from his own concerns? Or if, as most historians have assumed, he was only a 'front man' for others, whom did he represent? In particular, whose interests were threatened by the composition of the court at that point?

A variety of answers has been given to these problems. Tout, in a rare lapse, doubted Haxey's right to be in parliament at all.[2] McKisack thought this petition was 'inspired, perhaps . . . by a group of disappointed prelates who had not gained access to the court, perhaps by a general clerical hostility to the king's alignment with the schismatic French'.[3] Steel assumed that sinister forces were behind Haxey, and proposed the three original Appellants.[4] With greater precision, Margaret Aston suggested that the Arundel brothers may have been the driving force behind the petition,[5] while R.H. Jones held the opinion that Richard himself put Haxey up to making this criticism, both to demonstrate his own power over parliament and as a warning to more serious ill-wishers.[6] Tuck, wisely, called for fuller investigation of this episode.[7]

Even if we cannot answer all the questions raised by this episode, we can say with certainty that Thomas Haxey was an interesting individual deserving further study, and, although much about his life still remains obscure, it seems worthwhile to set out what has been discovered about him so far. By this route we may be able to advance some more plausible theory to account for the contents of his petition, if not for the royal response.

Thomas Haxey was one of that remarkable group of king's clerks who came from south-east Yorkshire, north Lincolnshire and north-east Nottinghamshire and who were such successful careerists in royal service for over a century. First noticed by W.H. Stevenson, they were described by Tout, and their importance demonstrated by Hamilton Thompson. Later they were discussed in detail and many of them listed by John Grassi.[8] They included such men as William Melton and John Thoresby, both archbishops of York, and, in the later fourteenth century, the two John Walthams (the bishop of Salisbury and his namesake, an Oxford graduate) and the brothers John and Richard Ravenser. A number of these, including the most successful, had ties not only of geography but of kinship too; for example, Master John Waltham was a nephew of Archbishop Thoresby,[9] and the Walthams and Ravensers were cousins. Their collective grip on positions in Crown service, especially in the chancery, was remarkable. Indeed, the strong connection between south Yorkshiremen (and their north Lincolnshire relatives) and Crown service, which began during the career of Robert Burnell (d. 1292), was brought to an end only by the rebellion of Archbishop Richard Scrope in 1405.

Thomas Haxey was described on several occasions as being a Lincolnshire man; two of these occasions were in the autumn of 1382, just at the time, the evidence suggests, when he was entering Crown service.[10] That Thomas Haxey was indeed a north-east Lincolnshire man, originating from the large parish of Haxey in the Isle of Axholme,[11] we may surmise from three pieces of evidence. The first, his will, is the most important. It lists bequests to no less than eighteen parishes and we can identify professional connections with seventeen of them. The exception, and the last to be mentioned, is a bequest of ten marks to be distributed among the poor tenants of the Isle of Axholme and especially of the parish of Haxey.[12] The second clue lies among the Haxey parish deeds. One of these, dated 1385, includes among its witnesses 'dominus Thomas Haxey clerk', which would accord with other evidence of a local man beginning to make his way in the world.[13] The third piece of evidence dates from 1395 when Haxey was instituted to the Lincoln prebend of Scamblesby and Melton Ross, on which occasion he was represented by his proctor, John Fouler.[14] Since each prebendary was represented at institution by a different proctor, we may presume that John Fouler had some connection with Haxey. What is significant is that the Isle of Axholme, in which Haxey parish lay, was a wetland area until the seventeenth century, and we can see – again from the remarkable series of Haxey parish deeds – that 'Fouler' was a name characteristic of that parish.[15]

It is likely that sympathy for the poor of the parish of Haxey, remembered in his will, reflected Haxey's own humble origins. The will mentions two relatives, John de Bekyngham *alias* John del Bottery, and his nephew Thomas Takell', mason.[16] No other member of his family can be identified with certainty; early in 1383 the election of William Haxey as coroner of Lincolnshire was nullified because he was 'insufficiently qualified'.[17] Since this was shortly after Thomas Haxey is first sighted in London, and about the royal courts in particular, it is possible that Haxey was intervening on behalf of a relative who did not want the job. Yet, although his origins were obscure and relatively humble, Thomas Haxey himself was, at his death in 1425, a wealthy man and had been so for a number of years. How was this material success achieved?

The short answer must be 'through Crown service', though much about that service remains obscure. The earliest evidence for his being in the Crown's employ comes from the autumn of 1382: on 6 October a letter close addressed to the abbot and convent of Milton (Abbas), in Dorset, ordered them to confer a pension on Haxey since they were bound, on the election of a new abbot, to give a pension to a king's clerk in default of a benefice.[18] Two days later he was one of a group of mainpernors for the abbot of Newhouse (Lincolnshire), and he was again a mainpernor in the following month.[19] In December a recognizance for £19 13s 4d owed to Haxey was entered on the same rolls.[20]

This activity suggests that in 1382 he entered royal service and was using his position to make money, but what is not so clear is what his position was, since no evidence has been found that he was feed by the king in the early 1380s. In 1385 he was again described as 'one of the king's clerks' when the abbess and convent of St Mary's abbey, Winchester, were ordered to provide Haxey with a pension, in lieu of a benefice, to which he had been nominated on the recent promotion of the new abbess.[21] The term 'king's clerk' was an elastic one – John Wycliffe, for example, referred to himself as being 'in a special sense the king's clerk', though he was never regularly feed[22] – and is notoriously difficult to interpret.[23] It is possible that Haxey, while not directly employed by the Crown, was in the service of someone who was, or who stood high in royal favour.

A similar mystery surrounds the identity of Haxey's earliest patron. An obvious candidate would seem to be the lord of the Isle of Axholme, Thomas Mowbray, earl of Nottingham, but the only evidence to connect the two men dates from October 1396 when Mowbray, then captain of Calais, nominated Haxey and Sir William Bagot as his attorneys in England for one year.[24] Bagot was an adherent of the Mowbrays, but the recommendation of Haxey could well have come from Roger Walden, treasurer of Calais and one of Haxey's business associates.[25] Another candidate is Thomas Arundel. Dr Margaret Aston discovered that Haxey's earliest benefice, Pulham in Norfolk (1384), as well as Somersham, Huntingdonshire (1388), was obtained at Arundel's presentation.[26] If Haxey were indeed closely associated with Arundel, it would help to explain Richard II's violent reaction to the 1397 petition. But the evidence of Haxey's later career does not support the theory of a close link between the two men, for it was just as Arundel was twice obtaining the archbishopric of Canterbury (in 1397 and 1399) that Haxey was shifting the focus of his life to the diocese of York.

Some of Haxey's earliest business associates were Lincolnshire laymen: William Skipwith the younger, son of the common pleas justice, Albin de Enderby, a well-known county figure, and others with localized names such as John de Yerdeburgh, Thomas de Ormesby and William Friskenay.[27] The way to advancement may have lain through one of them or their patrons.

Yet perhaps the best possibility lies with the Waltham clan. The evidence here is specific, if later than we would like. In September 1386 the abbot of Selby appointed three proctors to represent him in the forthcoming parliament. One was John Waltham, the future bishop of Salisbury, at that time archdeacon of Richmond, and another was Thomas Haxey. The choice of Haxey is notable in view of his apparent lack of a Crown appointment at this date.[28] In the spring of the following year, Haxey was described as a clerk of Waltham, who was then keeper of the privy seal.[29] Finally, in September 1395 he was named as one of the executors of Waltham's will (seventh out of eleven).[30] It has not been possible to trace the connection between Haxey and this family further back than 1386; for example, Haxey was not mentioned in the will of Master John Waltham, brother of the future bishop, made in 1384,[31] nor in Richard Ravenser's will of 1385,[32] nor in John Ravenser's will of 1390.[33]

One way of tracing his patron would be through Haxey's coat-of-arms: or, three buckles in fess, sable.[34] Granting arms based on those of the patron was a way of rewarding men of humble origins who had risen to prominent positions,[35] but Bishop Waltham is the only one of Haxey's early associates whose arms are known, and the two coats of arms have no elements in common.

Once within the orbit of Crown favour, Thomas Haxey's ecclesiastical career gathered momentum. Royal nominations to forthcoming vacancies,[36] and to pensions,[37] were soon joined by presentation to benefices by prominent patrons. Thus, although his tenure of the London rectory of St Nicholas Cole abbey was brief (4 to 15 December 1384), it is surely significant that this was in the gift of the dean of the royal free chapel of St Martin-le-Grand.[38]

Meanwhile, Haxey was embarking on a parallel business career – a common sideline for a successful king's clerk. The *Calendars* of chancery rolls show him undertaking two money-making activities: money-lending, and mainperning. The close rolls record ten loans made by Haxey, either alone, or with one or more associates, between November 1382 and December 1387, the amounts involved ranging between 5 marks and 500 marks.[39] The first of these was in December 1382 when he lent £19 13s 4d to Roger Raulyn of Norfolk, and the second in October 1384 when he and Lambert Fermer, a former servant of the Black Prince, lent 20 marks to the chancery clerk, John de Leycestre.[40] Not all Haxey's business associates can be readily identified as clerks in Crown service, but they did include John de Lincoln of Grimsby, a distinguished king's clerk, William Ferriby, one of three Yorkshire clerks of that name identified by Dr Grassi, and Robert de Garton, who is described elsewhere as a 'clerk of Yorkshire'.[41] Twice Haxey acted in concert with George de Louthorpe, clerk, who is identified elsewhere as an associate of the Waltham–Ravenser family.[42]

Evidence for Haxey's activities as a mainpernor is less extensive, for only five cases are recorded on the close rolls, but they date from a similar period, October 1382 to September 1388, and once again a regional element is perceptible among his associates.[43] They included such Lincolnshire laymen as William Skypwyth the younger and Albin de Enderby of Somersby and Enderby, though the northern clerks, John de Lincoln and William Ferriby, were also among them.

The lessons to be drawn from these activities are two: that Haxey from 1382 was evidently a member of the powerful clan of 'northern' clerks who combined public service with private profit. The other is that this regional affiliation was a base from which could be forged business links extending over a wide area. Thus Haxey made loans to, and mainperned for, men whose property and security were located as widely apart as Norfolk, Middlesex and Wiltshire. More significant, perhaps, was that his range of business links included, from 1382, two men from Middlesex, and, from 1386, one from Leicestershire.[44]

At the same time, Haxey was making himself useful to the Crown. On 18 April 1385 he and John Elyngham, one of the king's serjeants-at-arms, were issued with £10 for their expenses and dispatched to Cornwall on a commission '*ad certos pisces regales vocatos whalles sive Graspeys*', and to arrest these for the king's use.[45] Both the west country connection and the association with Elyngham were renewed a year later when they were commissioned to enquire into an embarrassing case of wreck. A Genoese vessel, a '*tarita*', belonging to Antony Carlera and laden with a high-value cargo which included alum, dates, and spare parts for crossbows, had been wrecked at Blavet on the coast of Brittany, but was then plundered by the men of Dartmouth. This was only one of a series of such incidents; the sandbanks at Blavet proved the undoing of many a vessel, and the men of Dartmouth regarded the plunder of these wrecks as a local industry.[46]

The first mandate to look into this particular case was dated 28 February 1386 and was addressed to Haxey, Elyngham, the sheriff of Devon (Richard Whitley), and was headed by John Cary, chief baron of the exchequer.[47] Haxey's presence in this company is interesting, for the other three members of the commission held important posts either at Westminster, or Devon, or in Brittany, where Elyngham was serjeant of the town of Brest.[48] Yet despite such high-profile involvement, the case was not settled speedily, and a series of commissions and instructions was issued during the following twelve months.[49] Perhaps this was not surprising given the propensity of the men of Dartmouth to commit acts of piracy.[50]

The business was still proceeding[51] when Haxey was appointed to the post of keeper of the rolls and writs of the court of common pleas on 18 July 1387.[52] This was an important appointment since the keepers 'were appointed directly by the king, on the king's behalf'.[53] Haxey continued in this office until his disgrace early in 1397 – his successor, Master Robert Manfeld (surely a north Nottinghamshire man), being appointed on 8 February[54] – and he received his final payment, of six months' arrears of wages for the previous Michaelmas term, on 21 July 1397.[55]

The fee for this office, 10 marks a year, was comparatively modest, but the appointment transformed Haxey's ecclesiastical career. It was from that point that he began to collect cathedral prebends, starting with Tervin,[56] in Coventry and Lichfield, in 1388. The outline of Haxey's ecclesiastical career is already well known,[57] but two comments may be made about it. One is that not all his attempts at promotion were successful; thus, he seems not to have gained either the 'first vacant . . . dignity' in the college of Chester le Street, to which he was nominated in 1384, nor the mastership of Sherburn hospital which he was granted in 1388.[58] The other noteworthy point is that his tenures of the benefices with cure of souls which he obtained early in his career were suspiciously short. His tenure of Pulham lasted less than a year.[59] Later in 1384 he was rector of St Nicholas Cole abbey (as we have seen) for only eleven days. Presented to Topsfield, in Essex, on 26 January 1386, he had resigned by 8 June when his successor was appointed.[60] In 1388 his tenure of Somersham, Huntingdonshire, was of similarly short duration, since he exchanged it for North Crawley (Buckinghamshire) on 23 August; he had vacated Crawley by 8 November.[61] Two years later we see a similar burst of activity; presented to Histon St Andrew (in Cambridgeshire) on 2 October 1390, he exchanged it for the rectory of Great Linford, Buckinghamshire, on the 29th of the same month.[62]

Every two years – 1384, 1386, 1388, 1390 – he held one or two benefices in quick succession, and the suspicion must be that he was engaged, through these exchanges, in the dubious practice of benefice-broking. Much about this activity remains obscure, but it reached epidemic proportions in the later fourteenth century, and king's clerks were deeply involved in it.[63] Suspicion that sharp practice was involved in these transactions is increased when we note that some at least of these benefices were exchanged very frequently. St Nicholas Cole abbey, for example, had no less than five rectors in 1384.[64] Great Crawley had two rectors in 1384 and again in 1386, while Great Linford had a new rector every year from 1390 to 1393 inclusive. All these new incumbents acquired their benefices by exchange.[65] A goodly sprinkling of these passing incumbents are identifiable as king's clerks: John Mulsho at St Nicholas Cole abbey, Henry Malpas and William Selby at Great Crawley, Simon Gaunstede at Great Linford. Probably we should add to 'moneylender' and 'mainpernor' the title of 'chop-church' as a description of Haxey during much of the 1380s and 1390s.

Perhaps the most significant preferments for Haxey during these years continued and strengthened his ties with the areas near to his home territory at the southern limits of the northern province. Before 15 April 1388 he had acquired the prebend of Rampton in the collegiate church of Southwell, in north Nottinghamshire.[66] In 1392 he had an enforced stay in York; the royal courts were removed to York during the summer of that year, though were brought back to London before Christmas,[67] and in the next year Haxey was presented to Laxton church – also in north Nottinghamshire – by Sir Reginald Everyngham, a Howdenshire landowner.[68] Meanwhile, he continued to represent the abbot of Selby in parliament, 'a house fallen into penury', as his letters of appointment usually described it, so that by January 1397 he was appearing in parliament for at least the sixth time.[69]

Nor was Selby his only parliamentary client, for he represented John Buckingham, bishop of Lincoln, in 1393, and Richard Scrope, bishop of Coventry and Lichfield, in 1395.[70] Haxey, it would appear, was a man with exceptionally wide connections. By the mid-1390s he had built on his Lincolnshire contacts, both clerical and lay, and had links – if only of a formal kind – with three members of the episcopate, with two abbeys, Selby and Ramsey, which had presented him to a benefice,[71] the common pleas judges, Thomas Mowbray, earl of Nottingham, and such administrative high-flyers as Bishop John Waltham and Roger Walden.[72]

Meanwhile, the Crown was assisting Haxey's ecclesiastical career, and the pope had given his blessing not only to his pluralism but also to his benefice exchanging.[73] He was making considerable sums of money through his various activities. His only discernible enemy was the prior of Tickford, an alien priory in Buckinghamshire, but this was a quarrel which he had inherited from his predecessor as rector of Great Crawley.[74] It is entirely plausible to suggest that it was the wide circle of his friends which made him a good candidate for the placing before parliament of a petition which was so critical of the Crown.

This brings us to a discussion of the first parliament of 1397. It was summoned by writs dated 30 November 1396, convened on 22 January 1397, and it ended on 12 February.[75] From the scarcity of sources concerning this meeting, Tout argued that the parliament roll was either censored or was later deliberately tampered with to avoid unpleasant topics, and, he continued, 'The Chronicles have so little to say about this parliament that we might almost suspect a conspiracy of silence'.[76] This is surely too strong; the account in the parliament roll is extensive, covering, in the printed edition, nearly ten folio pages.[77]

This was the first parliament to be held since the conclusion of the 28-year truce with France and the king's marriage to the Princess Isabella in the previous year. Indeed, the new queen's coronation had taken place earlier that month, on 7 January 1397. If, as the Monk of Westminster had alleged in his comments on events a decade earlier, Richard's wish in making peace was to escape from the constant necessity for tax grants which war required,[78] then it was especially unfortunate that in this, of all parliaments, he asked for a subsidy. In the event, this was not granted, so Richard did not have things all his own way at this meeting, despite the renewal of indirect taxation and the legitimization of the Beauforts.[79]

The famous petition presented to the parliament of January 1397 had four points. The first complained that the statute concerning sheriffs and escheators was not being observed. This had stipulated that these officials should be sufficient persons in land or rent, and that they should not remain in office for more than a year. The second alleged that the Scottish Marches were being insufficiently defended against the incursions of the Scots, who were failing to observe the truces arranged between the two countries, with the result that the king's lieges were suffering; a remedy was sought for this. The third request was that the statute concerning the giving of badges and liveries should be observed.

Finally, the petition sought that the great cost of the king's household should be reduced, and that the number of bishops and ladies and their hangers-on at court should be lessened.

Richard's answers, apparently given in person, on Friday 26 January, were as follows. To the first, he said that the persons appointed were sufficient in power and loyalty, as reason demanded; and it seemed to him more profitable that people with experience should remain in office, if they were satisfactory, than that new and inexperienced officers should be appointed every year.[80] To the second, he promised that he would see to it that the lords would guard the Marches more effectively. No direct response to the third part is recorded, but this same parliament passed a statute on the matter whose wording closely resembles this part of the petition.[81] To the fourth, he replied with fury that the Commons had greatly exceeded their powers and had caused great offence to the king and had encroached on his regality. Parliament was to assemble again on the following Saturday morning when the Lords would tell the Commons what was the king's will in this matter. Meanwhile, he ordered Gaunt and Sir John Bussy, the Lincolnshire knight who was speaker in the parliament, to discover who had brought the bill before the Commons. The outcome is well known: the Commons cravenly put forward the name of Thomas Haxey and excused themselves of the offence they had caused. The Lords, for their part, declared retrospectively that it was treason to call for reform of the king's household.

Haxey's position was serious since the statute *pro clero* of 25 Edward III had removed benefit of clergy for treasons and felonies touching 'the King himself or his royal Majesty'.[82] Fortunately for him, the see of Canterbury had just been filled by the fearless and energetic Thomas Arundel, who received his bulls of translation and provision at his manor of Lambeth on 10 January. In the following three days the new primate was busy issuing commissions to a wide variety of subordinates, but between 14 January and 11 February he apparently broke off from his purely ecclesiastical duties to attend parliament.[83] Archbishop Arundel and the other prelates speedily sought, and obtained, pity and mercy for Haxey, and the custody of his person. Indeed, Haxey may already have been in Arundel's keeping by Wednesday 7 February, when he appeared before Gaunt and was condemned as a traitor.[84] The curious nature of Haxey's position is exemplified by the fact that on 25 February his estate as warden of the chapel of Lazenby (Yorkshire) was confirmed, and on 25 April he was confirmed in possession of his six other benefices.[85] Finally, on 27 May he was pardoned, and we are told that his pardon was at the request of 'the bishops and multitude of ladies' in the king's household;[86] this sounds like either a medieval joke – entirely plausible since medieval humour seems to have had a strongly macabre element – or evidence that the whole affair was an 'inside job'. The granting of his 66s 8d of back pay, on 21 July, is confirmation that the king bore Thomas Haxey no continuing grudge,[87] though he was not reinstated in his post at the common pleas, nor did he hold any other Crown office under Richard II.

Haxey's next move is not entirely clear. In March 1399 Thomas del Kirk, his servant, was paid 12d by Selby abbey for bringing a letter from Haxey. Later that year, we hear of him at his prebendal church of Rampton, for when the abbot of Selby sought his advice in September it was to Rampton that the messenger was sent.[88] On the eighth of the month Peter Talbot, the abbey's porter, was paid expenses in going to Rampton 'in order to speak with *dominus* Thomas de Haxay concerning business of the lord abbot'.[89] We can well imagine that this need for advice was occasioned by Henry Bolingbroke's recent invasion. Possession of his seven benefices was confirmed to Haxey in November, at the same time as many other king's clerks had their benefices confirmed.[90]

Though he never again occupied so conspicuous an office as keeper of the writs and rolls of common pleas, Haxey was referred to as a king's clerk several times under Henry IV, and in 1405 he was twice described as 'one of the clerks of Chancery'.[91] In October 1404 he represented both the chapter of Lincoln and the archdeacon of Lincoln in parliament,[92] and he acted as proctor for the abbot of Selby for the last time in 1406.[93] Still described as a king's clerk, he was commissioned, along with Master William Waltham, to enquire into an allegation of bastardy in 1412, but their investigations were to take place in York.[94] In fact, in the new century the focus of his life changed, if perhaps gradually, to the northern province. This phase of his life, which was longer than his fourteenth-century career and scarcely less interesting, is outside the scope of this paper. Thus, we have no space here to discuss Haxey the ecclesiastical administrator, the generous benefactor, the energetic builder,

Haxey the connoisseur of fine jewels and plate, nor to consider the remaining evidence for his career as a Crown servant; he apparently remained alert, vigorous, and financially astute until his death in 1425.[95]

Our examination of Haxey's career before 1397 has revealed a man who was, by worldly standards, successful and who enjoyed extremely wide contacts. Yet his earliest connections still elude us, nor do we know what education he received. Though he had no discernible legal training, Haxey must have been, in some sense, a lawyer. We have observed Haxey as a common law lawyer in the court of common pleas, perhaps even Haxey the civil lawyer, investigating cases of maritime law; in the fifteenth century we may observe Haxey the canon lawyer participating in, and perhaps directing, the affairs of the chapter, and even the diocese, of York.[96] His presentation to Brington, in Huntingdonshire, by Ramsey abbey in December 1396 suggests that he was seen as at least a potential adviser by the abbey, since in Ramsey's case the connection between the granting of benefices and the expectation of public service was a close one.[97] The abbey was embroiled in a 'long and costly dispute' with John Fordham, bishop of Ely, and it apparently enlisted Haxey's help for its cause; his condemnation early in 1397 upset their plans.[98]

So we may return to the famous petition of 1397 and speak with more confidence of the man who presented it, and thus of the reasons and men behind it. Haxey's generous treatment by Richard II, and especially the terms of his pardon, mean that we must take seriously the suggestion that the king himself was behind the petition, either because he wished to 'test the water' of public opinion, or because he wished to use a ruling that it was treason to incite criticism of the royal household as a future weapon against the Appellants.[99]

This theory is open to criticism for a number of reasons. The king's anger at the criticism of his household seems to have been genuine. '*Item al quart article, touchant le Charge de l'Hostiel de Roy, & la demuree d'Evesques & Dames en sa compaignie, Le Roy prist grandement a grief & offense*', says the parliament roll,[100] and there is no reason to doubt it. Richard was notoriously sensitive to any criticism of his court. Had he not declared in 1386, to a delegation from parliament, that he would not dismiss so much as one kitchen boy from his service? In suffering so extreme a penalty as condemnation for treason, Haxey was undoubtedly only one of a long line of victims of the explosive royal temper. And, we might add, criticizing the number of ladies in the royal household was surely remarkably tactless immediately after the coronation of a new queen. Also, a king trying to persuade parliament to make a grant of taxation – as Richard was concurrently trying to do – would surely have regarded any adverse comment on his household expenses as unwelcome in the extreme. Finally, general observation of despotic natures is that they prefer the fiction that they command total approval and support; whereas the matters raised in the petition contained various matters which seemed to the king to be against his regality and estate and his royal liberty.[101] We might add that if the whole affair had really been a convoluted court plot in which Sir John Bussy, the speaker, was acting as Richard's tool in manipulating the Commons, we might have expected some earlier evidence of connections between himself and Haxey. Although they had interests in similar areas of Lincolnshire and Nottinghamshire, none has as yet been found. The suggestion that the king wished to use the declaration of principle that calling for reform of his household was treason cannot be proven since this was not one of the charges brought against the Appellants later in the year.

Contrariwise, it is hard to see the hand of any of the senior Appellants behind any part of the petition. All three were named as triers of petitions and Warwick was certainly present at the parliament. He had private business of his own on that occasion, for the bishop of Llandaff accused him of illegally seizing the manor of Bishopston, in the Gower peninsula, during the last vacancy of the see. This petition was heard by the king and lords who found against Warwick; they deprived him of the property and fined him for contempt.[102] Arguably this case – only one of the occasions when judgement was given against Warwick or one of his supporters[103] – is of considerable political importance for it shows the king taking the legal offensive against his old enemy.

Similarly, it is impossible to envisage Haxey's parliamentary master, John de Shirburn, abbot of Selby, as the originator of the petition. He was scarcely by nature a political animal, for since his election in 1369 he is known to have attended parliament only twice. It is true that his reasons for non-attendance – the poverty of his house – were slightly unusual; the most common excuses were that an individual was either broken with age or wracked with infirmity, or that pressure of work prevented attendance.[104] But all such excuses should be regarded as conventions and treated with some scepticism.

Another problem concerning this petition is its structure, for very unusually it was in four parts. When the king asked John of Gaunt and Sir John Bussy who had dared to criticize his household by presenting such a bill to the Commons, Haxey's name was produced.[105] The other three parts were relatively uncontentious, so no name was called for; but this surely does not exclude the possibility that Haxey was the presenter of the complete petition. There is here a disagreement among historians which further research on the drafting of Commons' petitions may yet resolve.[106] Much seems to hinge on the translation of the word '*bille*', which can either mean 'bill' (written complaint) or 'petition'.[107] Here it is argued that the four-part petition should be viewed as a whole and, as will also be argued, Thomas Haxey's career links him with every matter that it raised.

Whether the petition was entirely the work of one man or was presented by a consortium of administrators and gentry, it is surely more reasonable to see it as a reflection of the concerns of Haxey and his associates than to look for its sponsors among leading 'political' figures. As Ramsay long ago observed, Haxey was 'an old pluralist and official, who knew exactly where to lay his finger on the weak points of the administration'.[108] We have seen that his collaborators were numerous and that they came, not from the ranks of the aristocracy, but from the gentry class and the ranks of the king's clerks. If the petition is examined in its entirety, we can see how it reflected widespread concerns characteristic of these groups. The first request, that the king should honour his obligation to change the personnel of the sheriffs and escheators every year, was surely a cry for less restrictive patronage at county level. This is just the kind of issue on which the likes of the Skipwith family (one of whom was a trier of petitions in this parliament)[109] and Albin Enderby would have felt strongly.

The request for better guarding of the Scottish Marches is less easily linked with Haxey and his friends. As we have seen, two nominations to benefices in Durham diocese were not effective, and in 1397 his most northerly connection was with the hospital or chapel of Lazenby, in north Yorkshire.[110] But although Haxey himself may not have had direct contact with the Scottish problem, he knew men who did. His early associate, Master John Waltham, was sent on an embassy to Scotland in 1383 and 1384, and must surely have discussed his experiences among his circle.[111] Of more immediate importance was a loan made early in 1396. Dated 7 January, a recognizance of this transaction was entered on the close rolls. The lenders were Roger Walden, Master William Waltham, Haxey and his old associate, George de Louthorpe. The borrowers were Ralph Neville, lord of Raby, and Thomas, Lord Furnival,[112] Sir Robert Conyers, Thomas de Claxton, Robert Coverham and Gilbert Elvet. The sum involved was 1,000 marks.[113] The purpose of the loan eludes us, but we can say with certainty that the borrowers were northerners; Ralph Neville (another trier of petitions in January 1397)[114] and Thomas Furnival were brothers, Gilbert Elvet became controller of the customs in Newcastle upon Tyne a year later,[115] and Robert Conyers was a Yorkshire knight.[116] Haxey thus had a proven link with a keeper of the Scottish Marches, if only of a financial kind.[117]

It is a commonplace to say that worries about the effects of the giving of badges and liveries were centred on the gentry class and were a point of friction between them and the aristocracy, and all readers of the Paston Letters know how difficult it was for minor gentle and professional families to assert their case in disputes involving members of the magnate class and their adherents. Such disputes most often involved property and they therefore came within the jurisdiction of the court of common pleas. Who was better placed to know about such disputes and the allegations of perversions of justice than the keeper of the rolls and writs of that court? Haxey, we may suggest, was the obvious person to act as a conduit for complaints on this matter. Like the fourth part of his petition, this complaint directly touched the king who was by now distributing his badge of the white hart.[118]

The parasitical bishops were probably of more immediate concern to Haxey and his close clerical friends, for Haxey was representative of a particular class of men, successful king's clerks. As we have seen, many had strong ties of geography, and even kinship, but once at Westminster they forged wide-ranging and changing networks of business and patronage. They combined public service with private profit, and both king and pope connived at their evasion of ecclesiastical regulations. These men essentially ran the country, and, for the time being, no one in political life could do without them. Many became extremely wealthy, and they almost monopolized the senior positions in the church. The greatest of them could expect to be rewarded with a bishopric.

In the 1390s, however, a worrying trend set in: the king began to fill bishoprics not with senior men from the administration, but with his personal servants. Starting in 1390 with the promotion of his confessor, Alexander Bache, to St Asaph, a series of promotions rewarded those about the king's person, several of them regulars.[119] Worse, in the 'general post' of the episcopal bench in 1396, occasioned in part by the death of Archbishop Courtenay, no administrative king's clerk was promoted. By contrast, the king's physician, Robert Waldby, was granted first Chichester (February) and then York (October). At the turn of the year, the same pattern was continuing with the translation of Robert Reade from Carlisle to Chichester, and the promotion of Thomas Merks OSB, a monk of Westminster abbey, to Carlisle. Senior administrators, of whom Haxey was but one, were watching their promotion prospects being stunted.

At the same time, the costs of the king's household and of his increasing retinue were rising. We now know that, and Haxey, the associate of both John Waltham and Roger Walden, successive treasurers, was in a good position to know it too.[120] Complaints about household extravagance and about the character of the court were not new, but a new urgency, if not bitterness, could well have been felt by some of Richard's servants. In considering the origins of the petition, Haxey's 'political' affiliations are probably less important than the widespread nature of his contacts, for they included critics of Richard such as Thomas Arundel, William Skipwith,[121] and the former Appellant Nottingham, and also those enjoying the royal confidence such as Bishop Waltham and Roger Walden. Indeed, Haxey's career serves to remind us that, just as the aristocracy, however divided on occasion, were essentially members of one family clan, so among those who mattered, both in central administration and in county politics, there were numerous networks and points of contact, so that links can often be traced between individuals who were apparently at loggerheads on political matters.[122] Allegiances and affiliations could also change.[123]

The petition presented to parliament by Thomas Haxey in 1397 formed a wide-ranging critique of Richard II's government; it should perhaps be seen as being administrative rather than political in tone, and Thomas Haxey viewed as the front-row spokesman for the back-room boys. As for the most celebrated section of the petition, the criticism of the costs of the ladies and the courtier bishops, this may have been merely the civil service's way of saying that the wrong men were getting the top jobs.

Notes

[1] Thanks are due to Drs Margaret Aston and Nigel Saul and to Professors Jim Gillespie, Ralph Griffiths and George Stow for their encouragement concerning this paper; to Dr Paul Brand for reading an early draft and giving expert help on the legal matters raised; and to Professor Brian Kemp for his careful critique of a later version.

[2] T.F. Tout, *Chapters in the Administrative History of Medieval England* (6 vols, Manchester, 1920–33), IV, pp. 18–19, though, characteristically, he has some very useful things to say about this parliament in general.

[3] M. McKisack, *The Fourteenth Century* (Oxford, 1959), p. 744.

[4] A. Steel, *Richard II* (Cambridge, 1941), p. 228.

[5] M. Aston, *Thomas Arundel* (Oxford, 1967), p. 365.

[6] *The Royal Policy of Richard II* (Oxford, 1968), p. 73.

[7] *Richard II and the English Nobility* (London, 1973), p. 182.

[8] J.L. Grassi, 'Royal Clerks from the archdiocese of York in the Fourteenth Century', *Northern History*, V (1970), 12–33, which also gives references to the works of Tout and Hamilton Thompson, and to the unpublished work of Stevenson.

[9] A.B. Emden, *A Biographical Register of the University of Oxford* (3 vols, Oxford, 1957–9), III, 1973–4; see also *The Register of John Waltham, Bishop of Salisbury, 1388–1395*, ed. T.C.B. Timmins (Canterbury and York Society, 80, 1994), especially the introduction and app. E (Waltham's will).

[10] *CCR, 1381–5*, pp. 217, 232; 8 October and 25 November 1382. The other occasion was 29 January 1384, ibid., p. 615.

[11] Haxey, one of eight parishes within the Isle of Axholme, had within its boundaries the hamlets of East Lound, Graizelound, Low Burnham, High Burnham, Westwoodside, Newbriggs, Upperthorpe, Nethergate, and Park: W.B. Stonehouse, *The History and Topography of the Isle of Axholme* (Gainsborough, 1837), p. 10.

[12] York Minster Library L2/4 (Reg. Wills I), f. 219ᵛ.

[13] Lincolnshire Archives Office (LAO), Haxey Parish Deeds no. 48. It is not known when Haxey entered holy orders, nor anything about his progress to the priesthood; the ordinations register of John Buckingham, bishop of Lincoln, 1363–98, has not survived.

[14] LAO Reg. 11, John Buckingham (Institutions II), f. 442.

[15] For example, nos 23, 27, 34, 40, 41, 44, 47, 52. I should like to thank Mr Nigel Colley of the Lincolnshire Archives Office for drawing my attention to this collection of documents.

[16] The bequests include disposition of land in both Rampton and Beckingham. It is likely that the Beckingham refers to the Notts. village of that name, some 7 miles north of Rampton, also in Notts. Both villages lie to the west of the River Trent. York Minster Library L2/4, (Reg. Wills I), f. 220.

[17] *CCR, 1381–5*, p. 198; 21 February 1383. Dr Brand suggests that this excuse was sometimes used by someone who did not want the job.

[18] *CCR, 1381–5*, p. 222.

[19] Ibid., 25 November, p. 232.

[20] Ibid., 13 December, p. 238.

[21] *CCR, 1381–5*, p. 625; 18 March.

[22] K.B. McFarlane, *John Wycliffe and the Beginnings of English Nonconformity* (London, 1952), p. 63.

[23] For a discussion of the difficulties in interpreting this description, see A. Hamilton Thompson, 'The College of St Mary Magdalene, Bridgnorth: Part II The Dean and Canons of Bridgnorth', *Archaeological Journal*, LXXXIV (1927), p. 27.

[24] Tout, *Chapters*, IV, 4 n. 2.

[25] *CCR, 1392–6*, p. 500; they were engaged in money-lending activities together since 7 January 1396.

[26] M. Aston, *Thomas Arundel*, p. 311.

[27] *CCR, 1381–5*, pp. 217, 232; 8 October and 25 November 1382.

[28] PRO, SC10 (Parliamentary Proxies), file 36, no. 1772.

[29] Tout, *Chapters*, IV, 19n.

[30] Grateful thanks are due to Mr T.C.B. Timmins, the editor of Waltham's register, for providing me with a copy of this will in advance of the publication of Waltham's register by the Canterbury and York Society: see above, n. 8.

[31] York Minster Library, L2/4, (Reg. Wills I), ff. 80v–81.

[32] Richard Ravenser's will was printed in *Memoirs illustrative of the History of the County and City of Lincoln* (Royal Archaeological Institute, London, 1850). I am much indebted to Mr T.C.B. Timmins for this reference, and for providing me with a copy of the text.

[33] York Minster Library, L2/4 (Reg. Wills I), ff. 107–8.

[34] *The Fabric Rolls of York Minster*, ed. James Raine (Surtees Society, 35, 1858), p. 204; they were placed in the windows of the newly built chapter library for which Haxey donated £26 13s 4d for the lead roofing in 1418.

[35] John Buckingham of Lincoln bore arms based on those of Thomas Beauchamp, earl of Warwick, his first patron. Both arms may be seen on the north wall of the Vicars' Court, in the close at Lincoln.

[36] *CPR, 1381–5*, p. 513: 'Nomination of the king's clerk Thomas Haxeye to William [Courtenay], Archbishop of Canterbury, for presentation to the first vacant canonry, prebend or other dignity in the collegiate church of Chestre-in-the-Strete [Chester le Street], Durham diocese', 2 December 1384. No benefice resulted from this nomination.

[37] *CCR, 1381–5*, p. 625: Nomination to the abbess and convent of St Mary, Winchester, 18 March 1385.

[38] G. Hennessy, *Novum Repertorium Ecclesiasticum Parochiale Londinense* (London, 1898), p. 345.

[39] *CCR, 1381–5*, pp. 238 (£19 13s 4d), 589 (20 marks), 607 (6 marks); *CCR, 1385–8*, pp. 143 (500 marks), 247 (5 marks), 252 (£300), 261 (20 marks), 442 (£200), 444 (£20), 449 (£40).

[40] *CCR, 1377–81*, pp. 238, 589; 13 December 1382, 31 October 1384. Fermer had been a yeoman of the Black Prince and went on to become Richard II's receiver of the chamber, 1387–91, Tout, *Chapters*, IV, 336, 337 n. 1; VI, 57.

[41] Tout, *Chapters*, VI, 315, for references; Grassi, *Northern History*, V (1970), pp. 29–30; *CCR, 1385–92*, p. 142.

[42] *CCR, 1385–9*, pp. 143, 261; *CCR, 1381–5*, p. 626.

[43] *CCR, 1381–5*, pp. 217, 232, 615; 8 October and 25 November 1382, 29 January 1385; *CCR, 1385–9*, pp. 126, 608; 10 March 1386, 2 September 1388.

[44] *CCR, 1381–5*, p. 232: William Yorke of Westminster and Nicholas Barbour of Middlesex; *CCR, 1385–8*, p. 126: William de Outheby of Leics.

[45] PRO, E403 (Issue Roll)/510 m. 32.

[46] M. Jones, 'Roches contre Hawley: la cour anglaise de chevalerie et un cas de piraterie à Brest, 1386–1402', *Mémoires de la Société d'histoire et d'archéologie de Bretagne*, LXIV (1987), 53–64. I am grateful to Professor Jones for giving me a copy of this article.

[47] *CPR, 1385–9*, p. 170.

[48] M. Jones, *Ducal Brittany, 1364–1399* (Oxford, 1970), p. 156.

[49] *CPR, 1385–9*, pp. 284, 320; *CCR, 1385–8*, pp. 226–7, 328.

[50] '*Quo in tempore naute de Dertemouthe ceperunt vij. naves magnas ac quatuor naves minores vino sale et aliis mercimoniis diversis onustas*', *Westminster Chronicle, 1381–94*, eds L.C. Hector and B.F. Harvey (Oxford, 1982), p. 320, *s.a.* 1388.

[51] *CPR, 1385–9*, p. 328, 5 July 1387.

[52] E403/518 m. 10.

[53] Introduction to the Standard List Set of the Rex Rolls, CP23 (by Dr David Crook), September 1992. Dr Brand has pointed out to me, however, that the precise nature of the keeper's post is unclear.

[54] *BRUO*, II, 1213–4.

[55] E403/555 m. 17. The list of rex rolls, C23, shows that Haxey held the post continuously, though there was an irregular start to his tenure of the office, *CPR, 1385–92*, p. 314.

[56] Though the form 'Tervin' is retained for ecclesiastical purposes, the modern spelling of the place-name, and river, is 'Tarvin'. Thanks are due to Professor Michael Jones for this information.

[57] It may be consulted in the *Dictionary of National Biography*, in *The Fabric Rolls of York Minster*, ed. J. Raine (Surtees Society, 35, 1858), pp. 203–6; and, for corrections, see 'Documents Relating to Visitations of the Diocese and Province of York, 1407, 1423', ed. A. Hamilton Thompson, *Miscellanea II* (Surtees Society, 127, 1916), pp. 295–6. I am grateful to Mr T.C.B. Timmins for this last reference.

[58] *CPR, 1381–5*, p. 513; 2 December 1384; *CPR, 1385–9*, p. 506; 13 September 1388. Both are in Co. Durham.

[59] Instituted 21 April 1384, Aston, *Thomas Arundel*, pp. 205n., 311.

[60] *CPR, 1385–9*, pp. 109, 154.

[61] Aston, *Thomas Arundel*, p. 311; LAO Reg. 11 (Buckingham, Institutions II), ff. 383ᵛ, 390ᵛ.

[62] *Fabric Rolls of York Minster*, p. 203; LAO Reg. 11, ff. 397ᵛ–398.

[63] A.K. McHardy, 'Some Patterns of Ecclesiastical Patronage in the later Middle Ages', in D.M. Smith (ed.), *Studies in Clergy and Ministry in Medieval England* (York, Borthwick Studies in History, 1, 1991), pp. 31–2.

[64] Hennessy, *Novum Repertorium Ecclesiasticum Parochiale Londinense*, p. 345.

[65] LAO Reg. 10, ff. 462–462ᵛ; Reg. 11, ff. 376, 383ᵛ(2), 397ᵛ–398, 399ᵛ, 403ᵛ, 407.

66 *CPR, 1385–9*, p. 433.

67 *CCR, 1389–92*, p. 467: 'To Thomas Haxey the king's clerk, keeper of the writs of the Common Bench: order to be in person at York on the morrow of St John Baptist to execute his office in the accustomed form, causing all writs etc. in his custody and which concern his office to be brought with him', 30 May 1392. *CCR, 1392–6*, p. 76: 'To the keeper of the writs of the Common Bench: order to be at Westminster on the octave of Hilary in order to exercise his office, bringing with him all writs, etc. which concern the same', 25 October 1392, York.

68 Aston, *Thomas Arundel*, p. 311. The Everingham family also held land at Ruskington, Lincs., Alan Rogers, 'Parliamentary electors in Lincolnshire in the Fifteenth Century: Part I', *Lincolnshire History and Archaeology*, 3 (1968), 58.

69 PRO, SC10 file 37 no. 1847; file 38 no. 1872; file 39 no. 1916; file 40 nos 1952, 1964. This is an artificial PRO class with many gaps and losses. The Selby material may be most conveniently consulted in J.H. Tillotson, *Monastery and Society in the Late Middle Ages. Selected Account Rolls from Selby Abbey, Yorkshire, 1398–1537* (Woodbridge, 1988), pp. 255–8.

70 PRO, SC10 file 38 no. 1872; file 39 no. 1944.

71 Brington, Hunts., 17 December 1396, Reg. 11, f. 284.

72 *CCR, 1392–6*, p. 500: Walden and Haxey, along with Mr William Waltham and George de Louthorpe, acted as money-lenders together in January 1395.

73 *Cal. Papal Pets.*, IV, *1362–1404*, p. 395: 'Dispensation to Thomas Haxey canon of Lichfield to receive and hold for three years two benefices with cure . . . and to exchange the same as often as seems good to him for two similar or dissimilar incompatible benefices', 2 Kal. December 1390.

74 The dispute was over the tithes of Little Crawley (Bucks.); Haxey was rector of Great Crawley, and the dispute had started in the time of his predecessor as rector, *CCR, 1389–92*, pp. 199–200, 551.

75 The handiest timetable of the events of this parliament is to be found in Aston, *Thomas Arundel*, pp. 363–4.

76 *Chapters*, IV, 15.

77 *Rot. Parl.*, III, 337–46.

78 *Westminster Chronicle, 1381–1394*, p. 204.

79 A very full account of this parliament, with references, is given by J.H. Ramsay, *The Genesis of Lancaster* (Oxford, 1913), II, 313–9.

80 This seems a reasonable argument, yet the charge of keeping sheriffs in office for too long was repeated in the 'Record and Process' of Richard's deposition. It was the eighteenth of the thirty-three accusations, and may be conveniently consulted in C. Given-Wilson, *Chronicles of the Revolution, 1397–1400* (Manchester, 1993), p. 178.

81 *Rot. Parl.*, III, 345.

82 L.C. Gabel, *Benefit of Clergy in England in the Later Middle Ages* (Smith College Studies in History, XIV, nos 1–4, 1928–9), p. 59.

83 Lambeth Palace Library, Register of Thomas Arundel (Canterbury) I, ff. 5 (receipt of papal bulls), 3v–4 (diocesan commissions dated 11, 12, 13 January), 6 (resumption of Canterbury business, 10, 11 February).

84 On 5 February the constable of Windsor castle was ordered to deliver Haxey to one of the king's serjeants-at-arms to be handed over to the custody of the archbishop, *CCR, 1396–9*, p. 34.

[85] *CPR, 1396–9*, pp. 88, 123. The other benefices were the prebends of Scamblesby (Lincoln cathedral), Rampton (Southwell college), Beminster Secunda (Salisbury cathedral), Tervin (Lichfield cathedral), and Brington church (Hunts.) in Lincoln diocese.

[86] *CCR, 1396–9*, p. 141.

[87] PRO, E403/555 m. 17.

[88] Tillotson, *Monastery and Society: Selby Abbey*, p. 70.

[89] Ibid., pp. 61, 70.

[90] *CPR, 1399–1401*, pp. 24–7. Haxey's ratification is on the last page.

[91] *CPR, 1401–5*, pp. 123, 489 (26 January 1405); *1405–8*, pp. 47 (8 August 1405), 227.

[92] PRO, SC10 file 42 nos 2076, 2086.

[93] Tillotson, *Monastery and Society: Selby Abbey*, p. 257.

[94] 29 October 1412, *CPR, 1408–13*, p. 475.

[95] I hope elsewhere to print his will and to discuss the second half of his career, along with his interests and benefactions.

[96] For Haxey in ecclesiastical administration, see York Minster Library, H 2/1, Chapter Acts 1410–1429, ff. 21ᵛff. He was appointed keeper of the spiritualities of the archbishopric following the death of Henry Bowet in 1423, Raine, *York Fabric Rolls*, p. 204.

[97] McHardy, 'Some Patterns of Ecclesiastical Patronage', pp. 26–7. His two predecessors at Brington were described as *magistri*, and before them came David Wooler, the distinguished chancery clerk, LAO Reg. 10, f. 293; Reg. 11, ff. 263, 284.

[98] *CPR, 1396–9*, p. 57.

[99] This last suggestion was made by Professor Brian Kemp to me in a recent letter.

[100] *Rot. Parl.*, III, 339.

[101] Ibid.

[102] *Rot. Parl.*, III, 337, 341.

[103] J.B. Post, 'Courts, Councils and Arbitrators in the Ladbroke manor dispute, 1382–1400', in R.F. Hunnisett and J.B. Post (eds), *Medieval Legal Records edited in Memory of C.A.F. Meekings* (London, 1978), pp. 290–301.

[104] Parliamentary Proxies, PRO, SC10; the Selby commissions, along with a list of parliaments for which the class provides no evidence, may conveniently be consulted in Tillotson, *Monastery and Society*, pp. 255–8.

[105] '*Et outre, le Roy entendant coment les ditz Communes fuerent moez & enformez par un Bille baillee a eux pur parler & monstrer la dit darrein article, si comanda a le Duc de Guyen & de Lanc' pur charger Mons'r John Bussy, Parlour pur les Communes, sur sa ligeance de counter & dire a lui de Noun de cellui qui bailla as ditz Communes la dite Bille*', *Rot. Parl.*, III, 339.

[106] My interpretation accords with that of Tuck, *Richard II and the English Nobility*, pp. 181–3, in viewing the petition as a whole. Professor Kemp represents those who think that Haxey had nothing to do with the other three parts of the petition.

[107] W. Rothwell, L.W. Stone, T.B.W. Reid (eds), *Anglo-Norman Dictionary* (London, 1992), p. 68; A. Harding, 'Plaints and Bills in the History of English Law, mainly in the period 1250–1350', in Dafydd Jenkins (ed.), *Legal History Studies 1972* (Cardiff, 1975), pp. 65–86.

[108] Ramsay, *Genesis of Lancaster*, II, 317.

[109] *Rot. Parl.*, III, 337, William Skipwith the younger.

[110] *CPR, 1396–9*, p. 88: 25 February 1397, ratification of the estate of Thomas Haxey as rector of Laxton, York diocese, and warden of Lazenby chapel, Durham diocese. Lazenby is near Northallerton, North Yorks.

[111] *BRUO*, III, 1974.

[112] A courtesy title: Thomas de Neville, second son of John de Neville, lord of Raby, had married Joan, the Furnevalle heiress, but was addressed in writs of summons to military service and to parliament, as 'Thomas de Nevil', G.E. Cockayne *et al.*, *Complete Peerage*, V (1926), 589.

[113] *CCR, 1392–6*, p. 500. The sum was repaid and acknowledged by Walden and Waltham.

[114] *Rot. Parl.*, III, 337.

[115] *CPR, 1396–9*, p. 78: 17 February 1397.

[116] Ibid., pp. 241, 243. The names of Claxton and Coverham also suggest Yorkshire connections.

[117] 'Ralph de Nevyll de Raby' was summoned to attend the first parliament of 1397, *Complete Peerage*, XII part. II (London, 1959), 544–5.

[118] I owe thanks to Dr Margaret Aston for drawing my attention to this point.

[119] Other examples included Tideman of Winchcombe O.Cist., the king's surgeon, Llandaff 1394, Worcester 1395; John Burghill OP, the king's confessor, Llandaff 1396; see E.B. Fryde, D.E. Greenway, S. Porter and I. Roy (eds), *Handbook of British Chronology* (3rd edn, London, 1986), for lists of bishops, and Chris Given-Wilson, *The Royal Household and the King's Affinity* (Yale, 1986), pp. 179–83, for comment on the changing nature of the episcopate.

[120] Given-Wilson, *Royal Household*, p. 79.

[121] Justice Skipwith and his two eldest sons, William and John, 'were prominent among the Lincolnshire gentry who took oaths in March 1388 in support of the Lords Appellant', J.S. Roskell, Linda Clark, Carole Rawcliffe, *The Commons, 1386–1421* (History of Parliament, Stroud, 1992), IV, 388–9. John Skipwith was sheriff of Lincs., 1394–5.

[122] A further good example is John Scarle, another Lincolnshire man, who was both clerk and then keeper of the rolls of parliament (1384–97) and chancellor of the county palatinate of Lancashire (1382–94).

[123] A notable example is Sir John Bussy, the speaker, who was chief steward of the duchy of Lancaster, *c.* June 1394–March 1398, ibid., II, 450.

6

RICHARD II: CHIVALRY AND KINGSHIP

James L. Gillespie

Richard II is usually cast as a man out of touch with the ideals and values of his own time. Such a perception is summarized by Richard H. Barber: 'Edward II, who despite his bodily strength preferred menial occupations to knightly ones, and Richard II, with his highly developed aesthetic sense and love of refinement . . . could not share their interest with their barons and courtiers; and on their barons their power ultimately rested'.[1] A new twist was added by Richard H. Jones who argued that Richard II was a theorist of absolutism born before his time. Yet even Jones recognized that the Ricardian programme of kingship was designed 'to perfect the strength of medieval kingship by the employment of ideals and devices which preserved a strict inheritance from the old intellectual and social structure'.[2] Among the most basic values of the old intellectual and social structure was the code of chivalry and the related, albeit distinct, ideal of the crusade. Both chivalry and crusading were much sinned against in the later Middle Ages, but the values and the ideals they represented still captured men's minds – and their hearts. The successor of the founder of the order of the Garter and the son of the Black Prince could scarcely escape exposure to these ideals. Richard, in fact, embraced them as essential components in what has been described as his 'passion for the pageantry of kingship'.[3]

The young king's upbringing was entrusted to two paragons of the chivalric traditions of the Black Prince, Guichard d'Angle and Simon Burley. Guichard, a knight whose chivalric reputation had been earned throughout Europe, was intended to be Burley's senior partner. He first served the Valois kings as seneschal of Saintonge, where he distinguished himself in 1346 before St Jean d'Angely in combat against the English. D'Angle's martial prowess earned him the additional title of captain in Saintonge beyond Charente from John II. He was taken prisoner by the English in 1351, but he was released in 1353, and

later fought for the French at Poitiers, where he was left for dead. The
Frenchman's gallantry at Poitiers left an impression on the English. Chandos
Herald's Life of the Black Prince paid tribute to this chivalric warrior: 'Then
behold there came spurring a valiant and doughty knight, by name Guichard
d'Angle; he never lagged behind, but smote with lance and sword in the middle
of the press.' The French defeat seems to have placed Guichard's Poitevin
estates under English lordship. The ever chivalrous John II ordered Guichard to
go to La Rochelle and take an oath of fealty to the king of England. He would
be as loyal – as *preux* – to his new lord as he had been to the king of France. By
1363 Guichard had joined the English banner, and the Black Prince made him
marshal of Aquitaine, a clear tribute to his chivalric and martial talents. Later,
Guichard served as joint-marshal for the prince's army in Spain. He
distinguished himself at Nájera, and escorted Don Pedro to Burgos after the
battle. The Black Prince's trust in Guichard was again demonstrated in 1369
when he was sent to Rome to negotiate with the pope on the prince's behalf.

On his return journey from Rome, he was forced to elude the French by
disguising himself as a poor chaplain; he was received at Angoulême by the
Black Prince 'with great satisfaction and joy'. Guichard then joined the earl of
Pembroke's expedition to Anjou, and he was with Sir John Chandos on Sir
John's fatal sally from Poitiers. A bas-relief on the wall of the church at
Mortemer represents Chandos dying in Guichard's arms. In fact, Guichard was
not present at the moment of Chandos's death, but the relief indicates the very
close association these two great captains enjoyed in the popular mind. In 1370
Guichard joined the Black Prince at the siege of Limoges. In 1371 he served in
Aquitaine with the duke of Lancaster, and he helped to arrange Lancaster's
marriage with Constance, eldest daughter of Pedro of Castile. This paragon of
chivalric prowess was inducted into the order of the Garter in 1372. He
returned to the continent and was taken prisoner off La Rochelle by a superior
force of Spaniards on 22 June 1372. He was released in 1374. Such was the
chivalric and martial career of the man to whom the young Richard, prince of
Wales, was entrusted 'by the accord of all the lande, to be instructed in noble
vertues'. Guichard's personal services were recognized by Richard II with a
grant of the earldom of Huntingdon – for life only – on 16 July 1377. The term
of the new earl's life had nearly expired; he was dead by 4 April 1380.[4]

Simon Burley survived longer, and was to be a major influence upon the young king. His prowess and service to the Black Prince and to Richard clearly commanded respect. He seems to have begun his career as a protégé of his learned kinsman, Walter Burley, who had served as tutor to the Black Prince. Simon retained an interest in scholarship, but he chose to follow a military career. His first martial venture came when he was still in his early teens. He shared in the naval victory of Espagnols-sur-Mer, fought near Winchelsea in 1350, when a fleet commanded by Edward III attacked and destroyed some Spanish vessels which had been preying upon English shipping. In 1356 Burley was noted by Froissart among Edward III's attendants on the king's abortive expedition from Calais to aid King Charles the Bad of Navarre. By 1364 he had taken service with the Black Prince in Aquitaine. Simon was sent on an embassy to Pedro of Castile in 1366, and he shared in the great victory of Nájera in the following year. Like Guichard d'Angle, he was among the select group singled out by Chandos Herald for their gallantry on the Spanish campaign. Burley had earned his accolade in a daring reconnaissance sortie prior to the great battle during which he captured a knight who had been in command of the night watch of Henry of Trastamara's army. In 1369 Burley was taken prisoner by the French, to the great grief of the Black Prince, by whom, Froissart says, with a warm eulogy on Sir Simon's valour, he was highly valued. Liberated in 1370, he rejoined his master for the siege of Limoges. Burley became a valued adviser and diplomat in Richard II's reign, and he was closely involved in negotiating the king's first marriage. His prowess was rewarded with the Garter in 1381. He served as constable of Dover castle and participated in the Scottish campaign of 1385. It is significant that Richard II quite probably intended to bestow d'Angle's old earldom on Sir Simon as one of the attendant creations marking that campaign. Burley was by then, however, too closely identified with the Ricardian court and his elevation was thwarted. He was a leading target of Richard's foes in the crisis of 1386–8, but his chivalric reputation still commanded respect. Sir Simon's execution in 1388 split the Lords Appellant as the earls of Derby and Nottingham supported the pleas of Queen Anne to save her husband's valued mentor and supporter.

What little evidence we have suggests that Richard's education was conventional, albeit not distinguished. Such an education under the supervision of tutors such as Guichard d'Angle and Simon Burley could hardly fail to impart an appreciation of chivalric matters to the young pupil.[5] The continental witnesses to Richard's reign were far more impressed by Richard's chivalric character than were the English chroniclers. Richard was influenced by the attitudes and styles of the French and Burgundian courts. His attempts to emulate his continental neighbours included the code of chivalric values that so impressed these foreign observers of the king. The sympathies of Jean Créton, the French squire who accompanied Richard's second Irish expedition, as well as those of the monk of St Denys and the anonymous author of the *Traïson et Mort de Richart Deux* are strongly Ricardian. Jean Froissart, the great chronicler of chivalry, may have had doubts about the king's policies, but he has nothing ill to say of Richard's character. Froissart mourned the king's death.[6] Less well known is the tribute to Richard's chivalric character penned by Christine de Pisan after Richard's fall when there were no rewards to be gained by flattery:

> A chevalier wearing a crown
> In a place near the sea
> On the one hand, I heard him renowned
> Very highly for taking up arms
> Willingly, he was praised
> For being *preux*, a true Lancelot
> It was said of him, without fault,
> In matters of arms and battle,
> Notwithstanding that, more than a year ago I have seen
> Fortune greatly harmed him
> So that, I believe, if I am not mistaken
> Even his own people imprisoned him
> But I don't know the cause
> Because I have given his plight very little thought.

Christine thought of chivalry not of politics, and she was equally generous in her praise for her son's benefactor, that Ricardian stalwart John Montagu, earl of Salisbury. Even Thomas Walsingham had some praise for the young king's courage during the Peasants' Revolt: 'The king himself sent out daily to

Blackheath . . . a soldier among soldiers . . . he liked to be seen with the army and to be recognized as lord by his men.'[7] Richard II had his chivalric moments in the eyes of others: how did he see himself?

Richard did patronize knightly pursuits. The degree to which such interests were genuine or merely politic can never be assessed, but the key rôle of chivalry within Richard's kingly persona is plain. The royal interdiction for political reasons of the judicial duel at Coventry in 1398 between the dukes of Hereford and Norfolk, which had promised to be the chivalric event of the reign, had obscured the king's earlier interest in jousts and tournaments. The chronicles record Richard's presence at two jousts with both chivalric and diplomatic implications. In 1384 the English squire John Walsh defeated and slew his Navarrese opponent in the lists at Westminster in the presence of the king and the duke of Lancaster. Richard was so pleased with Walsh's performance that he knighted him, and rewarded him with rich gifts. In May 1390 Sir David Lindsay of Glenesk, the future earl of Crawford, upheld the honour of Scotland in a passage of arms with John, Lord Welles. Lindsay unseated Welles, but the Scot was accused of having tied himself on his horse. Sir David rushed to King Richard to seek exoneration. The king judged Sir David blameless. The contest was resumed, and Lindsay won the day.

> Schir Dauid de Lyndissay on þis wise
> Fulfillyt in Lundynge his iourne
> Withe honore and wiþe honeste,
> Before Richarde þe Secunde Kynge,
> þat had Englande in governynge,
> And in his flowris was regnande
> In to þe kynrik of Inglande.

Richard had also done himself honour by serving as a fair judge.[8]

Richard himself was never the jouster that his grandfather had been. In comparison with the reign of Edward III, references to royal jousting are sparse, but Richard did at least attempt to conform to chivalric norms. The Westminster chronicle recounts that Richard sought release from the Appellant crisis by spending the entire autumn of 1388 hunting and by celebrating

Christmas at Eltham 'with numerous tourneys'. In 1390 the king was awarded the honours of the first day of a three-day tournament at Windsor. Richard also organized the great Smithfield tournament in October the same year. This gathering of chivalry at Smithfield offered both English and foreign guests a symbolic confirmation of Richard II's renewed grip on the reins of kingship after the Appellant interlude. The selection of Smithfield as the site for the event may well have been intended to restore the bonds between the king and London; it would certainly impress – and enrich – the citizens. The formality of the occasion would also serve to emphasize the right order of society as Richard led the English host into the field. Even in the final years of his reign when the king was attempting most forcibly to implement his own concepts of kingship, the very time at which he halted the duel at Coventry, Richard's tailor, Walter Rauf, was ordered to make a number of doublets, cloaks, and shoes for the king's use at 'tournaments and jousts'.[9]

In the final crisis of Richard's life there are indications that the king – like his old foe, the earl of Arundel – attempted to defend his honour and his life through a challenge to personal combat. The *Traïson et Mort* was not an eyewitness account of the events associated with Richard II's incarceration in the Tower of London in 1399, and its author wrote with a French chivalric bias. None the less, it recounts Richard's attempt to confound his accusers through an appeal to personal combat: '. . . this will I prove, and fight four from the best of you, and there is my pledge . . .'. That Richard would offer such a challenge – or that he could be portrayed as having made such an offer – is evidence of the vitality of chivalric values in the final pageant of Ricardian kingship. How real Richard's desire for actual combat was cannot be known; the challenge itself was symbolic. It does, however, accord with what we know of the king's rage during his captivity, and would confirm a channelling of such personal emotions within the chivalric conventions of the age.[10]

The king's expenditures and goods provide further evidence of Richard II's commitment to chivalric activities. The accounts of the wardrobe, great wardrobe and the issue rolls of the exchequer are replete with entries connected with chivalric and martial activities. The issue rolls for the tenth year of the reign, for example, record an expenditure of 20 marks for a sword purchased by the king. While again falling short of the expenditures of Edward III, Richard's attention to hunting and falconry, those ancillaries of the martial arts, is revealed in the issue rolls through an entry for a hunting knife and a bow and through an expenditure of £77 13s 4d for falcons in 1399, at a time when the king had other heavy financial demands. The wardrobe accounts also mention hunting knives and apparel.[11] Clearly, Richard was overly punctilious about his attire, but the attire in question also suggests at least a degree of royal involvement in the activities appropriate to the fashion. This was the case with his desire to be properly dressed for tournaments; it was also the case with his desire for proper surcoats. The king's armourer, William Snell, received several payments throughout the reign for his work with the king's embroiderer, fashioning heraldic surcoats designed to be worn over armour 'both for war and peace for the body of the king'. Richard's love of sartorial display was firmly rooted in the chivalric ideal of magnificence. The king's self-perceived rôle as the arbiter of fashion may well have influenced his perception of himself as the arbiter of law, as the visible trappings of kingship were internalized. For Richard II the symbolic was often the real. It is also revealing that the account book of Simon Burley's nephew, Baldwin Radington, the controller of the wardrobe, lists expenses of £226 17s 11½d in connection with the celebration of the feast of St George, the great celebration of the order of the Garter, in 1396; the expenses listed for the Christmas 1395 celebration were £208 15s 5½d. Finally, the inventory of the goods and chattels of Richard II found in Haverford castle after his fall included six *penselx* of St George and five banners of diverse arms.[12]

Richard II's genuine interest in heraldry is well known. Quite apart from the Scrope–Grosvenor controversy over the right to bear the arms *azur a bend or*, which raged during the reign with little royal involvement, Richard made use of heraldry as well as badges of maintenance to express his political aims. The king's artistic tastes have led historians to search for an intellectualized theory of kingship behind such a programme; those who have experienced politics in the age of television should be aware that images can be symbolically manipulated without profound intellectual insight. Richard II seems simply to have exploited the visual impact of conventional symbols to win what support he could. Thus, when the king prepared to lead his first army on an expedition to Scotland in 1385, he was careful to secure the highly revered banner of St Cuthbert for his journey. St Cuthbert's banner was joined by thirty-eight standards of the king's arms and no less than ninety-two of the arms of St George delivered from the privy wardrobe. Richard II clearly appreciated the importance of chivalric display.[13]

A much more personal and more eloquent expression of heraldic politics was Richard's assumption of the arms of St Edward the Confessor. The symbolism was designed to impress not only the wild Irish who held the Confessor in high regard, but also the none too docile English, with the special sanctity of the king's position as the Confessor's heir. Richard's use of St Edward's arms on his first Irish expedition is well known, but there is evidence to indicate that the king already had begun to impale his arms with the Confessor's before the death of Queen Anne in 1394, since her arms appear (in at least two surviving examples) impaled with those of Richard and the Confessor.[14] The symbolic conjunction of Richard and St Edward is again emphasized by the impaled arms on the reverse of the heavenly panel of the Wilton Diptych, and it was, of course, immortalized in Richard's selection of his final resting place adjacent to the Confessor's shrine. It is not necessary to mistake Richard II for either Sir Lancelot or Giles of Rome to recognize that the heir of Edward III both appreciated and manipulated chivalric ideas and ideals.[15]

The manipulation of chivalric ideals, as well as Richard II's often elusive but usually conventional participation in the chivalric ethos, is displayed in the application of crusading themes. The chivalric and the crusading ideals were not identical. They have different roots, and they extend into diverse social, political and intellectual realms. None the less, crusading provided one of the most central – and most noble – expressions for the chivalric ideal. It has become common wisdom to deprecate the vitality and the sincerity of the crusading ideal in the late Middle Ages. For Huizinga crusading vows had become a fanciful and over-sentimental ritual of a decadent chivalry, while Terry Jones has argued that crusading was but a chivalric sham to conceal greed and political ambition. Before dismissing the crusading ideal, we would do well to reflect upon Christopher Tyerman's observation: 'Salvation, honour, wealth and a good fight were complementary incentives, not mutually exclusive. The combination of fusion of motives makes a great deal of psychological and historical sense. Most contemporaries, at least those who actually became crusaders, would have had difficulty in seeing much contradiction among them.' For Richard and his subjects, the crusading ideal and the concepts of chivalry it expressed were as real as were the very obvious debasements of the ideal.[16]

The manipulation of the crusade as a device in the prosecution of the war with France and the politics of the Great Schism was plain in the two English crusades, to Flanders in 1383 and Castile in 1386. Both crusades were born amid the political and financial struggles of Richard's court; both were nurtured by Urban VI's desire to end the schism by force; and both were brought to fruition by the ambitions of their respective leaders, Bishop Despenser of Norwich and John of Gaunt. The king himself did not play a leading rôle, but he was not averse to using crusading ideology to secure political and diplomatic objectives.

Men who joined the Flanders crusade were identified as being 'in the king's service' on the patent rolls. Bishop Despenser drew £37,475 7s 6d from the exchequer to finance his crusade, and the Crown provided the bows and arrows required. The crusade confined its attacks to fellow Urbanists. It proved a political and military disaster, and it was brought to a quick end through the intervention of Richard's new chancellor, Michael de la Pole. Many, including Froissart, were repelled by the hypocrisy of the Flanders crusade, but the potent imagery of the crusade could still move the dour Walsingham to write of the attack on Gravelines: 'Our men . . . having the banner of the Holy Cross before them . . . thought that victory in this cause was glory but death reward . . . those who suffered death would be martyrs . . . and thus the blessing of the cross was achieved, and the *crucesignati* gloriously captured the town and there destroyed the enemies of the cross so that not one of them remained alive.' For Thomas Walsingham, the lustre of the ideal might be dimmed, but it could never be extinguished by the realities of the manipulation.[17]

The Castilian crusade was very much the personal venture of John of Gaunt and Richard II played only a secondary rôle. Richard recognized his uncle's claim to the throne of Castile, and cooperated in the procurement of a parliamentary grant. The crusade soon ended in a diplomatic settlement with Castile, but even then the *Westminster Chronicle* could describe the Castilians 'as being in the truest sense enemies of Christ's cross'.[18]

It was Gaunt's son, Henry of Derby, who made the greatest personal and political capital out of the chivalric spirit of the crusade. Bolingbroke won notoriety with contemporaries and historians for his two Prussian crusades of 1390 and 1392. When no *reysas* was forthcoming in 1392, Henry proceeded to Jerusalem. Bolingbroke, of course, was not the only Englishman to take the cross against the Slavs in Richard's reign. In addition to the risible *reysas* of the duke of Gloucester in 1391 which got no further than Scotland, the future Ricardian earls of Somerset, Salisbury, and Worcester all joined Baltic crusades in the 1390s. That such magnates should seek the honour of being *crucesignati* is an indicator that the honour – abased as it might be – still mattered.[19]

The fight against the Moslems and the quest for the Holy Land retained their appeal for English chivalry. Bolingbroke was denied a safe-conduct to pass through France to join the duke of Bourbon's assault on Tunis, but Bolingbroke's half-brother, John Beaufort, did participate along with at least seven distinguished English knights. Two of these knights had served Richard II as chamber knights since 1381, and a third, John Cornwall, was to be retained for life by the king in 1397. The two chamber knights, John Clanvow and William Neville, were members of that small and influential circle of Lollard knights found at Richard's court. Richard II aided another of the English crusader knights, Henry Scrope, son of Sir Stephen Scrope, with his expenses in returning from Africa. Neville and Clanvow did not long remain in England after their return. They died within days of each other in the vicinity of Constantinople in October 1391, two of many Englishmen who died in the east during Richard II's reign in a continuing pursuit of crusading and chivalric ideals. Their Lollard sympathies make the deaths of these two especially revealing of the pervasive vitality of crusading among English chivalry; their association with the Ricardian chamber is equally indicative of the desire of the court to continue to be perceived as supportive of the ideal.[20]

Richard II certainly had not been an active crusader but nevertheless he was an active player in the politics of crusading ideology. J.J.N. Palmer has demonstrated the importance of the crusade in the diplomacy with the French court designed to achieve both peace between the two realms and an end to the schism that divided Christendom. Philippe de Mézières, founder of the order of the Passion which was intended to meld crusading and chivalric ideals, and the leading crusade propagandist of the time, directed his *Epistre au roi Richart II* in 1395. The *Epistre* urged the need for peace between Christian realms in order to defend Europe from Islam. In the face of opposition from Gloucester and Arundel to his French peace policy, Richard welcomed the letter. 'Peace and the healing of the schism would allow him greater freedom to secure his position within his kingdom without any loss of face; indeed the reverse.' The image of a crusader also bolstered the king's efforts to project himself in his Irish lordship as a lion of justice in the tradition of St Louis and on the continent as a potential candidate for the crown of the Holy Roman Empire.[21]

It was once thought that the Wilton Diptych was the iconographic embodiment of this crusading image within Ricardian kingship. Such an interpretation can no longer be championed, but Richard did lend his diplomatic support to the efforts to launch a crusade to Hungary. John of Gaunt was to lead the English host, and Gaunt had drawn almost £10,000 from the exchequer in the year from 26 February 1394 to 1 March 1395. Palmer speculates that although these disbursements were for other services, their magnitude and priority were intended to aid Gaunt in financing the crusade. This expedition was to have been part of a first sortie to clear the route for a second and greater army under the leadership of Richard II and Charles VI to liberate Jerusalem. Richard would thus take his rightful place alongside his famous lion-hearted namesake.[22]

This grandiose plan came a cropper in the face of political and diplomatic realities. The initial expedition was delayed for a year; Gaunt, as well as the duke of Burgundy, were forced to forego their participation in the crusade. Thus, English participation in the débâcle at Nicopolis was minimal. There was certainly no support from the king or his court as the attention of Richard II was called nearer home.[23] Throughout the late fourteenth century crusading fervour rose and fell in inverse proportion to the exigencies of the Hundred Years' War and domestic upheavals. The dream gave place to more sordid realities, but the dream of the crusading hero was still an important component in Richard's image of kingship. Crusading and chivalry were not the same thing, but they appealed to similar social and political sensibilities.

Just as Richard II was not a great crusader, he was not a great knight. Yet, the chivalric values of knighthood were an essential ingredient of Ricardian kingship. To pursue this point, it is useful to examine Richard's conferment of knighthood. Historians have made it appear that only the Black Death could rival knighthood as an affliction to a fourteenth-century gentleman's fortunes. No doubt knighthood carried with it disagreeable obligations. Yet prestige was vital in late medieval society, and the material benefits available to a knight dubbed by the king were not inconsiderable. Richard could and did exempt those whom he knighted from the onerous duties of local government associated with the honour.[24]

The king made use of knighthood as part of his martial policies. When he undertook his Scottish campaign, Richard II not only created three new peers (there might have been five if the claim that Simon Burley and John Nevill were created earls of Huntingdon and Westmorland, though they were unable to secure recognition for these titles, is accepted), he also 'dubbed knights in an uncomparable multitude' on his entry into Scotland.[25] The prestige of the expedition and its leader were thus enhanced by a chivalrous gesture that also served the political agenda of the king.

Richard II, the first English ruler since John to visit Ireland and the only monarch before Victoria to visit the island twice, also made use of chivalrous patronage in his efforts to restore his Irish lordship. The king had demonstrated his appreciation of the good service performed in the Irish wars by Geoffrey de la Vale by dubbing him a knight banneret in 1389. Vale had been an active opponent of Art MacMurrough, the putative king of Leinster, since the first year of the reign. An even clearer indicator of the use of chivalric bonds to enhance the king's position in Ireland was the knighting of the great Anglo-Irish lord, James Butler, third earl of Ormond. When Butler came of age, he was requested to come to England to do homage to the king for his lands. The earl attended parliament where, on 9 November 1385, 'Lord James earl of Ormond received the girdle of knighthood from the king'.[26] Richard would make even more direct use of knighthood in the course of his visits to his Irish lordship.

The first Irish expedition was designed to assert Richard II's lordship over all the peoples of the island. The culmination of this enterprise was the submission of the great Irish chiefs, and the king's attempt to secure their loyalty to the English lordship. Once again chivalry was to play a rôle in this process.

Froissart recounts that Richard II wished to confer knighthood upon four Irish kings: O'Connor, O'Neill, O'Brien and MacMurrough. This account contains a number of chronological and topographical inaccuracies, but the tale has a basis in fact. The four kings were invited to Dublin and given over to the tutelage of Sir Henry Christede who had acquired a mastery of Irish during a long period of captivity. It was Christede's task to familiarize the wild Irish with English courtly manners. As part of his tutelage, Christede explained to the kings the full meaning of knighthood:

> Thane I demaunded if they wolde not gladly receyve the order of knyghthode, and that the kyng of Englande shulde make them knyghtes, accordynge to the usage of Fraunce and Englande, and other countries. They answered howe they were knyghtes allredye. . . . But than I sayd, that the knyghthode that they had taken in their youthe suffyced not to the kynge of Englande, but I sayde he shulde gyve thym after another manner . . . that it shulde be in the holy churche, whiche was the most worthyest place.

The four kings were further instructed by the earl of Ormond: 'Than he entered lytell and lytell to speke of the order of chivalry, whiche the kynge wolde they shulde receyve. He shewed it them fro poynt to poynt, how they shulde behave themselfe, and what parteygned to knyghthode.' All of this effort culminated in the knighting of the four kings by Richard II at Dublin. Richard II seems to have knighted three Anglo-Irish members of his army on the same occasion. The dubbing of Thomas Ourgham, Johnathas de Pado and his cousin John de Pado served to emphasize the new brotherhood-in-arms between English and Irish.[27]

Following the ceremony, a great banquet was held. The usual reading of Froissart would indicate that the king shared his table with the new knights (*S'assirent ce jour a la table du Roy Richard d'Angleterre*), a gesture of friendship to the king's new companions-in-arms which he might hope would be reciprocated. A variant reading which was printed by John Anstis from a lost manuscript would suggest that the new knights first served the king as a mark of respect to the man who had guided their progress in arms (*Et servent ce jour a la table du Roy d'Angleterre*). Whether the Irish were served or themselves served at this chivalrous feast, the practical intent of attaching the new knights to the king was clearly served.[28] These efforts at chivalric politics culminated in a much more securely documented series of dubbings as Richard was preparing to leave his lordship:

> on the 1st day of May, 1395, on a ship of the Lord King called the Trinity, then in the port of Waterford, in the presence of the notary and others, the King being there in person together with the bishops of Chichester and Lismore-Waterford, there came Turloch O'Conor Don of Connacht, William de Burgo, and Walter Bermingham (who formerly, it was said, were rebels against the King), who came on board and lying prone there did obeisance. So the King, seeing that they had come to him and desiring that they should not leave him without some gift or honour, created them and belted them knights, and as token of that Order, admitted them to the kiss of peace and granted each of them a sword to be honourably used. And immediately thereupon the lords Henry Percy and William Arundel, knights, placed gilded spurs upon their heels as token of that order. Then the said Turloch O'Conor Don, William de Burgo, and Walter Bermingham paid the honour due to such a king, kneeling and with uplifted hands.[29]

The failure of Richard's chivalric policy for Ireland was one of mistaking symbolic obeisance for genuine obedience.

The king, therefore, was compelled to return to Ireland in 1399. Less was accomplished in his lordship on this occasion although a great deal transpired in his kingdom. As he had on the Scottish campaign, Richard took advantage of the occasion to bestow knighthoods. After the first martial action, '. . . he sent for the son of the Duke of Lancaster, a fair young and handsome bachelor, and knighted him, saying, "My fair cousin, henceforth be *preux* and valiant, for you have some valiant blood to conquer". And for his greater honour and satisfaction, he made eight or ten other knights . . .'. Créton had no interest in the supporting cast of knights, but Thomas of Otterbourne suggested that one of the other knights was the son of the duke of Gloucester who failed to survive the expedition.[30] The son of the countess of Salisbury is yet another likely candidate. The king clearly hoped to bind these young nobles to him through chivalric and martial ties, and Henry V was to demonstrate a measure of posthumous gratitude to the man who had given him arms when he had Richard II reinterred in Westminster Abbey.

Richard did not confine his dubbings to the scions of English noble houses. Chivalric patronage could also play a useful rôle in diplomacy. On St George's Day 1390 the king not only knighted the earls of March and Stafford, he also joined with them Alphonso de Villena, son of the count of Dénia. The count of Dénia was the leading Aragonese supporter of the Trastamaran interest in Castile. He had been captured by the English at Nájera in 1367, and had been forced to leave his son in England as a hostage. Dénia failed to pay his ransom, and he led the pro-Castilian Portuguese forces at the battle of Aljubarrota in 1385. His son, none the less, seems to have behaved admirably during his enforced stay in England. The king's bestowal of knighthood on Alphonso thus appears to be a reward for the youth's exemplary chivalrous conduct as well as a means by which the loyalty of a potentially valuable future player in the affairs of the Iberian Peninsula might be wooed.[31]

In 1398 Richard stretched out a chivalric hand to Byzantium. The Emperor Manuel II Palaeologus had sent a deputation headed by his Genoese-born son-in-law, Hilario Doria, to the English court to seek financial help for the blockaded city of Constantinople. The king urged his subjects to donate, and Richard himself gave 40 marks. In fact, little if any cash reached Constantinople, but Richard gave symbolic chivalric support for the cause of fighting the Turks by knighting one of the ambassadors, probably Doria, during his birthday celebration at Lichfield on 6 January 1399. What better way for Richard to express his Epiphany to the emperor of the East.[32]

Richard made conscious use of chivalric display in his diplomacy. The clearest example of this was the great tournament at Smithfield in the autumn of 1390. This was designed as both a complement and an offset to the great French tournament at Saint-Ingelvert at which the English had been the chief guests. On this occasion, Richard snared a valuable guest. William of Bavaria, count of Ostrevant, unable to resist the lure of the joust, ignored the advice of his father, Albert, duke of Bavaria, and proceeded to England. Froissart describes, with his usual zest, Ostrevant's cordial reception, the brilliance of the jousts, balls and banquets, and finally the investiture of the count at Windsor with the Garter. Although William made no formal commitments to the English, the French were upset by his actions. In the aftermath of the celebrated resignation of Enguerrand de Coucy from the order of the Garter, acceptance of this English chivalric device could only be interpreted as an indicator of unwillingness to bear arms against the order's sovereign.[33]

The count of Ostrevant was joined in the ranks of the knights companion of the Garter in the same year by William, duke of Guelders and Juliers, another potentially valuable friend for England. William had agreed in 1387, at the prompting of the duke of Gloucester and the earl of Arundel, to defy Charles VI and Philip of Burgundy and to give his homage to Richard II in return for an annual pension of £1,000. The English, who had their own problems in 1388, failed to support the duke in his war with Burgundy, and Richard's bestowal of the Garter may be seen as an attempt to make amends for that failure. His honour assuaged, William remained a loyal, albeit over-zealous, supporter of the English cause. Ostrevant's father Albert, duke of Bavaria and regent of Holland, was finally induced to receive the Garter in 1397. Albert had chosen Burgundy over England in 1385. He was, however, a nephew of Edward III, and chivalric honour was now employed by Richard II to reinforce consanguinity.[34]

The Garter was the ultimate chivalric honour which Richard could bestow upon a subject as well as a foreign friend. Once again, the king attempted to use his chivalrous patronage to personal and political advantage on the domestic as well as the diplomatic stage. The very restricted membership – twenty-five knights companion and the sovereign – made the Garter highly coveted; it also restricted Richard's prodigality. The men elected to the order prior to 1383 bear less interest since the young sovereign's personal input into the electoral process was slight. Still, Simon Burley, his brother John and his nephew Richard were all elected in the first years of the reign. The king's uncle and later foe, Thomas of Woodstock, was not elected until 1381. Anthony Tuck notes that Thomas may have already developed a sense of grievance that 'his earldom and his admission to the Order of the Garter were unduly delayed'.[35] Each of the Burleys, in any case, fits the profile of the Garter knights elected in Edward III's reign; they had all won their spurs in the French wars.

Richard was more clearly the moving force in the election of his boyhood companion, Thomas Mowbray, earl of Nottingham, in 1383, and the election of his great favourite, Robert de Vere, earl of Oxford, in the following year. These two knights were of impeccable lineage, but neither had the sort of martial reputation upon which the award of the Garter had been predicated. This must have galled the earl of Arundel, destined to be Richard's most obstinate foe, who remained outside this great company of chivalry in spite of his martial adventures at sea.[36] Vere's scandalous marital adventures – he divorced Edward III's granddaughter in favour of a Bohemian serving lady of Queen Anne – can hardly have helped the situation.

The knights honoured with the Garter in the period 1386–8 were supporters of the Lords Appellant, and they were a more martial group. The earl of Arundel received his Garter at last in 1386. In view of his later career as a Ricardian stalwart, it is interesting to note that the future earl of Gloucester, Thomas Despenser, was elected to the order of the Garter under Appellant sponsorship in 1388. With Richard back in the saddle, John, Lord Beaumont received the Garter in 1393. Beaumont had been a loyal supporter of the king during the Appellant crisis; Richard had stayed with him in 1387 at the outset of his journey from Westminster to escape the supervision of the commission appointed by parliament 'to amend the administration'. The Appellants expelled John from the household, but he demonstrated his bravery and value by serving as warden of the west March with Scotland while keeping out of the Appellants' way. Richard, therefore, rehabilitated him at the first opportunity.[37]

Clearly, the Garter was a chivalric reward and reinforcement for a loyal servant of the king. In 1394 another loyal friend of Richard, Sir William Scrope, joined the ranks of the knights companion. One of the gallant supporters of the king's Irish expedition, Sir William Arundel, was elected in 1395. Arundel was a relative, but not a friend, of the earl of Arundel. He served as a king's knight, and he shared in the spoils of his kinsman's fall. The king wooed Henry of Derby's illegitimate relations and paid court to John of Gaunt through the selection of Sir John Beaufort, afterwards marquess of Dorset, as a knight companion in 1396. Beaufort replaced Beaumont both in the ranks of the order and later as constable of Dover castle, a vital post for the defence of the kingdom. In 1397 Richard's nephew, Thomas, earl of Kent, and his close supporter in these final years of the reign, John, earl of Salisbury, received their Garters. Both men were to lose their heads on 7 January 1400 in the aftermath of an abortive coup designed to restore Richard II. Philip de la Vache, the final knight companion elected under Richard II, had served the king as a chamber knight since at least 1378, and he had been a receiver of the chamber under Edward III. Philip, however, provided his most notable service to the king on 17 September 1397, when he and Sir Simon Felbrigg served as pledges for the prosecution of the appeal lodged against the duke of Gloucester. Both men received their Garters after this date. Vache replaced Gaunt in the ranks of the knights companion; the succession to Gaunt's dukedom proved insoluble until the duke of Lancaster became king.[38] Richard and his foes clearly made political capital out of chivalric prestige associated with admission to the order of the Garter.

Richard, in the finest chivalric tradition, also paid court to the noble ladies of his realm through the distribution of the robes of the order of the Garter. Richard was the first king to bestow such marks of honour upon women on an appreciable scale, and he remained the most prodigal monarch in his distribution of these robes until the practice was discontinued by Henry VIII. Since the distribution of robes to ladies was not limited by the statutes of the order, the king was freer to exercise his personal choice in the selection of ladies to be so patronized. The king rewarded some thirty-six noble ladies in this fashion, well over half the total of ladies who are recorded as receiving the robes of the Garter in the Middle Ages. As has been demonstrated elsewhere, Richard II made political use of this custom to honour ladies and to win their husband's support.[39]

The Garter, of course, was less personally associated with Richard than the badge of the white hart. It is probable that the king first distributed his famous livery at the Smithfield tournament. While the distribution of such devices did not imply the same chivalric bonds as did the bestowal of membership in an order of knighthood, the knightly concept of brotherhood-in-arms still made such grants diplomatically desirable. Thus, the white hart soon found its way to Richard's Spanish friends. A privy seal writ dated 2 July but without regnal year declares that the king has granted twelve ladies, twelve knights, and ten squires licence 'to wear and use our livery of the stag, each according to his/her estate, in the manner and style as it is used within our realm of England'. The king also ordered harts fabricated of gold. One of these was given to the archbishop of Cologne in 1398; a second was sent to the Byzantine emperor in the following year. But the king did not stop at mere mortals in his distribution of the white hart: in the right panel of the Wilton Diptych, there is an angelic host bedecked in Richard's livery surrounding the Virgin and Child as they present a banner designed to inspire chivalric gallantry in a kneeling Richard who appears in the left panel. The king patronized ladies and angels as well as gentlemen with the white hart.[40]

Chivalry, in fact, provided an indispensable element in the patronage as well as the diplomacy of Richard II's reign. As Maurice Keen has reminded us, 'Social precedence and honours were quite as essential to the nobility as wealth was.' For a late fourteenth-century English king, the way to generate support lay not in the abandonment of chivalrous values, but in a renewed appeal to the traditional values of loyal and faithful service found in the chivalric ethos. The key lay in associating knightly loyalty with loyalty to the prince-patron, a recurring theme of late medieval chivalric literature. Clearly, such a simplistic concept was breaking down under complex social and economic tensions, but the ideal still served to motivate men. Even more primitive notions of personal brotherhood-in-arms still had an appeal. Sir Robert de Vere KG was led to assure Sir Simon Burley KG: 'I will never forsake you. Are we not companions?'[41]

Such concepts of personal comradeship had a special appeal to the man who was to end his life as the simple knight Sir Richard of Bordeaux, a man with no surviving siblings, no children, and only a child bride. 'Richard II would seem to have cared deeply for several women . . . but the strength of his very personal friendships for Robert de Vere, for his cousin Edward, at times for Thomas Mowbray and perhaps for Simon Burley and John Holland were primary political factors in his reign. The "plot" of the political history of late fourteenth-century England was conceived like that of contemporary English fiction to be a conflict of loyalties . . . The political party had not yet been thought of. The conflict between the king and groups of the magnates can hardly have been considered a constitutional issue, for there was no constitution, only groups of precedents pointing different ways. Feudalism had been dead since 1290. The transition from feudalism to political party was the affinity, and this had brought with it a new and complex network of loyalties.'[42] This network of loyalties remained based, however, on chivalrous values. No doubt Richard, his rivals, and the clients of both frequently sinned against the chivalric code and debased it through patronage, but an ideal that is tarnished has not been repudiated. Only the continued worth of the ideal allows for its debasement.

Notes

[1] R.H. Barber, *Edward, Prince of Wales and Aquitaine* (New York, 1978), p. 238; see also A.R. Myers, *England in the Late Middle Ages* (Harmondsworth, 1952), p. 35. This picture of Richard is admirably recounted in G.B. Stow, 'Richard II and the Invention of the Pocket Handkerchief', *Albion*, vol. XXVII (1995), 221–2.

[2] R.H. Jones, *The Royal Policy of Richard II* (Oxford, 1968), p. 7.

[3] J. Evans, *English Art* (Oxford, 1949), p. 83.

[4] G.E. Cockayne, *Complete Peerage of England, Scotland, Ireland, Great Britain, and the United Kingdom, Extant, Extinct or Dormant* (new edn, 12 vols, London, 1910–59), VI, pp. 650–3; G.F. Beltz, *Memorials of the Order of the Garter* (London, 1841), pp. 73, 182–7; *The Cronycle of Sir John Froissart*, trans. Lord Berners (4 vols, London, 1814–16), I, p. 483; Chandos Herald, *Life of the Black Prince*, eds and trans. M.K. Pope and E.C. Lodge (Oxford, 1910), p. 145; *La Vie du Prince Noir by Chandos Herald*, ed. D.B. Tyson (Tübingen, 1975), pp. 77, 81, 111, 137, 164; Bibl. Nat., Fonds Fr., 23592, f. 7, for the reference to King John II's order to Guichard to give his oath to the king of England; R.F. Green, *Poets and Princepleasers: Literature and the English Court in the Late Middle Ages* (Toronto, 1980), p. 75.

[5] Beltz, *Memorials*, pp. 285–9; *DNB*, eds L. Stephen and S. Lee (new edn, 22 vols, Oxford, 1908–9), III, pp. 373–4; *La Vie du Prince Noir*, pp. 117, 118, 137. See N. Orme, *From Childhood to Chivalry* (London, 1984), and *Education and Society in Medieval and Renaissance England* (London, 1989); G.O. Sayles, 'King Richard II of England: A Fresh Look', *Proceedings of the American Philosophical Society*, vol. CXV (1971), 28; G.B. Stow, 'Chronicles Versus Records: The Character of Richard II', *Documenting the Past*, eds J.S. Hamilton and P.J. Bradley (Wolfeboro, New Hampshire, 1989), p. 156; G.B. Stow, 'Richard II in Jean Froissart's *Chroniques*', *Journal of Medieval History*, vol. XI (1985), 342. Sir Richard Abberbury, another loyal servant of the Black Prince, had been the young prince's master prior to his accession. Abberbury continued to serve Richard II as a chamber knight and he was one of the members of the court expelled by the Lords Appellant in 1388. This suggests that Abberbury shared the values and outlook of Sir Simon Burley. The Austin friar Robert Waldby, who had received his doctorate from Toulouse, served as the director of the prince's academic studies. Waldby would later provide Richard II with loyal service as his physician and as archbishop of Dublin and of York. N. Orme, *Education and Society*, p. 160; W.J. Courtenay, *Schools and Scholars in Fourteenth-Century England* (Princeton, 1987), p. 159; F. Roth, *The English Austin Friars, 1249–1538* (2 vols, New York, 1961–6), I, pp. 86–7. R.F. Green, 'King Richard's Books Revisited', *The Library*, 5th series, vol. XXXI (1976), 235–9, has demonstrated that the lists of the king's books found on the memoranda rolls are books inherited from Edward III, which 'tell us little if anything about Richard's personal tastes in literature'. The effort to make use of the lists on the memoranda rolls

was undertaken in E. Rickert, 'King Richard II's Books', *The Library*, 4th series, XIII (1933), 144–7, and in R.S. Loomis, 'The Library of Richard II', *Studies in Language, Literature and Culture of the Middle Ages and Later*, eds E.B. Atwood and A.A. Hill (Austin, Texas, 1969), pp. 173–8.

⁶ G.B. Stow, 'Chronicles Versus Records', pp. 170–2; (*Œuvres de Froissart*, ed. K. de Lettenhove (25 vols, Brussels, 1870–7), XVI, 234.

⁷ *Le livre de la mutacion de fortune*, ed. S. Solente (4 vols, Paris, 1959–66), II, 12 (I owe the translation to Dr Maryann Weber, SND); *Œuvres Poetiques de Christine de Pisan*, ed. M. Roy (3 vols, Paris, 1886–96), I, 232–3; Thomas Walsingham, *Historia Anglicana (Hist. Angl.)*, ed. H.T. Riley (2 vols, London, 1863–4), II, p. 14. The translation of Walsingham is from N.B. Lewis, 'The Last Medieval Summons of the English Feudal Levy, 13 June 1385', *EHR*, vol. LXIII (1958), 11 n. 4.

⁸ *Chronicon Henrici Knighton*, ed. J.R. Lumby (2 vols, London, 1889–95), II, 204; *Knighton's Chronicle, 1377–1396*, ed. G.H. Martin (Oxford, 1995), p. 334. On Walsh, see *Hist. Angl.*, II, 118, and *Westminster Chronicle, 1381–1394*, eds L.C. Hector and B.F. Harvey (Oxford, 1982), pp. 104–6, which do not mention Walsh's knighthood; *The original chronicle of Andrew of Wyntoun*, ed. F.J. Amours (6 vols, Edinburgh, 1903–14), VI, 359–62; for Lindsay's safe-conducts see *Calendar of Documents Relating to Scotland*, ed. J. Bain (4 vols, Edinburgh, 1881–8), IV, p. 89. I owe the Wyntoun reference to Professor Anthony Goodman. Richard was present in 1380 at the judicial combat in the case of Annesley *v.* Catreton, but, given his youth, this tells us little. G. Neilson, *Trial by Combat* (London, 1890), pp. 171–7; *Issues of the Exchequer*, ed. and trans. F. Devon (London, 1837), p. 233. For a general discussion of the topic, see J.L. Leland, 'The Court of Chivalry under Richard II' (unpub. typescript). Dr Leland kindly provided me with a copy of his paper.

⁹ *Westminster Chronicle*, pp. 375–7; *Œuvres de Froissart*, XIV, 262. S. Lindenbaum, 'The Smithfield Tournament of 1390', *Journal of Medieval and Renaissance Studies*, vol. XX (1990), 1–20, presents a careful study of the event from the perspective of London, but her conclusion that Richard II intended – but failed – to produce a pageant of social integration must be viewed with some scepticism. Richard supported the natural orders of society, and, as Lindenbaum notes, everything at Smithfield was designed to confirm that impression. Yet one may wonder whether Richard and the citizens of London could have understood, yet alone implemented, all the subtleties detected in Lindenbaum's analysis. PRO, E101/403/19, f. 42.

¹⁰ *Chronique de la Traïson et Mort de Richart Deux Roy Dengleterre*, ed. B. Williams (London, 1846), p. 218.

¹¹ *Issues of the Exchequer*, pp. 226, 233, 261, 263; W.P. Baildon, 'A Wardrobe Account of 16–17 Richard II', *Archaeologia*, vol. LXII (1911), 498. See also M.H. Keen, *Chivalry* (New Haven, 1984).

¹² PRO, E101/400/20 m. 3; 401/4 m. 3; 401/14 mm. 1, 3; 402/12 m. 4; 403/10 pp. 13r, 22r (see also p. 34 which resolves all the mysteries of Ricardian finance); C.S. Nicewarner, 'A Study in the Reign of Richard II: The Account of Baldwin Raddyngton, 1395–1396' (unpublished University of Maryland Ph.D. thesis, 1977), pp. 163, 195, 362, 386; PRO, E101/355/13; F. Palgrave, *The Antient Kalendars and Inventories of His Majesty's Exchequer* (3 vols, London, 1836), III, 359. My thanks to Mr Ian Pierce for the interpretation of *hucs*. See P.J. Eberle, 'The Politics of Courtly Style at the Court of Richard II', in *The Spirit of the Court*, eds G.S. Burgess and R.A. Taylor (Cambridge, 1985), pp. 168–78.

¹³ *Extracts from the Account Rolls of the Abbey of Durham*, ed. J.T. Fowler (3 vols, London, 1898–1901), II, 441; see also ibid., III, 593 (my thanks to Professor Goodman for these references); PRO,

E101/403/23 m. 3; *Westminster Chronicle*, p. 124; N.B. Lewis, 'The Last Medieval Summons', pp. 25–6.

[14] J.L. Gillespie, 'Richard II's Knights: Chivalry and Patronage', *Journal of Medieval History*, vol. XIII (1987), 145; J. Harvey, *The Black Prince and His Age* (Totowa, NJ, 1976), pp. 150–1.

[15] On Richard II's use of symbols, see R.H. Jones, *Royal Policy*, p. 167, and E.H. Kantorowicz, *The King's Two Bodies* (Princeton, 1957), p. 38 n. 18.

[16] M.H. Keen, *Chivalry*, pp. 44–63; J. Huizinga, *The Waning of the Middle Ages*, trans. F. Hopman (London, 1938), pp. 92–3; T. Jones, *Chaucer's Knight* (London, 1980), pp. 34–63; C. Tyerman, *England and the Crusades, 1095–1588* (Chicago, 1988), pp. 288–9.

[17] *CCR, 1381–5*, pp. 280, 290, 305; *Issues of the Exchequer*, pp. 222–3; *Hist. Angl.*, II, 88–9; C. Tyerman, *England and the Crusades*, pp. 333–9.

[18] *Westminster Chronicle*, p. 195.

[19] F.R.H. du Boulay, 'Henry of Derby's Expeditions to Prussia, 1390–91 and 1392', in *The Reign of Richard II*, eds F.R.H. du Boulay and C.M. Barron (London, 1971), pp. 153–72; *Expeditions to Prussia and the Holy Land Made by Henry Earl of Derby*, ed. L.T. Smith (London, 1894); on the question of the relationship of *reysas* to crusade, see W. Paravicini, *Der Preussenreisen des Europäischen Adels* (Sigmaringen, 1989).

[20] *Chronique du religieux de Saint-Denys*, ed. L. Bellaguet (6 vols, Paris, 1839–52), I, p. 668; K.B. McFarlane, *Lancastrian Kings and Lollard Knights* (Oxford, 1972); W.T. Waugh, 'The Lollard Knights'; *Scottish Historical Review*, vol. XI (1914); E. Siberry, 'Criticism of Crusading in Fourteenth Century England', in *Crusade and Settlement*, ed. P.W. Edbury (Cardiff, 1985), pp. 127–8, which presents a perhaps over-enthusiastic corrective to previous views on the unacceptability of crusading; S. Dull, A. Luttrell, and M. Keen offer a careful study of Clanvow and Neville, 'Faithful Until Death; The Tomb Slab of Sir William Neville and Sir John Clanvowe, Constantinople 1391', *Antiquaries Journal*, vol. LXXI (1992), which raises doubts as to their presence in Africa. Dr Luttrell was kind enough to allow me to use this article prior to publication and to provide useful suggestions on the subject of crusading in Richard II's reign. For the tradition of English crusaders in the fourteenth century, see also A. Luttrell, 'English Levantine Crusaders: 1363–1367', *Renaissance Studies*, vol. II (1988). For Clanvow, see R.F. Green, *Poets and Princepleasers*, pp. 6, 65, 110, 130, 196.

[21] J.J.N. Palmer, *England, France and Christendom, 1377–1399* (London, 1972), pp. 180–210; É. Perroy, *L'Angleterre et le grand Schisme d'Occident* (Paris, 1933); Philippe de Mézières, *Letter to King Richard II*, ed. and trans. G.W. Coopland (Liverpool, 1975).

[22] The importance of the Wilton Diptych in this context has been advanced by M.V. Clarke, *Fourteenth Century Studies*, eds L.S. Sutherland and M. McKisack (Oxford, 1937), pp. 286–92; J.J.N. Palmer, *England, France and Christendom*, pp. 242–4; and C. Tyerman, *England and the Crusades*, pp. 297–300. The argument that Richard is being presented with a crusading banner is refuted by E.L. Scheifele's study which is to appear in *Richard II: Power and Prerogative*, eds A. Goodman and J.L. Gillespie (Oxford, forthcoming).

[23] C.L. Tipton, 'The English at Nicopolis', *Speculum*, vol. XXXVII (1962), 528–40, presents a strong case against any major English involvement. Tipton argues that the only English involved were a group of English Knights of St John who fought with their brother knights of this crusading order.

[24] For example, Sir George Felbrigg, *CPR, 1385–9*, pp. 12, 18.

25 *Knighton*, p. 206; C. Given-Wilson's essay in *Richard II: Power and Prerogative* (forthcoming).

26 W.A. Shaw, *The Knights of England* (2 vols, London, 1906), I, 126; J. Anstis, *Essay upon the Knighthood of the Bath* (London, 1725), app. XXXI; *CPR, 1385–8*, p. 539; *Rotulorum Patentium et Clausarum Cancellariae Hiberniae Calendarium* (Dublin, 1828), I, 104, 129, 138, 146, 147; *CPR, 1381–5*, p. 330; J.A. Tuck, 'Anglo-Irish Relations, 1382–1393', *Proceedings of the Royal Irish Academy*, vol. LXIX(C) (1970), p. 22 n. 50.

27 *The Cronycle of Sir John Froissart*, trans. Lord Berners, IV, 4; A. Cosgrove, *Late Medieval Ireland, 1370–1541* (Dublin, 1981), pp. 24–5.

28 J. Anstis, *The Knighthood of the Bath*, app. XXXIII.

29 E. Curtis, *Richard II in Ireland* (Oxford, 1927), pp. 186–7.

30 Jean Créton, 'A French Metrical History of the Deposition of Richard II', ed. and trans. J. Webb, *Archaeologia*, XX (1824), 29–30; Thomas Otterbourne, 'Chronica Regum Angliae', in *Duo Rerum Anglicarum Scriptores Veteres*, ed. T. Hearne (London, 1732), p. 206. I hope to publish a translation of Otterbourne.

31 W.A. Shaw, *The Knights of England*, I, 127; J. Anstis, *The Knighthood of the Bath*, app. XXXII; P.E. Russell, *The English Intervention in Spain and Portugal in the Time of Edward III and Richard II* (Oxford, 1955), pp. 98 n. 2, 105, 394–5; *CPR, 1377–81*, p. 546; *CPR, 1391–6*, pp. 318, 323, 324, 330.

32 PRO, E404/16/373; J.W. Barker, *Manuel II Palaeologus (1391–1425): A Study in Late Byzantine Statesmanship* (New Brunswick, 1969), pp. 180, 474; D.M. Nicol, 'A Byzantine Emperor in England: Manuel's Visit to London in 1400–1401'; *University of Birmingham Historical Journal*, vol. XII (1970), 206–7. Nicol (p. 207 n. 6) made use of the Hearne (Oxford, 1729), p. 148, text of the *Vita* to point up a contradiction with the continuator of Higden's *Polychronicon*, ed. J.R. Lumby (9 vols, London, 1865–6), VIII, 506. The *Polychronicon* stated that it was the 'brother' of the emperor of Constantinople who celebrated Christmas with Richard II. Nicol says that the *Vita Ricardi Secundi* stated that it was Manuel himself. The new edition, *Historia Vitae et Regni Ricardi Secundi*, ed. G.B. Stow (Philadelphia, 1977), p. 151 reads, *frater imperatoris Constantinopol*.

33 J.J.N. Palmer, *England, France and Christendom*, p. 185; M.H. Keen, *Chivalry*, pp. 200–18; H. Wallon, *Richard II* (2 vols, Paris, 1864), II, 37–40; G.F. Beltz, *Memorials*, p. 339; *Œuvres de Froissart*, XIV, 225–60.

34 J.J.N. Palmer, *England, France and Christendom*, pp. 58, 91–2; G.F. Beltz, *Memorials*, pp. 367–8; J. Anstis, *Register of the Most Noble Order of the Garter* (2 vols, London, 1724), I, 56; *Foedera*, VI, 533, 537, 574; E.H. Fellows, *The Knights of the Garter, 1348–1939* (London, n.d.), p. 69; A. Goodman, *The Loyal Conspiracy* (London, 1971), p. 59; *CPR, 1385–9*, p. 310; *1391–6*, p. 315.

35 J.A. Tuck, *Richard II and the English Nobility* (London, 1973), p. 9.

36 *Historiae Vitae et Regni Ricardi Secundi*, pp. 57, 100; 'Dieulacres Chronicle', eds M.V. Clarke and V.H. Galbraith, in *Bulletin of the John Rylands Library*, vol. XIV (1930), 45.

37 J.L. Leland, 'Richard II and the Counter-Appellants' (unpublished Yale University Ph.D. thesis, 1979), p. 21; A. Goodman, *The Loyal Conspiracy*, pp. 53–4; T.F. Tout, *Chapters in the Administrative History of Medieval England* (6 vols, Manchester, 1920–33), III, 418; G.F. Beltz, *Memorials*, p. 346; J.L. Gillespie, 'Dover Castle: Key to Richard II's Kingdom?', *Archaeologia Cantiana*, vol. CV (1988), 192–3; *Rotuli Scotiae in Turri Londinensi et in Domo Westmonasteriensi Asservati, 1291–1516*, ed. D. Macpherson et al. (2 vols, London, 1814–16), II, 94.

[38] *CPR, 1396–9*, pp. 24, 175, 207, 216, 256, 262, 289, 314, 354; G.F. Beltz, *Memorials*, p. 355. Sir William Arundel's wife also received Garter robes. J.L. Gillespie, 'Ladies of the Fraternity of Saint George and of the Society of the Garter', *Albion*, vol. XVII (1985), 268.

[39] Ibid., pp. 259–78.

[40] J.L. Gillespie, 'Richard II's Knights', p. 152; idem, 'Richard II's Cheshire Archers', *Transactions of the Historic Society of Lancashire and Cheshire*, vol. CXXV (1975), 5; M.H. Keen, *Chivalry*, p. 183; G. Mathew, *The Court of Richard II* (London, 1968), p. 145; J. Anstis, *Register*, II, 114n.a.; PRO, E403/556/14; 561/14; G.B. Stow, 'Richard II and the Invention of the Pocket Handkerchief', pp. 229–30. A surviving white hart badge is pictured in *Age of Chivalry: Art in Plantagenet England, 1200–1400*, eds J. Alexander and P. Binski (London, 1987), p. 524, no. 725 (my thanks to Dr Nigel Saul for this reference).

[41] M.H. Keen, *Chivalry*, p. 47; Sir John Froissart, *Chronicles*, ed. and trans. T. Johnes (2 vols, London, 1844), II, 267.

[42] G. Mathew, *The Court of Richard II*, p. 143.

7

RICHARD II: KING OF BATTLES?

James L. Gillespie

Among the character flaws enumerated to explain Richard II's failures, perhaps none is more commonly accepted than the king's lack of military prowess. The champion of the introduction of the handkerchief has never been confused with his lion-hearted namesake! Thomas Rymer epitomized the popular view of Richard II's reign: 'A Reign which affords but little Matter that may shine in History, and cannot boast of any one great and distinguish'd Captain, any one memorable Battle, not one important Siege [*sic*]; no Proceeding to St. *Paul's*, no *Te Deum* for Victory'.[1] Anthony Steel personalized the martial shortcomings of the reign through his claim that Richard's physical inability to meet the martial standards of his father, the Black Prince, was a component of the king's psychological trauma; Gervase Mathew's survey of court life under Richard stated that 'unlike his father and his grandfather he never jousted'.[2] Richard's curmudgeonly contemporary, Thomas Walsingham, completed the picture of Richard's court for later generations when he wrote in 1387 of chamber knights 'more devoted to Venus than to Mars, more valiant in the bedroom than in the field, armed with invective rather than the lance, quick to talk but slow in the performance of the arts of war'.[3] All things considered, it would seem that a reflection upon the military aspects of Richard II's reign would be rather like a study of Margaret Thatcher's Marxist ideals.

All things, however, have not been considered. T.F. Tout argued that from the time of Richard's first Irish expedition, 'Richard's autocracy began to clothe itself in military garb'.[4] It is salutary to note that the army assembled for this expedition was one of the largest armies led by a fourteenth-century English monarch, and that if Richard won no victories in France, he did command three military expeditions against England's Celtic foes. If Walsingham had unkind words for Richard's knights, he was no more impressed with the knights who surrounded the former crusader and jouster, Henry IV. He thought these Lancastrian stalwarts 'more like Dionysus than Mars, more like Laverna than Athena'.[5] True, Richard II was not the military hero his father and grandfather had been, but this unhappy comparison, coupled with the ultimate failure of his reign, has caused scholars to neglect the military aspects of Ricardian kingship. The concomitant flaw in the scholarly portrait of Richard II has been the assumption that an effete king must of necessity have been an intellectually astute individual.

The military failures of Edward II and the triumphs of Edward III provide contrasting but compelling evidence for the continued importance of martial ability to fourteenth-century English kingship. From the duke of Gloucester to twentieth-century scholars, Richard II's military interest and ability have come under severe attack. The king's failure to pursue the French war with vigour completely overshadowed his martial ventures in the British Isles for contemporaries and historians alike. The failure of Richard II to establish a credible military reputation among his contemporaries can be quickly conceded and the negative consequences of that failure are not to be denied. Richard's military expeditions and their relationship to his conception of kingship none the less require examination.[6]

As prince of Wales, the young Richard had been groomed to follow in the footsteps of the Black Prince. In Edward III's last year, plans were undertaken for a major expedition against the French after the expiry of the general truce on 24 June 1377. The captains for this expedition were to include the exiled Duke John de Montfort of Brittany with 300 men-at-arms and 300 archers, John, duke of Lancaster with 500 men-at-arms and 500 archers, and Thomas of Woodstock, the future duke of Gloucester, with 150 men-at-arms and a like number of archers. The largest contingent of 600 men-at-arms and 600 archers was to be under the command of Richard, prince of Wales. This was part of 'a brilliant army of 4,000 warriors and 70 ships, led in person, nominally by the Prince of Wales, actually by the Duke of Lancaster'. Richard drew wages of £631 11s 8d at the exchequer on 17 June; John of Gaunt received £666 13s 14d on the same day, perhaps an indication of the true order of precedence for the expedition. The exchequer had also issued payments for ships and messengers.[7] This was as close as Richard would ever come to command against the French. The expedition was halted by Edward III's death on 21 June, and Richard was carried to higher responsibilities after this abortive military apprenticeship.

Richard would not take the field until 1385, and it would then be against the Scots, not the French. The French were involved, however. Flanders had been secured for Philip the Bold, Charles VI's uncle, and the French planned an assault on England from the Flemish port of Sluys. The Scots were to join the assault from the north, and to stiffen this northern assault Jean de Vienne, admiral of France, was sent to Scotland with a band of 1,300 men-at-arms and 250 crossbowmen in May 1385.[8]

The autumn parliament of 1384 had provided two subsidies to organize an expedition under Richard's command, but that army was to go to the continent. By the summer of 1385, Richard or, more likely, John of Gaunt had decided that an expedition against the Scots would be a more suitable theatre. The northern threat could be removed with a surgical strike before the French could effectively mobilize their force at Sluys. It was a gamble, but a sensible gamble. The way of Scotland would also allow Gaunt a quicker return to his own military ambitions in the Iberian peninsula while allowing him to effect a reconciliation with the royal court where relations had been strained. Such a switch in theatres would, however, necessitate the remission of one of the subsidies. Whether Lancaster had initiated the idea of Scotland or not, Richard adopted it as his own; he claimed that the remission of the subsidy was done 'by his own special act without the council or any other intervening'. 'At last, men thought, the son of the Black Prince and the grandson of Edward III would show the martial spirit of his race, and would display against an alien and an enemy the courage which for a moment had cowed the rebels at Smithfield. Summoning his levies to meet him at Newcastle on July 14, Richard prepared to invade Scotland in force.'[9]

Indeed, it was to be an invasion in force. Richard intended that both the Scots and his English subjects should be impressed by the display of the third largest English army assembled in the fourteenth century. An army of this size required a major financial and recruiting effort. Thus, writs of summons were issued on 4 June to thirty-six ecclesiastical tenants-in-chief and on 13 June to fifty-six lay tenants-in-chief for a general feudal levy, the last summons of the feudal army in English history. Modern scholars have noted the financial motives behind the summons. N.B. Lewis argued that the obligation was levied as a means of forcing the leading magnates to act 'as involuntary contractors for the royal army' and of forgoing the customary regard or bonus above the contractual wages paid to those who served in the host, an expense which Richard could ill afford after the remission of the subsidy. J.J.N. Palmer has countered that the primary motivation was rather to provide a justification for the levy of scutage which might have raised £12,000, but which was blocked by strong opposition. The financial arguments are obvious and compelling, as they must have been to Richard and his counsellors. Equally compelling, albeit less tangible, would have been the imagery of the newly matured king summoning all the feudality of England to come not only *cum servitio debito* but *quanto potentius poteritis* for his first venture in the field.[10]

The king's use of the clergy in his first military campaign is once again interesting in both a practical and a symbolic sense. Richard was to be the leader and defender of all in his realm, and he was able to command the resources of the Church in his support. Both France and Scotland were also adherents of Avignon. The feudal summons of the ecclesiastical tenants-in-chief was not unusual. The king, however, issued a writ of array to Bishop Wykeham of Winchester ordering the bishop 'to arm and array all abbots, priors, men of religion and other ecclesiastical persons of his diocese' in order to defend the Isle of Wight against invasion by the French. Such arrays included clergy of every grade, and they bore no relation to feudal tenure. They were the equivalent of the arrays of lay subjects under the provisions of the statute of Winchester. As the royal army moved north, the southern flank was to be protected at least in part by an army of local clergy loyal to their *patria* and their king.[11]

The army that was actually assembled at Newcastle upon Tyne and described by the contemporary Order of Battle has long been recognized to be typical of the contract armies of the fourteenth century rather than of the feudal host.[12] The huge retinue of John Gaunt comprised somewhere between a quarter and a third of the entire force. Yet if the force had a strongly Lancastrian base, it also reflected the organizational and military potential of Richard's household. Lewis commented on these men: 'Some of these are explicitly described in the [issue] roll as king's squires, sergeants-at-arms or yeomen; others, without being so described are known to have been "king's knights" or knights of his chamber; while others, again, are described as holding or are known to have been holding, offices of varying degrees of importance in the administrative departments, chief

among them the king's secretary, Richard Medford, and the controller of the
wardrobe, Baldwin of Raddington.' In fact, seven of Richard's administrative
officers (the chancellor, treasurer, keeper of the privy seal, secretary, steward of
the household, under-chamberlain of the household, and controller of the
wardrobe) commanded between them 450 men-at-arms and 550 archers, nearly
10 per cent of the entire host.[13] Among the personnel who accompanied the king
were thirty-five archers of the Crown whose wages were paid by Ranulph de
Hatton, clerk of the privy wardrobe at the Tower of London; the issue roll
indicates payment for the wages of forty archers of the Crown as well. The privy
wardrobe also supplied weapons for the enterprise, and it paid expenses to the
master of *Le George* of Dover for shipping supplies to Berwick.[14]

The expedition itself failed to live up to the careful preparations, which also
included the earliest extant code of discipline for an English army.[15] The
normal formation of three battles was adopted, the centre under the king being
augmented by two wings. Tout accepted Sydney Armitage Smith's suggestion
that 'To prevent the factions of politics being carried into the field, friends were
separated, and enemies were thrown together'. This view, however, is difficult to
sustain. An examination of the Order of Battle reveals an array based on
principles of military tactics and chivalric precedence. It was not, therefore, a
matter of Ricardian policy that 'Lancaster marched with the Earl Marshal in
spite of the enmity that existed between the duke and the young courtier'.[16]
That there were personal and perhaps political rivalries within the host had
already been amply demonstrated by the murder of the courtier Ralph Stafford
by Richard's half-brother, John Holland, as the army was being assembled. John
Leland has argued that this murder had great political significance; it has little
military significance, however, in spite of the possible disappointment of
Holland over Richard's grant of the marshalship to Mowbray.[17]

Richard pursued his foes for about a week, 'giving free and uninterrupted
play to slaughter, rapine and fire-raising all along a six-mile front'. The king
then put Melrose abbey to the torch in spite of the pleas of Lancaster, who felt
indebted to the Scots for the refuge they had provided him during the Peasants'
Revolt. Newbattle abbey and Holyrood suffered the same fate as the army
advanced on Edinburgh.[18] These burnings serve to illuminate Richard's
character. They reveal a headstrong ruler determined to exact vengeance on the

Scots for their raids into England. Later, Richard would feel contrition for his actions: a warrant of 15 October 1389 to the chancellor authorized letters allowing the abbey and convent of Melrose an abatement of 2s a 'saak' on the custom of Scotch growth sent by them to Berwick to the number of 1,000 'saaks', as an alms from the king for the destruction and burning sustained by the abbey when he was there with his army.[19] The king's actions in Edinburgh would also prove revealing.

Although the English army occupied Edinburgh, the Scots had not been brought to battle. John of Gaunt wished to continue the pursuit across the Forth into Fife and Strathmore much as he had done the year before when he had led a smaller expedition beyond Edinburgh to the Forth estuary. Richard, with perhaps more vehemence than was necessary, rejected the duke's counsel; he argued that it would be foolhardy to advance into barren territory where resupply by sea would be difficult. 'Though you and the other lords here might have plenty of food for yourselves, the rest, the humbler, and lowlier members of our army, would certainly not find over there such a wealth of victuals as would prevent their dying of hunger.' Richard told Gaunt that the duke could march on if he wished, but 'I and my men are going home'.[20] Gaunt then backed down and agreed to return with the king. Quite apart from the remarkable concern, without any suggestion of egalitarianism, for the ordinary soldier that would later endear the king to his Cheshire guard, Richard's decision was militarily sound, though he received little credit for it from contemporaries or modern historians. The king had broken the threat to his northern border, and he had inflicted serious damage on the Scots. There would be no real threat from the north for the next three years. There was little to gain and much to lose by pursuing the Scots into the Highlands as autumn approached. Froissart averred that the king's refusal to proceed north had been influenced by his great favourite Robert de Vere, and the poor reputation of this royal adviser has discredited the advice tendered. Vere's motive may well have been to discredit Lancaster in his nephew's eyes, but whatever the motive the advice was sound. Even the bad can give good advice![21]

The campaign taken as a whole also reveals a grasp of strategy and the will – perhaps even the courage – to carry it out. The king refused to be deflected by a diversionary thrust undertaken by Jean de Vienne into the West March.

Richard had taken measures to strengthen the defences of Carlisle with cannon the previous December, and he relied on local levies to repulse the attack.[22] In the end, Vienne did little damage. The much more significant gamble of leaving England's southern coast exposed was also militarily justified, but it was politically foolhardy.[23] The king had appointed his old tutor and the chamberlain of his household, Sir Simon Burley, as constable of Dover castle on 5 January 1384. Dover was the key to the defence of the southern littoral which Burley organized before his departure for Scotland.

The evidence demonstrates that Burley fulfilled his responsibilities in the defence of Kent conscientiously. The accounts of Ranulph de Hatton, the clerk of the privy wardrobe, show that Sir Simon and his nephew, Baldwin de Raddington, had taken care to supply and garrison Dover castle. Simon had also secured a patent of 11 April 1385, empowering him to organize the region's defence and to evacuate inhabitants to the castle and towns in the face of the French threat; a patent of 22 June 1385 authorized the constable to receive for the king's use the armour and artillery of Dover castle held by his predecessor's executors.[24] As matters degenerated at home and abroad, however, mistrust of Burley grew.

The French invasion never materialized; the only result of all the preparations was a small raid on the Isle of Thanet during which the vill of Stonar was burnt. Yet, this minor incident was taken as proof of Burley's treachery. Although Sir Simon's strategy of sacrificing Thanet to concentrate upon the defence of Sandwich was eminently sensible, Kent's leading historian could still speak four centuries later of the fate of Stonar as the result of 'the treachery of Sir Simon of Burley'.[25] How much more must this accusation of treachery have appealed to Burley's contemporaries. This mistrust came to haunt Simon and his king in the Appellant crisis.

Richard's first military campaign had produced no victories to impress his subjects with his martial prowess. His own venture into Scotland had lasted barely a fortnight; the king was back in Newcastle on 20 August.[26] On 21 August Richard attempted to secure the northern border by concluding an indenture 'whereby the Earl of Northumberland, John "sire de Neville", Roger "sire de Clifford", Henry Percy, warden of Berwick-on-Tweed, and Sirs Thomas Swynburne and Richard Tempest, wardens of Roxburgh castle, agreed to attend the king for twenty-nine days from Friday following, viz., the earl with 260 men-at-arms and 520 archers, on the east March, Sir Henry Percy with 100 men-at-arms and 200 archers beyond his garrison, Thomas and Richard with 40 men-at-arms and 80 archers beyond their garrison, and Neville and Clifford on the west March with 200 men-at-arms and 400 men-at-arms (half of whom to be in Carlisle, besides the garrison), and with Clifford at Brougham [Burgham] 30 men-at-arms and 60 archers besides its usual garrison. The pay to be two parts in money and the third in victuals at a fair price. Two-thirds of the force shall be strangers to the Marches.' An account dated 23 July 1386 of John Hermesthorpe, who would be appointed as a war-treasurer by the Cambridge parliament in 1388, notes additional supplies and funds sent to strengthen the Scottish Marches. John Derby, clerk, who had been on the Scottish expedition, played a key rôle in supplying weapons for both Berwick and Bamburgh castles from the stores of the privy wardrobe.[27]

It may have appeared to contemporaries, as it did to Tout, that 'the Scots campaign was not a success'.[28] The king, however, had achieved and carefully defended his military objective. Ironically, his failure was a failure to project the politically powerful image of the victorious warrior king. Richard II would not take the field again for nearly a decade. His martial reputation would suffer the same inglorious fate in Ireland that it had endured in the Scottish campaign.

Why would a monarch who never raised a sword to win fame and glory in France risk life and reputation in Ireland? The two Irish expeditions of 1394–5 and 1399 are much more clearly Richard II's own doing than the Scottish campaign, and as such they reveal much about Richard's martial talents and even something about his larger conception of kingship. Once again, many modern English historians share the prejudice of Richard II's contemporaries against Ireland, and the king's Irish campaigns have been dismissed by scholars from Sir John Davies to Anthony Steel as of little military or political consequence save in the loss of Richard's English throne. Recent historians based in Celtic lands, joined by Anthony Tuck, fortunately have begun to reassess these campaigns.[29]

Richard's motives in undertaking these expeditions were probably mixed, and, as with any mortal, the king's views and policies were altered by time and circumstances. The claim that Richard first went to Ireland as a diversion from his grief over Queen Anne's death has been laid to rest. Ireland had long been a source of concern and an object of royal policy. The Irish great council had asked the king personally to restore his lordship as early as 1385. Richard had attempted to install Robert de Vere in Ireland in his stead. Vere was created marquess of Dublin in 1385 and duke of Ireland the following year. Ever conscious of chivalric symbolism, Richard attempted to replace the royal arms with the newly created escutcheon of the marquess.[30] Since Vere was also installed as justice of Chester, there may well have been an attempt by Richard to establish a personal following on the Celtic fringe, but since the Lords Appellant had other plans, the extent of Richard's and Vere's Irish ambitions cannot be known. Ireland, however, was on the king's mind.

In the aftermath of the Appellant crisis, the king again associated Ireland with his earldom of Chester through the appointment of Vere's former deputy, the Cheshireman Sir John Stanley, as justice of Ireland. Stanley's indenture of 31 July 1389 allowed him a retinue of 5 knights, 94 men-at-arms, 300 mounted archers, and 100 foot archers, which was adequate for defensive purposes, but hardly an impressive retinue. Of more interest is a clause freeing Stanley from office in the event of an expedition by the king or another member of the royal family.[31] Richard clearly saw the need for the reassertion of authority in Ireland, but he did not yet have a clear idea of how to accomplish it. The king toyed with the idea of establishing his recalcitrant uncle, the duke of Gloucester, but Gloucester's efforts to mount an expedition came to nought. After he had received 9,500 marks to assemble an expeditionary force, Gloucester's appointment as lieutenant of Ireland was cancelled in July 1392.[32] The lordship, in dire straits, awaited rescue.

The king was willing to undertake the rescue for several reasons. Financial incentives may have played a rôle. The *Annales* claimed that while Ireland had produced £30,000 per annum in the time of Edward III, it now cost the exchequer £20,000 a year. The figures are inflated, but the perception is valid. Vere's grant had stipulated that once he had pacified the lordship, he would pay 5,000 marks a year to the exchequer and Gloucester's 1392 indenture had projected that Ireland could be made self-supporting within three years. Édouard Perroy tried to place the expedition in the context of an assault on the Clementist Irish. While over half of the thirty-three Irish sees were in the hands of native Irish bishops in the late fourteenth-century, the English-Urbanist clergy controlled the real wealth and power of the Irish Church. Defence of the Church, therefore, may have provided an emotional and symbolic justification for armed intervention, but it was not a major motive for the undertaking. Richard, always sensitive to the symbolic, made little public use of this theme. Both wealth and Clementists could be found in greater abundance in an attack on France.

Tout argued that Richard intended to use the Irish expedition as the recruiting ground for a military autocracy at home. This is, however, to read history backwards. Indubitably, the first Irish expedition revealed to the king the military potential of his household, and this may well have had some residual impact on the king's subsequent attempt to develop his own private retinue in England in 1397. It was not a primary reason for leading troops to Ireland in 1394. J.F. Lydon has summarized the reality of the situation: 'The plain fact of the matter is that Richard had very little choice but to lead the armed might of England against Ireland if he wished to hold on to his lordship there. And unless we understand that we will never fully appreciate the proper extent of his achievement in Ireland. For that achievement was primarily a military one and not, as it is often depicted, a diplomatic or a political one.' The lordship was in dire shape. Communications between the lordship's administrative centres of Carlow and Kilkenny, the centre of the Butler earldom of Ormond, could only be kept open through the payment of black rents to Art MacMurrough Kavanaugh. Such was the hard reality of the situation.[33]

Richard II, of course, was also concerned with image. If the Scottish expedition had been the début of the young warrior king, the first Irish expedition came to be predicated upon the image of the king wielding the sword of justice, an image that came more and more to dominate the campaign. This image has some chivalric overtones. The hagiographic chivalric tract, *Le Livre des faicts du Mareschal de Boucecaut*, which was designed to set a model of chivalry before the age includes a chapter which describes 'how the marshal follows the rule of justice'. The real roots of the image, however, are founded upon theories of kingship. It is very doubtful that Richard was a serious student of Giles of Rome. None the less, Simon Burley did own Giles's *De Regimine Principum*, which taught that the prince must strive to bring peace and security to all his realm. Giles's contemporary, John of Paris, referred to the prince as '*Justitia animata*' and as the guardian of what is just, and Albert the Great had demanded that the king be the 'living and vigilant Justice'. Richard need not have parsed out all the implications of these writers to have appropriated the vivid imagery they offered him. That he had accepted such imagery is suggested in one of the articles of his deposition: '[Richard] expressly said, with an austere and determined countenance, that the laws were in his own mouth or, occasionally, in his own breast . . .'. The king's fanciful flirtation with election as Holy Roman Emperor in 1397 may also in part have been based upon an image of himself as lawgiver to many peoples which the Irish expedition had nourished. Certainly as Richard's Irish adventure progressed, he saw himself more and more as the lion of justice for both English and Irish subjects.[34]

Justice carried a sword, however, and 'the first point in Richard's programme of reform was the application of military force'. The king demonstrated considerable acumen in the preparation of the military expedition. He began to assemble transport in June. The task was entrusted to a group of royal sergeants-at-arms, men of some standing in the royal household who received daily wages of 1s and an annual allowance for robes. John Orwell, a sergeant-at-arms who slept outside Richard's chamber, joined by John Michael, Gilbert Manfield, Hugh Sprot, John Mosdale, Richard Hembrigg and John Helmsdale, divided the coast of England among themselves in a series of commissions to seize ships to make ready for 'the king's intention . . . to go to Ireland shortly in person with a sufficient armada for its peace and good government'. These men managed to assemble a fleet of more than 500 vessels at Milford Haven.[35] When the fleet arrived in Waterford, the sergeants-at-arms served as paymasters along with John Spencer, clerk, with funds provided by John Stacy, the cofferer, and John Carp, the keeper of the wardrobe. Arms for the force were provided by the privy wardrobe. A clerk and a valet were sent from the Tower of London to Dublin castle with a store of arms to be held until the king should need them. The great wardrobe was called on to provide suitably impressive garments for the king, the earls of Rutland, Huntingdon, and March, Lord Beaumont, and Sir Thomas Percy for the expedition.[36] Transport and supply were very much household enterprises; so was provision. Baldwin Raddington, controller of the household, and John Stanley were sent to Ireland with the new treasurer of Ireland, the bishop of Meath, at the end of July to ensure food and shelter for the army's arrival. The importance of, and potential difficulties involved in, this task were emphasized by the retinue of 293 household personnel who accompanied them.[37]

The host itself reflected this same household tincture, although there has been a tendency to overestimate the household character of the rank and file. There were some unlikely soldiers, such as Ralph Repington, a clerk of the kitchen, who received wages of war for himself and an esquire who accompanied him; one wonders how much combat duty Ralph saw or expected to see. Modern generals have military staff assigned to their personal comfort and so did medieval monarchs. One may also doubt the fighting fitness of John Rose, a squire of the chamber who had served Edward III and who received wages of war for himself and two archers from the wardrobe for service in Ireland. Chris Given-Wilson has shown that even within the king's own retinue of 79 knights and 182 esquires there were 'nearly 100 of the senior members of the retinue who were not retained by the king'. Richard augmented his permanent household with those men he had retained throughout the realm. Writs of 1 July had directed each of the sheriffs to summon every one of the yeomen and archers of the Crown holding royal wages and fees to report for service in Ireland.[38]

The household remained the driving force behind the organization of the expedition, but the military operations were undertaken by a collection of commanders drawn from a broader base. It is true that several retinues were commanded by men with household offices, such as Richard's half-brother and chamberlain, the earl of Huntingdon, the under-chamberlain and future earl of Wiltshire, Sir William Scrope, and the steward of the household, Sir Thomas Percy, the future earl of Worcester. Yet, with the possible exception of Percy, the ties of these men with the household were but a minor component in a broader spectrum of royal favour. Two bishops associated with the royal household also joined the expedition: the bishop of Llandaff, who had served as Richard's physician, and Bishop Richard Medford, Richard's former secretary, who had been imprisoned by the Appellants; they were accompanied by a retinue of 6 men-at-arms and 8 mounted archers. The troops under the direct command of the king and the household were augmented by over 700 men commanded by Roger Mortimer, earl of March and Ulster, the greatest English landholder in Ireland and the man with the greatest vested interest in the success of the expedition, as well as by troops led by those younger nobles to whom Richard was especially close: the earls of Rutland and Nottingham, Thomas Holland, the heir of the earl of Kent, and Sir Thomas Despenser, the future earl of Gloucester. Richard had clearly created a force much more open to his personal direction than the force he had led to Scotland a decade earlier. The real rôle of the household was to serve as a nerve-centre for this force. The king was able to revitalize the wardrobe as an instrument of military organization amenable to his personal supervision in the best tradition of Edward I. Furthermore, the first Irish expedition did undoubtedly solidify bonds of brotherhood-in-arms among those who would be his strongest supporters in the final power struggle of the reign.

The only wild card in the deck was the duke of Gloucester. Gloucester, perhaps too dangerous to leave behind or perhaps retaining residual Irish ambitions, travelled separately to join his royal nephew in early November with a retinue of 100 men-at-arms and 300 archers.[39] The total force assembled at Waterford was indeed impressive – Richard intended to impress and to awe the Irish. Froissart, too, was impressed: 'It is not recorded in living memory that a king of England ever undertook an expedition on so large a scale, and with so many men-at-arms and archers, against the Irish.' The Irish were awed: 'The king of England came to Ireland with an immense force, including English and Welsh, and such a fleet did not come to Ireland since the Norse fleets came.' Even the Anglo-Irish took note: '*Anno* 1394, Richard II king of England came with a great multitude of ships and armed men.'[40] James Lydon calculated the total size of the army as between eight and ten thousand men. Critics have complained that Lydon's estimate of 2,000 Irishmen available to augment Richard's English host is overly generous, and Lydon has since retreated to a figure 'over 6,000' for the entire army. The wages of war recorded in John Carp's wardrobe account amount to £28,718 15s, a sum that certainly speaks of a force of some magnitude, and G.O. Sayles deemed it one of the largest English armies assembled in the fourteenth century.[41]

Although there were no great battles, Richard effectively utilized this force to achieve his military objectives. He had landed at Waterford on 2 October, a very late date to begin a campaign, but one carefully chosen. To succeed in Ireland, the king first and foremost had to bring Art MacMurrough to ground. MacMurrough, self-styled king of Leinster, challenged the heart of the English lordship, and he was a mobile and elusive foe in the rough and heavily wooded Leinster terrain. The Irish double-headed axe was deadly in the guerilla skirmishes from ambush that characterized the local style of combat. Richard's counter was the mounted archers who could match MacMurrough's men in mobility and whose fire power could keep the Irish axemen at bay. Such tactics would only be effective once the summer foliage and undergrowth were gone. In fact, the king had to remain in Waterford for an additional fortnight to allow nature to complete her work before setting out on 19 October for Jerpoint, where he awaited Gloucester's arrival. Richard then began to use his heavily armed troops to create a ring of wards around MacMurrough's lands to pin Art down. The fleet was used to blockade Leinster and deny MacMurrough supplies. The king made use of mounted archers to pursue and harass his enemies. The earls of Nottingham and Rutland seem to have commanded mobile strike forces that harried the Irish by burning villages and rounding up cattle so that MacMurrough was deprived of resources. On one such raid Nottingham nearly grabbed the brass ring:

And on another 'journey' he broke in upon him, and if he had not been foreseen, he would have found the said MacMurrough and his wife in their beds. But they, being told of the affray, escaped with great difficulty and at such short warning that they were very nearly taken. And among other things was found a coffer belonging to the said MacMurrough's wife, in which were certain articles of feminine use, but of no great value. And among other things was found the seal of the said MacMurrough, with the inscription around it: SIGILLUM ARTHURII MACMURGH DEI GRACIA REGIS LAGENIE. And when the said Earl M[arshal] failed to take MacMurrough, he was sorely vexed thereat, and determined to punish him, and had his house burned, which was in the said wood of L., as also some fourteen villages round about the said wood, and had four hundred cattle driven away with him.[42]

The tightening noose worked. On 7 January 1395 MacMurrough met with Nottingham and agreed to submit to Richard II.

Richard's successful military campaign against Art MacMurrough led to a series of submissions by the other Gaelic chiefs, including the submission of the O'Neills of Ulster after a great gathering of Irish leaders at which O'Brien, O'Connor and MacCarthy had argued against submission. As Froissart astutely observed, 'But when the Irishmen saw the great number of men at war that king Richard had in Ireland this last journey, the Irishmen advised themselves and came to obeisance'. Tout and Steel misled modern students of the reign concerning the significance of the king's military policy. As Anthony Tuck said, 'In military terms, the campaign was a remarkable success'.[43] Richard had succeeded in using military means not to destroy his foes, but as a means of imposing a political solution.

Richard's Irish policy hit the shoals through political failures. The king tried to effect a political solution based on his image as the dispenser of justice. He was a willing recipient of Niáll Mor O'Neill's plea that the king should act as 'shield and helmet of justice between my lord the Earl of Ulster and me', and O'Kelly's plea that he was 'expecting recompense and grace from your Highness'. Richard emphasized the honour and the grace that could be found in submission to a king. As Dorothy Johnston notes in relation to the process of submission, 'Use of the medieval idiom of kingship is most apparent in the repeated references to divine grace'.[44] Perhaps most significant was the king's promise to do justice to MacMurrough's claim to the barony of Norragh in right of his Anglo-Irish wife, Elizabeth de Veal. While insisting that MacMurrough evacuate lands he had unjustly seized from the Anglo-Irish, Richard offered Art and his men the king's good lordship. Under the terms of an indenture made by MacMurrough and the earl of Nottingham, who was also lord of Carlow and who acted on behalf of the king, Richard took Art's men into his own army and promised to pay them from his household. The Leinster Irish were to aid the king in further military action which the submissions of the other Gaelic chiefs made unnecessary. The indenture, however, was still considered binding in July 1395 when arrangements were made for the payment of fees under the terms, and there was even concern in England that Richard II would make use of Irish troops at home (as James II would later do).

There was perhaps an anticipation of the king's private Cheshire retinue. The king hoped to build up a body of loyal Gael subjects by providing them with justice and good lordship in his lordship of Ireland.[45] At least one Irishman, O'Connor Donn was given letters patent granting him the right to English law and access to the lordship's courts.[46] Sadly, however, there are always Irishmen who fail to appreciate the benefits of English justice. When Richard returned to England in May 1395, Mortimer and the Anglo-Irish pressed the Gaels who now lacked Richard's mediation. The king had been guilty of political naïveté. He confused the images of the good lord and dispenser of justice with political reality; he confused the promises of the Gaels with facts. Yet, short of complete military conquest, the cost of which no English ruler with the possible exception of Oliver Cromwell has been willing to countenance, Richard had succeeded militarily.

The king did in fact make provision to defend his gains. He attempted to check Mortimer's power through a division of authority between Mortimer, whom Richard appointed as lieutenant, and William Scrope, who served in the household-based office of chamberlain of Ireland as well as that of justice of Leinster, Munster and Louth. Mortimer and Scrope served with a combined retinue of 1,000 men.[47] Such a large force demonstrates a continued commitment to pacification. The relationship between the lieutenant and the justice was clarified more fully in a patent of 25 September 1396 which reappointed the earl of Ulster as lieutenant. Mortimer was given supreme authority in Ulster, Connaught and Meath as well as the right to make war on such rebels as might invade the earl's lordships in Leinster, Munster and Louth. In these latter regions the earl was to take counsel with Scrope who was given primary authority for those parts. Mortimer was apparently not overly happy with these limitations. On 26 September, after a curious blank of approximately four inches on the roll, a second patent, joined with the first by a bracket with the marginal notation 'for the Lieutenant of the King in Ireland', declared that it was the king's intention that all documents which passed under the great seal of Ireland in the king's absence should be sealed by the sole testimony of Mortimer as the king's lieutenant in Ireland, as fully as in times past notwithstanding the powers granted Scrope in Leinster, Munster, and Louth. Sir William Scrope in any case had returned to England, leaving his kinsman,

Sir Stephen Scrope, as his deputy.[48] Sir William remained responsible for Irish hostages held on the Isle of Man. Stephen was to enhance Richard's image as the just lord; he was given power to issue pardons to both English and Irish to bring about peace. The patent again carefully attempted to enumerate the judicial powers of both Stephen and Roger Mortimer, albeit these details are omitted from the *Calendar of Patent Rolls*. The key phrase is 'our lieges Irish as well as English'. After his return to England, Richard even attempted to order the earl of Desmond to control the abuses of his Fitzgerald cousins against the king's lieges, a noble but probably symbolic gesture.[49] The king had also looked to the military defence of his lordship.

Prior to embarkation for England, Richard and Sir William Scrope established a series of semi-permanent wards in Leinster in order to perpetuate the successful strategy of the campaign. These wards were set up by 25 April 1395 and were placed under the command of Stephen Scrope. Originally there were seven wards, including one at Cork under the titular command of the earl of Rutland but effectively integrated with the other six. These defensive enclaves could also be used to launch small strike forces such as Richard had employed. Gradually, the strength of the wards was reduced, and Scrope himself took command of a larger strike force as the Gaels became more aggressive. The system, none the less, continued to function until Scrope and his retinue were recalled to England in 1397 to take part in the political battles looming there. 'It appears, therefore, that Richard's Leinster settlement survived, to some extent, the two years following his departure.'[50]

Even in Ulster, Richard attempted to preserve the image of the just lord. He promised to deal with O'Neill's grievances and 'to return you to unity and concord with the Earl of March'; he ordered the earl to restore tranquillity.[51] For Mortimer tranquillity meant Anglo-Irish conquest, and for O'Neill peace meant loss of respect among the Gaels in Ulster. The Ulster settlement never had a chance. The earl of March himself (wearing only the linen dress of an Irish chief) died in battle at Kellestown near Carlow.[52] The fruits of Richard's first Irish expedition had withered.

To save Richard's lordship, title, policy, and image, a second military expedition was required. English historians, aware of the disastrous results of the second Irish campaign and not valuing the Irish lordship, have generally held with Tout that this was the act of a 'fatuous king . . . for revenging the death of Roger Mortimer'. Richard's actions on the Scottish campaign and in domestic politics certainly reveal that he could be stubborn and vengeful. These personality traits unquestionably played a large rôle in his refusal to be turned from Ireland by the political situation in England as well as in the tactics adopted on the campaign, but the necessity for the expedition had been recognized since the winter of 1397. From a military perspective, such an expedition was indispensable.[53]

The second expedition was a smaller affair and even more closely organized by and around the household than the first had been. The figures for Richard's retinue are incomplete, but of the 49 surviving names of knights and bannerets, 6 were knights of the chamber and an additional 30 had been granted fees earlier as king's knights; of the 62 esquires, 46 were household esquires and 2 others had earlier been retained by the Crown. The privy wardrobe sent considerable stores of arms to Dublin including 1,500 bows, with large quantities of arrows and bowstrings as well as 32 cannon, cannon stones, and gunpowder. Shipping was again assembled by royal sergeant-at-arms such as Richard Kays; the king's clerks John Newbold and John Spencer served as the wardrobe's paymasters for the mariners. John Macclesfield, controller of the wardrobe, delivered a series of standards of royal arms and the arms of St George for the expedition. Since Richard intended to defeat rather than woo MacMurrough and the Gaelic chiefs, the royal arms replaced those of St Edward the Confessor which had been featured in the pageantry of the first expedition. The king, however, always concerned with image and appearance, did take his embroiderer to Ireland.[54]

The yeomen of the Crown were again summoned by writs to the sheriffs. There was also a strong Cheshire contingent in which archers predominated. In addition to the king's permanent guard of some 300 Cheshire archers, Robert Parys, the chamberlain of Chester, received wages for 10 knights, 10 men-at-arms and 900 archers.[55] The disparity of archers again indicates that Richard had a grasp of how to fight in Ireland. The magnate component of the host was on a much reduced scale. The duke of Exeter brought a retinue that included 100 mounted archers as well as masons and carpenters; the duke of Aumale was followed by 40 men-at-arms and 600 archers; the earl of Worcester came with

40 men-at-arms and 100 archers, the earl of Gloucester brought a retinue with an additional 100 archers, and the earl of Salisbury was of course present with his retinue.[56] Although the magnate retinues were small and led by an inner circle of family and loyal courtiers, they were – except for Worcester's six-month indenture – retained for an entire year.[57] The king seemingly planned a long campaign with a small and loyal force. The total host was under 5,000 strong. Finances probably limited the size of the royal army in any event as Richard's expenditures had severely taxed his revenues in his last years, leading to dangerous financial expedients.[58]

The finances of this expedition raise further questions. The king clearly did take a significant store of the crown jewels as well as royal treasure with him to Ireland. As both Walsingham and the articles of his deposition charged, Richard had maintained a private hoard of Fitzalan treasure at Holt castle, and he had likewise sent a store of arms to Holt from the privy wardrobe. The king seems to have wished to create financial wards from which he could supply his armies. The crown jewels were fungible and hence a useful tool in military finance as Edward III had already demonstrated.[59] The chamber, the most personal of royal financial departments, was solvent in Richard's final years, and it is likely that the king invested chamber funds in his Irish army. There is a very fragmentary account which records the expenses of the receiver of the chamber for the maintenance of servants and horses and the custody of the royal jewels in Ireland. When the king left Ireland, he left a store of £14,148 16s at Trim which had been deposited by the king's chamberlain, Stephen Scrope.[60] Richard was clearly willing to commit his most personal resources to his Irish lordship; the full extent of that commitment can no longer be known.

The aborted campaign is outlined by the French squire, Jean Créton, who accompanied the expedition. The royal army landed at Waterford on 1 June 1399. The king had remembered the value of archers in an Irish campaign, but he had abandoned the advantages of an autumn offensive. Richard waited for his cousin Aumale for six days before deciding to move inland to Kilkenny, where he had to wait a further fortnight for the duke. The king was by now impatient to engage Art MacMurrough in a decisive battle. Richard, therefore, marched the whole army through Wicklow. MacMurrough refused battle, preferring a strategy of guerilla attacks which were both damaging and frustrating. The army reached Dublin on 1 July without achieving battle. Richard then sent the earl of Gloucester to try to negotiate a new submission from MacMurrough, but in a meeting described and illustrated by Créton, MacMurrough declared: 'I am the rightful king of Ireland, and it is unjust to deprive me of what is my land by conquest.' When Richard heard this, he paled with anger, put a rather modest price of 100 marks on Art's head, and swore to burn him out of his wood. The king took the field again, but once again attempted a quick, direct assault rather than the carefully coordinated tactics used on the first expedition. The army wound up back at Waterford without the showdown Richard sought.[61] This angry and dogged defence of his position in his Irish lordship against the affronts of MacMurrough should dispel any belief that Richard II abandoned his English throne a few short months later, *hilari vultu* as the Lancastrian account claimed. It was at Waterford that the king received the news that the exiled duke of Lancaster had returned to England for a far more serious showdown.

The second Irish campaign was summed up by the fifteenth-century assessment that Richard 'lytill or noone esploit dit'. Yet even on this occasion, the *Annals of Loch Cé* declared that 'MacMurrough was much weakened . . . a great many of the Saxons fell and many of MacMurrough's hired kerns and four chiefs of Leinster'.[62] Even under the stress of a challenge to his throne, Richard did not entirely abandon his military responsibilities to his lordship. Apart from the money, arms, and hostages, including Bolingbroke's son, deposited at Trim, the king left the retinue of his lieutenant and nephew, the duke of Surrey, consisting of 2 bannerets, 14 knights, 134 squires and 800 archers, under the command of Surrey's younger brother, Edmund of Kent.[63] Richard saw the Irish expedition as unfinished business when he departed the lordship.

Indeed, the king delayed his departure from Ireland with fatal consequences. Salisbury was sent ahead to rally forces in north Wales and Chester while the king gathered and organized the remainder of his army in Waterford for a crossing to south Wales. He is generally said to have fallen victim to either the treachery or incompetence of the duke of Aumale.[64] In hindsight, the strategy certainly was a dismal failure, but militarily it made sense: 'A proposal to concentrate an army in Cheshire where Richard was popular, in a county from which he had drawn his formidable archers, had a great deal to commend it.

Another force, sent eastward through Glamorgan to menace Lancaster's communications, was a threat that the usurper could not disregard. Any hostile advance upon Chester would almost inevitably be delayed and Salisbury given more time to build up a strong force. A great deal depended upon Aumale's skill and resolution. The plan had its risks: but was any other conceivable plan without risks? Historians know that both York and Aumale turned traitor: Richard did not possess their hindsight. Maybe he should have known Aumale too well to have trusted him, but he had no reason to suspect York who had been for many years his faithful servant in war and peace and had served as keeper of England during the king's absence on previous occasions. Had he suspected his uncle and his cousin his plans would have been very different.'[65] The duke of York did in fact rally some forces to resist Lancaster. Once again, only in hindsight can historians condemn York as a coward and a military incompetent. Both York and Richard have been harshly judged because of Richard's final defeat.[66]

The date of Richard's departure from Ireland, and almost everything that happened to the king and his army until Richard fell into the hands of his cousin and supplanter have been the source of much historians' ink. It is unlikely that the puzzle can ever be solved. Did the 'panic-stricken king' desert his army or did the army desert the king? James Sherborne's examination of the events in south Wales led him to conclude that Richard had contributed to his own downfall by leaving his army to seek out Salisbury's no longer extant host.[67] Richard II fought no battles in defence of his throne. Rather did he allow himself to be lured from a defensible position at Conway castle to negotiate with Lancaster who made the king his prisoner. Richard chose to rely upon the symbolic power of his kingship, and he held to his faith in that power even as a captive in the Tower of London.[68]

The king certainly hoped to shore up his power through the genuine potential for military and political action represented by his household and affinity, but he also relied heavily upon his rôle as an anointed monarch. In the showdown, his affinity was not strong enough to overcome his enemies. Richard was left only with the imagery of kingship for his defence. He never fully mastered the pragmatic necessity of real force as an underpinning for the power of imagery.

This failure cost the king his throne as well as his martial reputation. Military imagery none the less was an essential feature of Ricardian kingship. No one can claim Richard II was a great warrior, but he did demonstrate strategic sense in both Scotland and Ireland which historians have been slow to credit. Sir Richard of Bordeaux used military force as a tool, not an end. He never fought in France; and he used a handkerchief![69] His critics have looked no further.

Notes

[1] *Foedera*, VII, 183.

[2] A.B. Steel, *Richard II* (Cambridge, 1941), p. 41; G. Mathew, *The Court of Richard II* (London, 1968), p. 22.

[3] Thomas Walsingham, *Historia Anglicana (Hist. Angl.)*, ed. H.T. Riley (2 vols, London, 1863–4), II, p. 156.

[4] T.F. Tout, *Chapters in the Administrative History of Medieval England* (6 vols, Manchester, 1920–33), III, p. 487.

[5] *Hist. Angl.*, p. 259.

[6] M.H. Keen, *Chivalry* (New Haven, 1984), pp. 1–18; K.B. McFarlane, *England in the Fifteenth Century* (London, 1981), pp. 1–43; J.M.W. Bean, *From Lord to Patron: Lordship in Late Medieval England* (Philadelphia, 1989), pp. 1–9, 231–7. (Ricardians will have to excuse Bean's identification of Aubrey de Vere as duke of Ireland and commander at Radcot Bridge found on p. 162!) For a general overview of royal armies, see A.L. Brown, *The Governance of Late Medieval England, 1272–1461* (Stanford, California, 1989), pp. 85–99.

[7] A.F. Alexander, 'The War with France in 1377' (unpublished University of London, Ph.D. thesis, 1933), pp. 43, 388–9; PRO, E403/462 mm. 15–16; R.H. Jones, *The Royal Policy of Richard II* (Oxford, 1968), pp. 82–3.

[8] See H. Wallon, *Richard II* (2 vols, Paris, 1864), I, 238–40, for the discomfort of the Frenchmen in Scotland.

[9] *Foedera*, VII, 471–2; S. Armitage-Smith, *John of Gaunt, Duke of Lancaster* (London, 1904), pp. 293–4.

[10] N.B. Lewis, 'The Last Medieval Summons of the English Feudal Levy, 13 June 1385', *EHR*, LXXIII (1958), 1–25; J.J.N. Palmer, 'The Last Summons of the Feudal Army in England (1385)', ibid., LXXXIII (1968), 771–5.

[11] C.B. McNab, 'Obligations of the Church in English Society: Military Arrays of the Clergy, 1369–1418', in *Order and Innovation in the Middle Ages: Essays in Honor of Joseph R. Strayer*, eds W.C. Jordan, C.B. McNab, and T.F. Ruiz (Princeton, 1976), p. 298; C.F. Briggs, 'The English Clergy and the Hundred Years War, 1337–1389' (unpublished University of Edinburgh M.Litt. thesis, 1988).

[12] S. Armitage-Smith, *John of Gaunt*, pp. 437–9; N.H. Nicolas, 'An Account of the Army with which King Richard the Second invaded Scotland, in the ninth year of his Reign', *Archaeologia*, XXII (1828), 13–19.

[13] N.B. Lewis, 'The Last Medieval Summons', pp. 7–8.

14 PRO, E101/400/22. The archers of the Crown are listed on m. 2. This list largely corresponds with those men who received patents as archers of the Crown between 20 August and 19 October 1385. Two of the archers who accompanied the king were hold-overs from Edward III's reign, while four men who received patents in the aftermath of the expedition were not included among the thirty-five archers listed. Thomas Hornington was among the thirty-five, but he never received a patent. For prosopographic detail on the archers of the Crown, see J.L. Gillespie, 'The Cheshire Archers of Richard II' (unpublished Princeton University Ph.D. thesis, 1973), pp. 194–245.

15 *The Black Book of the Admiralty*, ed. T. Twiss (4 vols, London, 1871–6), I, p. 453.

16 S. Armitage-Smith, *John of Gaunt*, p. 295; T.F. Tout, *Chapters*, III, 395 n. 1; A. Goodman, *The Loyal Conspiracy* (London, 1971), p. 157; *Westminster Chronicle, 1381–1394*, eds L.C. Hector and B.F. Harvey (Oxford, 1982), p. 124.

17 J.L. Leland, 'Richard II and the Counter-Appellants' (unpublished Yale University Ph.D. thesis, 1979), pp. 57–69.

18 *The original chronicle of Andrew of Wyntoun*, ed. F.J. Amours (6 vols, Edinburgh, 1903–14), VI, 315.

19 PRO, C81/508/5579; *Calendar of Documents Relating to Scotland*, IV, 88.

20 *Westminster Chronicle*, p. 131.

21 H. Wallon, *Richard II*, I, 245; S. Armitage-Smith, *John of Gaunt*, pp. 296–7; A. Goodman, *John of Gaunt: The Exercise of Princely Power in Fourteenth-Century Europe* (London, 1993); H.F. Hutchison, *The Hollow Crown: A Life of Richard II* (New York, 1961), pp. 90–100; J.A. Tuck, *Richard II and the English Nobility* (London, 1973), pp. 97–8; A. Steel, *Richard II*, p. 105.

22 PRO, E101/40/6 m. 10; *Calendar of Documents Relating to Scotland*, IV, 76.

23 J.S. Roskell, *The Impeachment of Michael de la Pole, Earl of Suffolk in 1386* (Manchester, 1984), pp. 187–9.

24 PRO, E101/400/22 mm. 4–5; 400/27 mm. 15–20; C. Given-Wilson, *The Royal Household and the King's Affinity* (New Haven, 1986), pp. 64–5; *CPR, 1381–5*, p. 533; *1385–9*, pp. 1, 175; *CCR, 1385–9*, p. 77.

25 'William Thorne's De rebus abbatum Cant.', in *Historiae Anglicanae Scriptores Decem*, ed. R. Twysden (London, 1652), cols. 2181–3; E. Hasted, *The History and Topographical Survey of the County of Kent* (2nd edn, 12 vols, Canterbury, 1797–1801), XII, 411–12; J.L. Gillespie, 'Dover Castle: Key to Richard II's Kingdom', *Archaeologia Cantiana*, vol. CV (1988), 186–8. On the defence of the southern coast, see J. Sherborne, 'The Defence of the Realm and the Impeachment of Michael de la Pole in 1386', in *Politics and Crisis in Fourteenth-Century England*, eds J. Taylor and W. Childs (Gloucester, 1990).

26 J.H. Ramsey, *Genesis of Lancaster, 1307–1399* (2 vols, Oxford, 1913), II, p. 224.

27 PRO, E101/73/2 no. 30; N.B. Lewis, 'The Last Medieval Summons', p. 16; PRO, E509 m. 24; E101/42/23 [Not dated in *Lists and Indexes*, vol. XI (London, 1900), p. 47. The first membrane is very badly damaged, but m. 2 is clearly dated 23 July 10 Richard II]; *CPR, 1385–9*, p. 283; *1388–92*, pp. 347, 519.

28 T.F. Tout, *Chapters*, III, p. 395.

29 J. Davies, *A Discoverie of the True Cause – Why Ireland Was Never Entirely Subdued . . . until His Majesties Happie Reign* (London, 1612), pp. 11, 44; A. Steel, *Richard II*, p. 209; D. Johnston, 'Richard II and the Submissions of Gaelic Ireland', *Irish Historical Studies*, vol. XXII (1980), 1–20.

30 *Statutes and Ordinances and Acts of the Parliament of Ireland: King John to Henry V*, ed. H.F. Berry (Dublin, 1907), pp. 485–7; J.A. Watt, 'The Anglo-Irish Colony under Strain, 1327–99', *A New History of Ireland: II: Medieval Ireland 1169–1534*, ed. A. Cosgrove (Oxford, 1987), p. 391; J.A. Tuck, 'Anglo-Irish Relations, 1382–1393', *Proceedings of the Royal Irish Academy*, vol. LXIX (C) (1970), 23–4; *CPR, 1385–9*, p. 78; *Reports from the Lords' Committees Appointed to Search the Journals of the House, Rolls of Parliament and Other Records for all Matters Touching the Dignity of a Peer* (5 vols, London, 1820–9), V, 716–17; J.J.N. Palmer, *England, France and Christendom, 1377–1399* (London, 1972), p. 166.

31 PRO, E101/68/11 no. 265.

32 PRO, E101/74/1; E403/538; BL, Add. MS 40859A; J.F. Lydon, 'Richard II's Expeditions to Ireland', *Journal of the Royal Society of Antiquaries of Ireland*, vol. XCIII (1963), 108.

33 J.F. Lydon, *Ireland in the Later Middle Ages* (Dublin, 1973), p. 106; E. Perroy, *L'Angleterre et la grand schieme d'occident*, pp. 97–9; J.A. Watt, 'The Anglo-Irish Colony', pp. 334–5; T.F. Tout, *Chapters*, III, p. 487; J.F. Lydon, 'Richard II's Expeditions to Ireland', p. 135.

34 'Le Livre de faictz du bon Messire Jehan le Maingre, dit "Boucicant",' in *Collection des Mémoires relatifs à l'histoire de France*, ed. C.B. Petitot (52 vols, Paris, 1819–26), VII, 205–7; R.H. Jones, *Royal Policy*, p. 156; E.H. Kantorowicz, *The King's Two Bodies* (Princeton, 1957), p. 153; W. Ullmann, *The Medieval Idea of Law* (London, 1946), pp. 50–2; *Rot. Parl.*, III, 419b; C. Stephenson and F.G. Marcham, *Sources of English Constitutional History* (New York, 1937), p. 252.

35 J.F. Lydon, *Ireland*, pp. 137, 140; C. Given-Wilson, *Royal Household*, p. 54; *CPR, 1377–81*, p. 410; *1391–6*, pp. 420, 518, 520–1. John Helmsdale is noted as a clerk in PRO, E101/41/33 m. 4.

36 PRO, E101/41/33 where Carp acts through John Judith. For additional information on shipping, see E101/41/26.

37 PRO, E101/69/1 nos. 283 (Raddington), 286 (Scrope), and 287 (Percy); E101/402/20; J.F. Lydon, *Ireland*, p. 140.

38 PRO, E101/402/15 no. 6; E364/38d; C. Given-Wilson, *Royal Household*, pp. 63–5, 174 n. 128 (the index is in error here in citing p. 172); T.F. Tout, *Chapters*, III, 487–90; *Foedera*, VII, 782; J.L. Gillespie, 'Richard II's Archers of the Crown', *Journal of British Studies*, vol. XVIII (1979), 19; idem, 'Richard II's Yeomen of the Chamber', *Albion*, vol. X (1978), 324.

39 PRO E/101/69/1 no. 289; H.F. Hutchison, *Hollow Crown*, p. 147; A. Goodman, *Loyal Conspiracy*, p. 62.

40 A. Cosgrove, *Late Medieval Ireland, 1370–1541* (Dublin, 1981), p. 18; BL, Add. MS. 4793 f. 74.

41 J.F. Lydon, *Ireland*, p. 142; idem, *Ireland in the Later Middle Ages*, p. 112; PRO, E101/403/1 m. 4; T.F. Tout, *Chapters*, III, 489; J.H. Ramsey, *Genesis*, II, p. 299, despaired of arriving at a figure ('Of Richard's force no estimate of any worth is forthcoming'). Professor Sayles's comment was offered in a private conversation with the author in 1970.

42 E. Curtis, 'Unpublished Letters from Richard II in Ireland, 1394–5', *Proceedings of the Royal Irish Academy*, vol. XXXVII (C) (1927), 279, 292–3.

43 J.F. Lydon, 'Richard II's Expeditions to Ireland', pp. 145–6; T.F. Tout, *Chapters*, III, 490; A. Steel, *Richard II*, p. 208 (Steel does admit in a note on p. 208 that he may have understated the case); J.A. Tuck, *Richard II*, p. 174; *Œuvres de Froissart*, ed. K. de Lettenhove (25 vols, Brussels, 1870–7), XV, 180.

44 E. Curtis, *Richard II in Ireland* (Oxford, 1927), pp. 122–3, 129–31, 203–4, 210–11; D. Johnston, 'Richard II', pp. 5–10.

45 BL, Hargrave MS. 313 f. 54; *CPR, 1391–6*, p. 682; A. Cosgrove, 'England and Ireland, 1399–1447', *A New History of Ireland: II*, p. 525; D. Johnston, 'Richard II', p. 15.

46 PRO, E163/7/12 no. 6; D. Johnston, 'Richard II', p. 13.

47 PRO, E101/69/1 nos 292, 293.

48 PRO, C66/344 m. 16; *CPR, 1396–9*, pp. 29, 174; T.F. Tout, *Chapters*, III, 491. Sir William was paid £12,185 11s 4d for wages of his retinue from the English exchequer. PRO, E364/31 m. 4d; 32 m. 8d.

49 PRO, C66/344 m. 20; *CPR, 1396–9*, p. 23; Add. MS. 24062, p. 122.

50 The accounts of the wages for wards and the names of the men who served are preserved in a beautiful document, PRO, E101/41/39, which the scribe took care to decorate with lilies in the left margin. D. Johnston, 'The Interim Years: Richard II and Ireland, 1395–1399', *England and Ireland in the Later Middle Ages*, ed. J.F. Lydon (Dublin, 1981), pp. 176–7, has made fine use of this document, but there are more blooms to be picked. PRO, E364/32 m. 8d; D. Johnston, 'The Interim Years', p. 178.

51 BL, Cotton MS. Titus B XI 1/7.

52 E. Curtis, *A History of Medieval Ireland* (2nd edn, London, 1938), p. 275.

53 T.F. Tout, *Chapters*, IV, 53; J.A. Tuck, *Richard II*, p. 210.

54 C. Given-Wilson, *Royal Household*, p. 221; PRO, E101/403/19 no. 49; 403/20 mm. 2–4; J.F. Lydon, *Ireland in the Later Middle Ages*, p. 122.

55 PRO, E403/562 mm. 10, 16; E364/37E m. 5v; J. Davies, *Discoverie of the True Cause*, p. 278.

56 PRO, E101/69/1 nos 296–301.

57 PRO, E101/69/1 no. 296; D. Johnston, 'Richard II's Departure from Ireland, July 1399', *EHR*, vol. XCVIII (1983), 793 n. 4, does not note this exception to the pattern of one-year indentures.

58 C. Given-Wilson, *Royal Household*, p. 79; C.M. Barron, 'The Tyranny of Richard II', *Bulletin of the Institute of Historical Research*, vol. XLI (1968).

59 PRO, E101/403/13 m. 6; C. Given-Wilson, *Royal Household*, pp. 180–1; J. Nichols, *A Collection of the Wills of the Kings and Queens of England* (London, 1780), pp. 191–202.

60 PRO, E101/403/21; E159/177 m. 19; D. Johnston, 'Richard II's Departure', p. 797.

61 Jean Créton, 'A French Metrical History of the Deposition of Richard II', ed. and trans. J. Webb, *Archaeologia*, vol. XX (1824), 298–309; E. Curtis, *Medieval Ireland*, pp. 275–6.

62 *Three Prose Versions of the Secreta Secretorum*, ed. R. Steel (London, 1898), pp. 136–7; D. Johnston, 'Richard II's Departure', 785 n. 1; E. Curtis, *Medieval Ireland*, p. 276 n. 2.

63 PRO, E403/562 (13 May); D. Johnston, 'Richard II's Departure', p. 801.

64 Jean Créton, 'French Metrical History', pp. 312–13; T.F. Tout, *Chapters*, IV, 59; M. McKisack, *The Fourteenth Century* (Oxford, 1959), pp. 492–3.

65 G.O. Sayles, 'Richard II in 1381 and 1399', *EHR*, vol. XCIV (1979), 824. A less favourable view of Richard's slow departure from Ireland is C.M. Barron, 'The Deposition of Richard II', in *Politics and Crisis in Fourteenth-Century England*, pp. 137–8.

66 PRO, E101/42/12 provides the names and provenances of those who brought forces to Richard's support. See also J.A. Tuck, *Richard II*, p. 218; J. Sherborne, 'Richard II's Return to Wales, July 1399', *Welsh History Review*, vol. VII (1975), 390–2.

[67] J. Sherborne, 'Richard II's Return', p. 402; J.H. Ramsey, *Genesis*, II, p. 355; M.V. Clarke and V.H. Galbraith, 'The Deposition of Richard II', in *Fourteenth Century Studies*, eds L.S. Sutherland and M. McKisack (Oxford, 1937), pp. 72–3.

[68] H.G. Wright, 'The Protestation of Richard II in the Tower in September, 1399', *Bulletin of the John Rylands Library*, vol. XXIII (1939), 151–65.

[69] See G.B. Stow, 'Richard II and the Invention of the Pocket Handkerchief', *Albion*, vol. XXVII (1995), 221–35.

8

THE OXFORD TRIAL OF 1400: ROYAL POLITICS AND THE COUNTY GENTRY

John L. Leland

In January 1400, King Henry IV came to Oxford to hold trials of the surviving members of a conspiracy which had nearly overthrown him early that month.[1] Most of the prominent leaders of the attempted insurrection – the recently demoted noblemen whose participation gave the attempted coup the name the 'Duketti Uprising' – had died during or immediately after the revolt without any formal legal process.[2] Now, however, the remaining participants were given conventional jury trials, though they were held by the court of the seneschal and marshal of the household.[3] This meant that these men, ranging from knights through squires to more obscure men, faced juries who often were their literal peers – knights and gentlemen whose activities at court, at war, and in county offices very much paralleled their own. The jurors and the defendants had shared many experiences in the service of Richard II, whom the rebels had tried to restore. From their past records, many of the jurors could quite easily have been among the rebels; many rebels, had they shown a little more discretion, might have been among the jurors. If the revolt had succeeded, King Henry himself might have been on trial. His fragile régime attempted to use the prosecution to extract specific political commitments from the jurors. The phrasing of the indictments repeated the official story of Henry's coming to the throne after Richard II *sponte voluntarie et absolute renunciavit et resignavit* the Crown on account of his *mala gubernatione*.[4] Many present must have known that Richard's abdication had hardly been spontaneous or voluntary in the usual sense of those terms. For many of these jurors, who had been retained to follow Richard for life or received other favours at his hands, and yet had later had their privileges confirmed by Henry, the question of where their loyalties lay must have been very real. By serving on these juries and voting to convict the rebels as traitors, they were in effect endorsing Henry's position.

There could be no doubt that the defendants had taken up arms against Henry, riding with banner flying in the mode of open war (as the indictment said),[5] and they were obviously traitors if Henry was indeed the true king.

Henry's kingship might have been in real doubt a few weeks before, when the rebellion was actually in progress, but by the time he came to Oxford he had clearly established himself as king *de facto*. It is not very surprising that the jurors generally returned the expected verdicts that the rebels were guilty of treason against Henry as their lawful ruler. It is more surprising that in one case they did not: Alan Buxhill the younger was acquitted. Although he was son of a noted Lancastrian knight, he was also the stepson of John Montagu, earl of Salisbury, a leader of the rebellion.[6] Acquittals in English treason trials in this period were unusual, especially when the rebel was actually taken in arms. It might be thought this was a calculated act of mercy by prearrangement with the king (who did pardon some other rebels),[7] but the king reacted to the verdict by saying that Buxhill would not be considered guilty of rebellion but should none the less be held prisoner in the Tower, which suggests the acquittal came as an unpleasant surprise to the presiding monarch.[8]

Presuming that the acquittal actually represented the honest opinion of the jury, it is very interesting to look further into the lives of the men who had the courage to render this verdict in the very face of their sovereign. This is more easily done because the jury involved seems to have been what American usage has called a 'blue-ribbon' jury; that is, its members were more distinguished than many of those in the other juries empanelled during these trials. The comparatively superior status of these men may have given them the self-confidence to defy the king, as well as the contacts with the previous Ricardian court which may have influenced their verdict. Some of them came from families with more than one generation of service to the deposed king.

The first juror, Sir Baldwin Bereford, was once in the retinue of Edward, prince of Wales, the father of Richard II, and although he also served the duke of Lancaster (Henry IV's father), he appears as one of Richard's knights, and in the first great crisis of Richard's reign, in 1387–8, when the hostile noble faction known as the Appellants took power, Bereford was among those required to abjure the court.[9] When one of King Richard's allies, Sir Nicholas Brembre, was executed by the Appellants, Bereford appears in the records interceding for

Brembre's servants (he may have married Brembre's widow as well).[10] He received many royal favours, including the keeping of Clarendon forest, in which he succeeded Alan Buxhill, the defendant's father of the same name.[11] There are references to both a Baldwin Bereford the elder and the younger in these records, but it is likely to be the juror himself who repeatedly served on official commissions in Oxfordshire, often together with others who took part in this jury: Thomas Barantyne, Thomas (de la) Poyle, John Drayton, Thomas Paynell and so on.[12] Like several of these men, he served on King Richard's first Irish expedition in 1394, when he nominated Barantyne as one of his attorneys.[13] When Richard's noble allies brought their own appeal against the former Appellants in 1397, Bereford's name was among those acting as pledges that these lords would maintain their appeal. (Many of these lords became leaders of the Duketti rebellion.)[14]

When Henry IV took the throne in October 1399, Bereford (like many other courtiers) promptly secured Henry's confirmation of previous grants from Richard,[15] but it would not be surprising if Bereford still felt some sympathy for the Ricardians. None the less, Henry seems to have trusted him, as Bereford was among those on the commission of array for Oxfordshire issued on 18 December 1399 (five of the jury members were on this commission).[16] His name also appears on a later commission of array to deal with the Glyndŵr revolt in 1403; but already in 1401 he had been given an exemption from serving on royal commissions due to his great age (following two earlier exemptions in Richard's reign) and by 1406 he was dead.[17] His career was almost purely that of a favoured Ricardian, yet he was willing to make some accommodation with Henry in the end.

Another man with strong Ricardian ties, but a bolder style, was the second juror on the list, Sir John Drayton. He appears as an esquire in the service of Thomas Holland, earl of Kent, King Richard's half-brother and father of the Thomas who was one of the leaders of the Duketti uprising. The Thomas whom Drayton served was marshal of England in 1380, and Richard confirmed Holland's grant to Drayton of the offices of sergeant-marshal and clerk-marshal of the marshalsea of the king's household.[18] A few years later, Drayton served on the 'crusade' led by Bishop Henry Despenser against the schismatic French in Flanders. Despenser was to be loyal to Richard in 1399, but it is perhaps not

fair to count the 'crusade' as a Ricardian link for Drayton, since in the
ignominious withdrawal of the Flanders expedition he was among the English
officers who took money from the French for yielding the last few English-held
towns. These commanders seem to have felt that it was not improper to take
French money for abandoning untenable positions, but the bishop and others
naturally disagreed, and Drayton and the other captains involved had to defend
themselves in parliament.[19]

After this inauspicious experience, Drayton spent a few years on local affairs,
but by 1385 he was a knight and the captain of the English castle of Guines on
the Calais frontier.[20] During the Appellant crisis, he seems to have been in
serious trouble, like many of those involved in King Richard's French policies.
On 19 March 1388, Drayton was given a pardon for all treasons in Calais,
Guines and England, and also for all debts owed to the king, but on 4 April he
received a special protection on grounds that he was coming to the council on
urgent business and feared arrest and loss of goods at the hands of his
enemies.[21] It is not entirely clear whether these enemies were personal or
political, but Drayton was certainly willing to take political risks: on 4 June he
acted as mainpernor for Richard Metford (or Medford), one of the king's clerks
imprisoned in the Tower. The highly political nature of this case is proved by
the special condition attached to Medford's release: he was to be 'sending
naught to the king for any business which concerns the king or the estate or
governance of the realm'.[22]

Besides the factional conflict, Drayton seems to have been involved in
monetary claims (as the fact that his March pardon was for both treason and
debt already suggested). On 20 July 1388, Drayton received an assignment of
£250 with the special provision, 'the king's will is that the assignment shall at no
future time be revoked'.[23] Royal favour, however, did not prevent Drayton's
imprisonment. His old patron, Thomas Holland, as lieutenant of the Tower,
was ordered by the council to receive Drayton in safe custody on 26 October
1388, and Drayton remained in the Tower until his brother William and others
mainperned for him on 11 February 1389.[24] One clue to the cause of this
episode may be the pardon given to Drayton on 27 December 1389, which says
that he was accused by Roger Walden, treasurer of Calais, of rebellion in
refusing to give up the custody of Guines 'when required by the king's writs and

mandates'.[25] Despite the pardon, Drayton's conduct at Guines was investigated by a powerful commission headed by the bishop of St David's and Henry Percy, earl of Northumberland, which was appointed on 1 February 1390.[26]

Thereafter, Drayton appears only as involved in local affairs until he was sent to the Tower again on 5 July 1393; this time the cause seems to have been merely a local land dispute.[27] There are several subsequent references to this case, including a complaint to parliament in 1394 in which Drayton alleged that he was unable to regain an estate by writ of novel disseisin because the opposing party was maintained by Sir William Bagot.[28] Bagot was one of King Richard's unpopular favourites, but this did not prevent Drayton from serving the king on his first Irish expedition in 1394, like Bereford and other future jurors.[29] The Bagot dispute continued until 1397, when Bagot and Drayton were exchanging recognizances.[30] Drayton, who seems to have been quite litigious, was involved in other disputes during these years. None the less, he again went to Ireland in Richard's second expedition of 1399, and while there served as attorney together with another future juror, Thomas Paynell.[31] Presumably, this Irish service meant that when Henry of Lancaster landed in England, Drayton was in the army which Richard tried to lead against the invasion. We know that this army rapidly disintegrated, but all we know of Drayton is that by December 1399, he was receiving a commission in Oxfordshire, where the next month he served on the jury that acquitted Buxhill.[32] This acquittal has the boldness characteristic of Drayton, and he may have been a major factor in the jury's decision. He and Paynell may have thought it best to return to Ireland after this, as on 9 February 1400 they again received letters of attorney to act in Ireland, but if he did go Drayton soon returned, for in the following year he was pursuing a case of debt in England.[33]

He does not seem to have been in government again until 1404, when he was both a tax collector and a member of parliament for Oxfordshire; in the same parliament the neighbouring seat of Berkshire was held by John Golafre (the younger), another former member of the same jury.[34] In 1407, Drayton witnessed a charter received by Golafre, and again served on a tax commission.[35] In 1410, Golafre and Robert James, another member of that jury, served on a commission about a complaint by Drayton that his enemies had besieged him in Nuneham, Oxon.[36] In Henry V's reign Drayton was in trouble again: on 17 May 1414 the sheriff was ordered to arrest him, but by the next month Drayton was himself on a commission about concealed lands, an unusually quick turn of the revolving door which often characterized royal relations with the gentry.[37] In 1415, Drayton was found still holding Nuneham – and holding it from the widow of William, earl of Salisbury (whose nephew John had been one of the 'Duketti', and Buxhill's stepfather).[38] The next year, Drayton committed an exploit mentioned in the *Victoria County History* and Preston's history of St Nicholas Church, Abingdon: in a dispute with the abbot of Abingdon, the old warrior built his own fort encroaching on the abbey's lands and fired arrows and cannon to disrupt the church's attempts to beat its bounds.[39] This seems to have been Drayton's last hurrah, as the next year he was dead.[40] As late as 1423, an inquest was still recording Drayton's arrangements for Nuneham, again involving John Golafre the younger as well as Thomas Chaucer, the poet's son, a major figure in the region under the Lancastrians (chiefly as an ally of Henry Beaufort).[41] Even the combative Drayton had apparently accepted the Lancastrians before his death.

It is difficult to distinguish the early career of the third juror, Sir William Lisle, as there were two men (uncle and nephew) of that name, but both had similar careers under Richard II; they were retained as king's knights, both served on Richard's second Irish expedition, and both had their grants from Richard confirmed by Henry IV in October 1399, very shortly after his accession.[42] On the whole, it seems likely that the knight voting for the acquittal in 1400 was Sir William Lisle the younger; when he received his protection to go to Ireland with Richard on 9 April 1399, the very next recorded protection was granted to Sir Benedict Cely (or Sely), later to be one of the 'Duketti' rebels brought before the court at Oxford.[43] Lisle the younger had also been granted his annuity from Richard to be paid by the bailiffs of the city of Oxford, so he is more probably the Lisle summoned to jury duty there.[44]

Apparently Lisle retained Henry IV's favour despite the jury's verdict, for in the next year William Lisle the younger not only received an order for payment of the arrears of his grant from Oxford, but was also granted a tun of wine a year. By 1402, William Lisle in Oxfordshire was serving on several commissions, including one to raise men against Glyndŵr's revolt in Wales.[45] Like Drayton, he helped to collect taxes, but he also had other responsibilities: he served as deputy to the marshal of England in 1409 while the latter was abroad, and as sheriff of Oxfordshire and Berkshire in 1411, escheator there in 1417–18, and sheriff again in 1420–2.[46] Meanwhile, William Lisle the elder was declining, giving up his various grants and finally being given a place at Windsor 'in consideration of his great poverty in his old age'. This place was granted to another poor knight in 1428, presumably when the elder William Lisle died.[47]

Sir Thomas Paynell, the next knight on the jury list, has already been mentioned as an associate of John Drayton's in Ireland. On the whole, he seems to have had a less colourful career than Drayton, but there are certain resemblances. In 1384, he appeared as a witness in two documents involving Sir Richard Abberbury (the elder) who, like Baldwin Bereford, was required to abjure Richard II's court in 1388 by the Appellants.[48] Lines were not so sharply drawn in 1384, however, as another party to one of these charters was Thomas Arundel, bishop of Ely, brother of the earl of Arundel who was one of the Appellants. After the earl was executed by Richard in 1397, the bishop became one of the leaders in the king's deposition. On the whole, it seems to be the Bereford/Abberbury link that explains Paynell's presence. The second document in particular, a quitclaim by the royal justice, William Shareshull, to Abberbury for land in Oxfordshire, is witnessed by a group of Oxford worthies, including not only Baldwin Bereford and Thomas Paynell but also Thomas Barantyne, who served on the 1400 jury with them.

Similar links to Abberbury and Oxfordshire occur for Paynell in 1386 and 1389 – unlike Bereford and Drayton, he seems to have avoided the ill effects of the Appellant crisis.[49] In 1390 he obtained a writ of *supersedeas* by making oath that he had not received a commission against rebels in Oxfordshire.[50] He did have at least an indirect political connection in 1395, when he was one of the mainpernors for Bernard Brocas, father of one of the 'Duketti' rebels.[51] Paynell thus seems to have been a more minor member of the same Oxford Ricardian group as Bereford and Drayton. As already noted, he served with Drayton in Ireland on Richard's last expedition, when he and Drayton served together as attorneys in Ireland for an English merchant. Paynell's connection with Ireland proved more lasting than Drayton's. In 1401 he was in England acting as attorney for a man in Ireland, but by 1403 he was back in Ireland acting as attorney for a man in England, and he was doing the same thing as late as 1418 and 1419.[52] So far as the available records go, this seems to have been his chief concern; he seems to have had no English career after his jury service, perhaps a sign that he was, like his comrade Drayton, one of those more active in opposing the royal will on that occasion.

Sir Peter Besiles, on the other hand, was only in the early stages of a very active career in the Oxford region when he served on the 1400 jury. This career had begun in 1384, when he proved his age and inherited the property of his father Thomas (strictly speaking, Peter was the heir of his elder brother John, who had died a minor).[53] Like Bereford and Drayton, he served on Richard's first Irish expedition in 1394, but unlike Drayton and Paynell he was apparently not on the second expedition in 1399.[54] He does not seem to have had any Ricardian grants to be confirmed by Henry IV, but Henry appointed him in December 1399 to the Oxfordshire commission of array, which, as already noted, included several of those who would be jurors together a month later: Bereford, Lisle, John Golafre (the younger), and Thomas Barantyne. The equivalent Berkshire commission included Drayton and another future juror, Edmund Spersholt.[55]

Whatever the feelings between some of these men and the new king, Peter Besiles for one really achieved more official recognition under Henry IV than he had under Richard. He was appointed justice of the peace in Berkshire on 16 May 1401, and repeatedly thereafter, whereas he had not served in this office under Richard.[56] He was also put on a commission against rebels in May 1402 and again in September 1403, at the height of the first great revolt against Henry, serving with Lisle, Golafre and Barantyne.[57] In 1404, he was a member of parliament for Oxfordshire, and in 1405 he was escheator there, an office he held again in 1414; meanwhile he was sheriff for Oxfordshire and Berkshire in 1409.[58] He often served on commissions with men who had been on the jury, particularly John Golafre the younger and Robert James, and these men appear to have known each other more informally as well. In 1410, Robert James made a grant to a group including Thomas Chaucer and John Golafre the younger, and it was witnessed by Peter Besiles, John Drayton and Edmund Spersholt, among others. All these save Chaucer had been on the 1400 jury, and several others present for the charter had been listed as potential jurors in 1400. Besiles and Drayton were also witnesses the following year, when Thomas Chaucer,

John Golafre and the rest re-enfeoffed Robert James.[59] In his later years (1418–20), Besiles often served on commissions to raise men and money for Henry V's expeditions, and he was still on the commission of the peace in 1422.[60] He died in 1424 but was long remembered: a distant relative gave a portrait of him to Christ's Hospital in Oxford as late as 1607.[61]

In contrast to the very full active career of Peter Besiles (only very selectively outlined here), the last two jurors given the title of 'knight' on the jury list were much less distinguished figures. Both were apparently too old and infirm by the time of the trial to be much involved in political activities. Thomas de la Poyle had succeeded to his estates as early as 1360, and was to die in 1402, only two years after the trial.[62] George Nowers lived until 1425, but by 1409 the sheriff was ordered to elect a coroner in place of Nowers, who was too sick and aged to serve, and in fact he rarely held office before or after that date.[63] Such appearances as George Nowers did make linked him to the group of Oxford Ricardians already defined above. In 1385, when he gave a quitclaim to his father's widow Alice, the witnesses included Richard Abberbury (not a juror in 1400 but a veteran courtier and associate of several of the jurors) and the juror Thomas Paynell, while in 1387 Paynell and Nowers served as witnesses to a grant by John, Lord Lovell to Abberbury. Almost the only time Nowers appeared on a commission, in 1418, it was one concerning wardships concealed from the king which reported that the heirs of John Drayton had been so concealed.[64]

Thomas de la Poyle was very different politically from the well-defined group of which Nowers was a minor member. While most of that group were identifiably on the king's side during the Appellant crisis, Poyle had his moment of political recognition when men like Drayton and Bereford were in trouble. Poyle served as a member of the Cambridge parliament of 1388, and in December 1388 he was made sheriff of Oxfordshire and Berkshire.[65] This was late in the Appellant period, when the political tide was already turning against the Appellants, but still some months before King Richard regained power in the spring of 1389. After that, Poyle served again in parliament in 1390 and on commission with his fellow jurors, Paynell and Barantyne, and may have gone on Richard's first Irish expedition in 1394, another point on which he resembled several other jurors.[66] In so far as he had a political attitude, the slim evidence would suggest it was much less Ricardian than that of most of the jurors, but by 1400 he may well have been too frail to take an active part in the jury's deliberations.

Although Nowers and Poyle were knights, they were only minor figures in Oxfordshire, some of the esquires whose names follow theirs in the jury list were actually more active participants in county official life. The first of these significant squires was Robert James. Unlike Thomas de la Poyle, who seems to have had no connection with the great de la Pole family, Robert James married Katherine, daughter of Edmund de la Pole, who was kin to Michael de la Pole, earl of Suffolk, one of the first major Ricardians attacked by the opposition.[67] In 1387, Earl Michael fled to his brother Edmund, then captain of Calais, for refuge, but Edmund unexpectedly turned him over to the Appellants. The James–Pole connection had been formed by 1383, before the earl's disgrace, but it continued after the Appellant crisis. During the crisis, Robert James apparently followed the Appellants with Edmund, and in 1390 he was once more working to secure his wife's inheritance from Edmund. By 1391 Michael de la Pole, the son of the earl (who had also sided with the Appellants), was giving a charter to Edmund de la Pole and others including Robert James, a transaction witnessed by Sir John Bussy, later one of Richard II's allies in the last phase of his reign (and one of the first men executed by Henry IV when he landed). Several contacts with the de la Pole family followed.[68]

Besides these links in high politics, he also had a local connection. On 29 October 1391, he served as mainpernor for Edmund Spersholt, who would serve with James on the 1400 jury.[69] His local duties, like those of Peter Besiles, were only beginning at the end of Richard II's reign. In 1398, Robert James was appointed to the relatively minor commission on mills, weirs, and other river obstructions in two counties, Berkshire and Buckinghamshire. In Berkshire he served with Richard Abberbury the elder, the old courtier whose links with other jurors have already been noted. In Buckinghamshire he served with Thomas Shelley, who may have become one of the 'Duketti' rebels.[70]

These links might explain Robert James's position on the Oxford jury that defied King Henry, but if so the defiance does not seem to have troubled the king. On 24 November 1400, the new king gave Robert James his first major office as escheator of Oxfordshire.[71] In 1402, James served on the commission to suppress claims that Henry IV had broken the promises he had made to obtain the throne. In this commission, James served with another of the jurors, John Golafre the younger. The same year he was a member of the parliament and was appointed sheriff on 29 November.[72] By 1404 there was an alliance of two of the powerful squires who had been on the 1400 jury: Reginald, son of the juror Thomas Barantyne, married Joan the sister of Robert James.[73] Thereafter, James continued to have a very active career, not only in Oxfordshire and Berkshire but in Buckinghamshire as well, representing the latter county in the Coventry parliament of 1404 and serving on the peace commission, and as escheator again in Oxfordshire 1406–7.[74] His link to Edmund Spersholt also continued, for in July 1408 Thomas Chaucer and Robert James received a quitclaim witnessed by Spersholt. Later on, James was escheator again in 1413 and 1415 and sheriff in 1416.[75] Like several other jurors, James served in 1419 on a commission to raise money for Henry V's wars. The Oxfordshire commission included his fellow juror, William Lisle the younger. Both James and Lisle served on another commission for a royal loan the next year. In the 1420s Robert James appeared in a series of local land transactions, and in 1428 he was sheriff of Oxfordshire and Berkshire once more. The next sheriff, Thomas Wauton, was accused of election fraud, and James was on a commission to investigate the charge.[76] The year 1430 saw a last link between James and John Golafre: both witnessed a charter by William, Lord Lovell to the archbishop of Canterbury. In February 1432, Robert James made some last property arrangements, and by the next month he was dead, leaving his property to his daughter Christina, widow of Edmund Rede.[77]

As was mentioned above, Robert James was allied by marriage with Thomas Barantyne, and the alliance was a logical one, since they were both among the squires whose official duties and landed property were greater than those of some of the knights with whom they served on the jury in 1400. The long-standing associations among these people are shown by one of Thomas Barantyne's earliest recorded appearances. In 1373, Baldwin Bereford made an exchange of property with John James (father of Robert James) which was witnessed by Sir John Golafre (the elder), Sir Richard Abberbury (the elder), Sir Thomas Besiles (father of Peter), Thomas Barantyne and many other Oxford gentry.[78] By 1380, Thomas Barantyne was a justice of the peace in Oxfordshire, and by 1383 he was sheriff there.[79] On 3 November 1385, Barantyne was again a witness, this time to a grant by Richard Felde of Wallingford to John James, with remainder to Robert James; other witnesses included Edmund de la Pole and Thomas Blount, probably the father of one of the 1400 rebels.[80]

In November 1386, as the Appellant crisis approached, Barantyne was made sheriff of Oxfordshire and Berkshire again, perhaps a sign that King Richard hoped for his support.[81] His continued contacts with the Ricardians are shown by a charter of 20 October 1387 in which Robert Symeon (also a juror in 1400) made a grant witnessed by Richard Abberbury (probably the elder – who abjured the court at the behest of the Appellants), Thomas Blount and Thomas Barantyne with other Oxford gentry who often appeared in the same group (such as Gilbert Wace).[82]

Barantyne appears to have been more flexible (or perhaps more powerful locally) than some of the other Ricardians in this group, for he continued to hold office despite the drastic political reversals of the next few years. There are some indications that he did have problems at this time. His appointment as escheator in Oxfordshire and Berkshire on 22 February 1388 (at the height of Appellant control) was vacated, and the man who did receive the position, John Thame, was ordered, on 4 April 1388, to give Adam Ramsey, the king's esquire, and his wife Isabel (widow of Edmund Malyns) land which Isabel had lately recovered in the king's bench from Thomas Barantyne and others as part of her dower.[83] None the less, on 30 November 1388, Thomas Barantyne became escheator in Oxfordshire and Berkshire after all, as well as a member of parliament (like Thomas de la Poyle for a different county); in 1389, as well as receiving many orders concerning his escheatry, he also was a justice of the peace together with his future fellow-juror Thomas Paynell. By 1390 he was no longer escheator, but he was still justice of the peace with Paynell and again MP with Poyle (both for Oxfordshire). Poyle, Paynell, and Barantyne were on a commission concerning felonies in Oxfordshire in September 1391, and from January 1392 Barantyne was escheator again.[84]

Barantyne's connection with the James family appeared once more when Ralph Stonor made a recognizance to Thomas Barantyne, John James and others on 22 September 1392.[85] In 1393, Barantyne and Paynell served together as knights of the shire for Oxfordshire in the same parliament in which

Edmund Spersholt represented Berkshire. In 1394 there were three commissions of the peace in Oxfordshire; in the first and third, Barantyne was included with Richard Abberbury, and in the second he appeared with John Golafre. Unlike many of the others on the 1400 jury (but like Robert James), Barantyne did not go to Ireland in 1394 on Richard II's first expedition, but he did serve as attorney for several men who did so, including Baldwin Bereford.[86] That same year he received appointment as ulnager for Oxfordshire, perhaps because of his brother Dru's mercantile career. In November of the same year Barantyne was made sheriff of Oxfordshire and Berkshire, which resulted in 1395 in his receiving a pardon for money owed as a result of the escape of prisoners from Oxford castle.[87]

On 20 January 1397, there arose another instance of the bonds among the Oxford gentry: Robert James made a grant to Edmund de la Pole, Thomas Barantyne and others, witnessed by John Drayton, his brother William, Edmund Spersholt and several familiar Oxfordshire names.[88] In the first parliament of 1397, whose importance to Richard II's plans is discussed elsewhere, Thomas Barantyne sat for Oxfordshire with John Abberbury, while Richard Abberbury the younger and Robert James represented Berkshire.[89] By November of that year, when Richard's triumph over the former Appellants appeared complete, the Oxfordshire justices of the peace were headed by Thomas Despenser, now earl of Gloucester, as Richard's ally and later to be one of the 'Duketti' rebels as Richard's would-be liberator; those serving with him included the old royalist Richard Abberbury the elder, Thomas Barantyne, and John Golafre the younger.[90] A commission on weirs in June 1398 again included these three, but in November 1399, after Henry IV had taken the throne, the new peace commission included John Drayton, Thomas Paynell and Thomas Barantyne – again showing the flexibility (or inescapable influence) that Barantyne had in 1388.[91] The ties among the jurors of January 1400 were demonstrated again in May of that year: Barantyne and Robert James witnessed a grant by William Lisle the elder to William Lisle the younger.[92] This must have been one of Thomas Barantyne's last acts, however, for on 25 August 1400 an order was given to the sheriff of Oxfordshire for the election of a new verderer in place of Thomas Barantyne, who was dead.[93]

One interesting fact about Thomas Barantyne did emerge posthumously: in 1416 his son Reginald inherited the property of the well-known London citizen Drew (or Dru) Barantyne, the brother of Thomas. It seems likely that Drew's support may have contributed to the success of Thomas's career. It may also have contributed to Thomas's transfer of loyalties to Henry IV, as Caroline Barron suggests that Dru Barantyne, who was mayor of London in the critical year 1398–9, was given a grant of tenements by the new king for facilitating the Londoners' support for Henry. If so, this was another abrupt reversal, as 'Drugo' Barantyne had appeared with Richard II when he required oaths to support the decisions of his 'revenge' parliament.[94]

Thomas Barantyne's career intersected that of Edmund Spersholt at several points, but there are other interesting intersections between Spersholt and the political world of his day. On 19 May 1389, just as Richard II was regaining his royal authority, Edmund Spersholt and John Drayton's brother William mainperned to free John Holcotes, one of the royal clerks imprisoned by the Appellants.[95] It will be remembered that the Draytons were also mainpernors for Richard Medford, another of these imprisoned royal clerks. Spersholt, too, was appointed sheriff of Oxfordshire and Berkshire in 1395, an honour he shared with many members of this unusually distinguished jury.[96] After that jury had done its duty, another document appeared which cast an interesting light on Edmund Spersholt's associations: on 6 July 1400 an exemplification was requested by the abbot of Westminster (described by Chris Given-Wilson as 'one of the ringleaders' of the 'Duketti' revolt, though Henry IV forbore to execute him)[97] of a charter of Roger Walden, 'late archbishop of Canterbury' – the man whom Richard II had intruded into the see when he attempted to remove Thomas Arundel, an attempt which failed when Arundel returned in triumph with Henry IV – himself another man sympathetic to the 'Duketti' rising. This charter granted Richard II himself land in Berkshire and Wiltshire, and was witnessed by Edmund Spersholt among others, thereby dramatically confirming his association with Richard's court in its most unrepentantly royalist phase.[98]

It is further interesting that in August 1400, Edmund Spersholt was among those appointed by Henry IV to look into the claims of his sister Elizabeth to property she said had been jointly enfeoffed to her and her late husband, John

Holland, earl of Huntingdon, who had died among the 'Duketti'.[99] It is debatable whether this should be considered an early service to Henry IV, or a last one to the old royalists. Thereafter, however, Spersholt seems to have settled down, like many of his fellow jurors, to loyal local Lancastrian duties, including a place on the commission of array in 1403 against the great Percy–Glyndŵr revolt, which might have been his best opportunity to show any lingering Ricardian sympathies – an opportunity he showed no sign of taking.[100] In this, however, he was no different from the rest of the jury, such as John Golafre the younger with whom Spersholt acted as a mainpernor in 1407, in one of his last recorded acts.[101] This John Golafre is probably to be identified with John Golafre, the son and heir of Thomas Golafre of Berkshire, who gave a quitclaim to Sir John Golafre on 12 July 1392.[102] John the knight was one of Richard II's 'more trusted chamber knights', according to Dr Palmer, and one of those who took a leading part in Richard's French negotiations, to which the Appellants were particularly hostile.[103] Hence, the elder Golafre, like Sir John Drayton, was in serious danger under the Appellants; according to Dr Palmer (following the chronicler, Knighton) this Golafre was sent to France in September 1387 with letters arranging a meeting with Charles VI; being charged with transmarine treason by the Appellants, he wisely stayed abroad until the crisis was over and he could return unmolested. Official records show that his imprisonment was ordered on 4 January 1388, at the same time that Richard Medford (for whom Drayton mainperned) and other Ricardians were ordered taken.[104] On 28 February 1389, however, he was being granted permission to bring some bales of cloth from Venice to England customs-free, suggesting that whatever the Appellants may have intended by their earlier order, he had in fact been able to stay safely abroad, as Palmer believed.[105] Thereafter, he resumed his usual round of duties and favours as a chamber knight.[106]

What the younger John Golafre was doing in those tumultuous times is not recorded, but after his appearance in 1392 his career seems to have followed the same pattern as his namesake's, though on a less ambitious scale. As John Golafre the elder was Richard's chamber knight, so John Golafre the younger was retained for life as the king's esquire, in December 1395.[107] The elder John Golafre was dead by 26 November 1396 (according to a regrant of an alien priory he had held), leaving as one of his executors the future juror Thomas

Barantyne (according to a release of 9 February 1397).[108] This is significant, because it permits a clarification of an important record. The younger John Golafre served as a MP for Oxfordshire in the second parliament of 1397 – often called Richard II's 'revenge parliament' – along with the future 'Duketti' rebels, Thomas Shelley, Thomas Wintershull, and Thomas Blount.[109] At the end of this parliament, a notorious commission was appointed to deal with the matter of the accusation of the duke of Hereford (later Henry IV) against Thomas Mowbray, duke of Norfolk.

The commission was a list of the most influential surviving peers, most of whom, naturally, were those most loyal to Richard, and hence future members of the 'Duketti' rebels, though it also included a few who later betrayed Richard in 1399, like the duke of Aumale (who allegedly also joined and betrayed the 'Duketti' plot), the earls of Northumberland and Worcester (who died in later revolts against Henry), the elderly dukes of Lancaster and York and the earl of March, who died in Ireland before Richard's deposition. It also included representatives of the Commons, headed by Richard's close allies, John Bussy and Henry Grene, whom Henry executed in 1399, and ending with John Golafre.[110] Although all those listed are described as 'knights', it seems clear that this must be understood as 'knights of the shire', as John Golafre the knight was dead and it was the younger Golafre, the royal squire, who was present in this parliament. Thus, he, like Edmund Spersholt and Baldwin Bereford, can be shown to have still been closely linked to King Richard in the last period of his 'tyranny'. It is not surprising that on 3 November 1397 he had been appointed sheriff in Oxfordshire and Berkshire, and on 18 April 1398 he received the verderership of Woodstock for life and £10 a year for life from the king's mills in Oxfordshire.[111]

What may be more surprising is how completely Henry IV seems to have accepted Golafre's status and *vice versa*. On 30 September 1399, when Henry was already effectively in power, Golafre was reappointed sheriff of Oxfordshire and Berkshire. In October of the same year, Golafre's money grants from Richard II were confirmed by Henry, and it appears that this was understood as confirmation of his status as a king's esquire.[112] If Golafre's participation in the acquittal of Buxhill was due to any regard for his former patron Richard II, it was not enough to disturb the new relationship with Henry IV, for in November 1400 Golafre was called a king's esquire when receiving a share in the keeping of the lands of one Thomas Poeur.[113] As he had sat in Richard's 'revenge parliament', so he also appeared in Henry's parliament in 1401, representing Berkshire.[114] It appears likely that in his area Lancastrian loyalties were mediated through the Beaufort connection, as Golafre, with his fellow jurors, Robert James and Edmund Spersholt, witnessed a charter by Henry, bishop of Lincoln on 10 March 1401, and Beaufort's kinsman and parliamentary ally, Thomas Chaucer was a major figure in this region.[115] In 1404, Golafre was on the commission to collect a subsidy, a rôle filled even by some of the jurors who had previously not received Henrician office.[116] The same year he was on the commission on weirs and, more importantly, served again as sheriff of Oxfordshire and Berkshire.[117] In December 1407, Golafre was in parliament for Berkshire again, this time with Edmund Spersholt, with whom he had acted as a mainpernor for William Broun in November, probably while both were in London for the parliament.[118] In 1408, and often thereafter, Golafre was a justice of the peace in Berkshire.[119]

This continued under Henry V, who also confirmed the letters of Henry IV regarding Golafre's money, and made him surveyor and controller of Woodstock for life.[120] It is worth noting that a pardon of 1414 refers to a remainder given to Golafre and Robert James in property formerly held by Philip de la Vache, another of the old courtier knights like the elder Golafre or Bereford (and, like Bereford, a pledge for the counter-Appellants in 1397).[121] In that year, Golafre the younger was again sheriff of Oxfordshire and Berkshire.[122] From 1417 he frequently appears with Thomas Chaucer, both on official duties and also in more personal associations, as in May 1420 when just the two of them received the keeping of a manor in Berkshire.[123] Thomas Chaucer has already been mentioned as a political ally of the Lancastrian–Beaufort connection: his father Geoffrey was the brother-in-law of Katherine Swynford, mother of the Beauforts. But it is worth adding that Geoffrey was also a friend of Philip de la Vache and the old Ricardian courtier group in general, so Chaucer and Golafre shared a mixed political history.[124] When Henry VI became king, Golafre's grants were confirmed once more, and his official duties were much the same. It is unnecessary to review in detail a career that lasted until 1441, but this should suffice to demonstrate both his strong early Ricardian links and his long subsequent Lancastrian service.[125]

Much less is known of the last man who follows Golafre on the jury list, but that little is sufficient to make his political allegiance more explicable than that of some better-documented figures. Robert Symeon appears as an esquire of the duke of Lancaster, John of Gaunt, in an indenture of 24 May 1390. His grant from Gaunt of the modest sum of 20 marks a year was confirmed on 27 April 1399 by Richard II as part of his energetic effort to take over the Lancastrian retinue.[126] Generally speaking, this effort failed to hold the loyalty of these men in the face of the challenge from the son of their former lord, and it is not in this case a matter for cynicism or surprise that Henry IV was able to retain Symeon as his esquire for the same sum his father had first granted and Richard had confirmed.[127] Under these circumstances, it is natural that Symeon was among the men Henry summoned to judge his enemies at Oxford, though it is more puzzling that he was on the jury that rendered one verdict of 'not guilty'. It may be that his low status meant that he was overborne by the better-established old Ricardians. Henry seems to have been pleased with his services, however, for on 7 February 1400, very shortly after the trial, Robert Symeon was given eight cows and seventy sheep forfeited by Thomas Despenser for his part in the rising – the only case where one of the jurors benefited directly from the suppression of the revolt.[128] After this promising beginning, however, Robert Symeon does not seem to have received any further office or favour.[129]

Reviewing the jury as a whole, it seems that it was made up of several diverse groups. The most notable at the time was probably the close-knit set of men with long court and county service and strong Ricardian associations, particularly Sir Baldwin Bereford and Sir John Drayton and, on a lesser level, Sir William Lisle, Sir Thomas Paynell, Sir George Nowers, and Edmund Spersholt. Most of these were older men whose careers lay behind them in Richard's reign, though many did go on to serve Henry IV. A second group, including Sir Peter Besiles and Robert James, had had little experience of office or profit under Richard, and went on to lengthy service and larger rewards under the Lancastrians. John Golafre the younger, despite his strong early Ricardian connections, seems to have effectively fallen into this category. Two minor figures, Sir Thomas de la Poyle and Robert Symeon, may have been more sympathetic towards Richard's opposition early on; for Symeon, the confirmation of Gaunt's grant by Richard II may have been the moral equivalent of the confirmations some of the Ricardians received from Henry IV, a prudential recognition of a new reality of power.

At Oxford in January 1400, just such a new reality confronted the gentry of Oxfordshire in the person of Henry IV. By and large, they pragmatically conformed to it; most of the rebels were found to be guilty, as indeed they were if Henry was the lawful king. But it is pleasant to record that these gentlemen of the jury were capable, whether out of a recollection of old loyalty to Richard or simple justice to a less deeply implicated defendant, to render one verdict of *non culpabilis*. It may not be too much to suggest that this small gesture was one of the steps towards the creation of that tradition of independent juries which has been regarded as one of the glories of the British legal system.[130]

Notes

[1] The primary record of these trials used here is PRO, E37/28: Marshalsea Court plea rolls. The first historian who cites this document is James E. Tyler, *Henry of Monmouth* (2 vols, London, 1838), I, 7 n. h. He, however, is only interested in the pardon to Ferrour (see below). He says that ' . . . during the insurrection headed by Wat Tiler . . . Bolinbroke was in the Tower of London, and owed his life to the imposition' [i.e. interposition??] of one John Ferrour of Southwark. This is a fact not generally known to historians . . . This same John Ferrour, with Sir Thomas Blount and others, was tried in the castle of Oxford for high treason, in the first year of Henry IV. Blount and the others were condemned and executed, but to John Ferrour a free pardon, dated Monday after the Epiphany, was given, 'our Lord the King remembering that in the reign of Richard II during the insurrection of the counties of Essex and Kent, the said John saved the king's life in the midst of that commonalty, in a wonderful and kind manner . . .' Tyler's account is cited in M.L. Bruce, *The Usurper King* (London, [1986]), p. 267, without reference to the original source. The pardon of Ferrour is also mentioned by H.F. Hutchison, *The Hollow Crown* (London, 1961), pp. 233–4; K.B. McFarlane, *Lancastrian Kings and Lollard Knights* (Oxford, 1972), pp. 18 and n. 1 (citing Tyler and the *Calendar of Patent Rolls*) and by Williams in his edition (see note 2), 246 note 1, directly from the original text. True to its reputation as a home of lost causes, Oxford had hitherto been a centre of sympathy for Richard: Oxfordshire had sent troops to fight against Henry when he had landed the previous summer in his bid for the throne (Anthony Tuck, *Richard II and the English Nobility* [New York, 1974], p. 215); Richard's counsellors, Scrope, Bussy and Green, had been there before they fled to Bristol where Henry had executed them (ibid., p. 216); the tournament at which Henry was to have been killed by the Duketti plotters was, according to Froissart, to have been held at Oxford (though others say Windsor) (Jean Froissart, *Chronicles of England, France and Spain*, trans. Thomas Johnes [2 vols, London, 1874], 2, 704–5), and one of the plotters, Sir Thomas Blount, was 'a knight of Oxfordshire' (Wylie, 1, 92). More accurately, he had ties there and in other counties.

[2] Accounts of the defeat of the rebels and the deaths of their leaders are given by Jean Créton, trans. John Webb, 'Metrical History of the Deposition of Richard II', *Archaeologia*, 20 (1824), 210–15; Thomas Walsingham, *Historia Anglicana* (Rolls Series, 28), part 1: 2: 243–5; *Chronique de la Traïson et Mort de Richard Deux Roy d'Engleterre*, ed. Benjamin Williams (London, 1846; reprint Kraus 1964), pp. 230–61; in a letter of Archbishop Arundel in *Literae Cantuarienses*, ed. J.B. Sheppard (Rolls Series, 85), 3, 73–75; in letters of Edmund Holland and John Norbury in *Anglo-Norman Letters*, ed. M.D. Legge (Oxford, Anglo-Norman Text Society, 3, 1941), pp. 86–7, 116–17; Adam of Usk, *Chronicon Adae de Usk*, ed. E.M. Thompson (2nd edn, London, 1904), pp. 41–2, 197–8; Froissart, pp. 704–7; *Rotuli Parliamentarum* (6 vols, London, 1767–77 [hereafter *Rot. Parl.*], 3, 459; *Eulogium Historiarum sive Temporis*, ed. F.S. Hayden (Rolls Series, 9, 1863), 3, 386; John Capgrave, *The Chronicle of England*, ed. Francis C. Hengeston (Rolls Series, 1858), 1, 275–6. Modern accounts include Henri Wallon, *Richard II* (Paris, 1864, 2 vols), 2, 352–9; J.H. Wylie, *History of England under Henry the Fourth* (London, 1884; reprint New York, 1969), I, 91–110; Anthony Steel, *Richard II* (Cambridge, 1941), p. 287; E.F. Jacob, *The Fifteenth Century* (Oxford, 1961), pp. 25–7; Charles Oman, *The Political History of England, 4 (1377–1485)* (London, 1906; reprint New York, 1969), pp. 161–4; J.L. Kirby, *Henry IV of England* (London, 1970), p. 88; A.L. Brown, 'The Reign of Henry IV' in *Fifteenth Century England, 1399–1509*, eds S.B. Chrimes, C.D. Ross and R.A. Griffiths (Manchester, 1972), pp. 3–6; Bruce, pp. 241–3, 267; *Calendar of Inquisitions Miscellaneous* (hereafter *CIM*, 7 (*1399–1422*), 26–79, 259–74, especially 29, 34, 38, 41–51, 65, 69–70, 259, 267; *Calendar of Fine Rolls* (hereafter *CFR*) *12 (1399–1405)*, 35–6.

[3] The sheriff, William Wilycotes, is ordered '*venire fac' coram senescallo et marescallo hospicii domini Regis apud Castr' Oxon. . . .*' juries of knights and other lawful men, PRO, E37/28.

[4] PRO, E37/28.

[5] '*vexillo explicato felonice et proditore insurrexerant*', PRO, E37/28.

[6] For Buxhill the elder, Joseph Dahmus, *William Courtenay, Archbishop of Canterbury* (University Park, PA, 1966), pp. 65–7; *CIM 3 (1348–77)*, 340–1; *Rot. Parl.*, 3, 10a, 40b; *Calendar of Patent Rolls* (hereafter *CPR*) *1377–81*, pp. 110, 199, 474, 469, 541, 557–8, 568; *Calendar of Close Rolls* (hereafter *CClR*) *1381–5*, pp. 6, 16, 21, 26, 82, 178. For the two Buxhills and Montagu, *CClR, 1381–5*, p. 276; *1399–1402*, pp. 38, 100, 154; *1402–5*, p. 100; *1405–9*, p. 90; *1429–35*, p. 166; *1435–41*, p. 178; *CPR, 1388–92*, p. 476; *1422–9*, p. 258; *1429–35*, pp. 96, 97.

[7] See the Ferrour case in n. 1; also, a large number of minor figures were pardoned, a fact noted by Kirby, p. 88, and by Wylie, 1, 106, and stressed by Brown, p. 5: he says the leaders of the revolt received the 'accepted penalty' in such cases, death, but 'At Oxford the overwhelming majority of the accused were merely imprisoned and told to have their friends seek a pardon for them from the king', citing E37/28 and *CPR*.

[8] '*predictus Alanus Buxhull . . . prodiciones et felonias quietus est . . . tamen . . . de causis dominum Regem specialiter movientibus, idem Alanus de mandato ipsius Regis committitur [ad] Turr' London.*' PRO, E37/28.

[9] Beeford's indentures with both the Black Prince and John of Gaunt appear in J.M.W. Bean, *From Lord to Patron* (Philadelphia, 1989), pp. 61 and n. 76, 255; *CClR, 1377–81*, p. 162; *CPR, 1377–81*, p. 209; *CClR, 1377–81*, p. 398; *CPR, 1381–5*, pp. 25, 45, 52, 111, 128, 272, 320, 376, 378, 468; *CClR, 1381–5*, pp. 265 etc., refer to Bereford as king's knight. The abjuration is discussed in my article, 'The Abjuration of 1388', *Medieval Prosopography*, vol. XV (1994), 115–38.

[10] Pardons to Nicholas Brembre's servants at the supplication of Bereford: *CPR, 1388–92*, pp. 377, 378, 384. On 17 February 1390, Bereford appears with his wife Idonia, the first name of Brembre's wife, in being granted substantial properties in London forfeited by Brembre. *CPR, 1388–92*, p. 194. He received another grant of Brembre property in 1396: *CPR, 1391–6*, p. 685; *CClR, 1392–6*, p. 456.

[11] *CPR, 1381–5*, pp. 128, 515, 519, 567, 564.

[12] *CClR, 1377–81*, pp. 242, 320–32; *CPR, 1377–81*, pp. 3, 327, 473, 628; *1381–5*, pp. 140, 195, 247; *1391–6*, p. 92. Two exemptions from service were granted to Baldwin Bereford under Richard II: *CPR, 1391–6*, pp. 57, 657, and a third under Henry IV: *1399–1401*, p. 223. *CClR, 1377–81*, p. 330, refers to Baldwin the younger and Baldwin the father, ibid., pp. 360–1, to Baldwin the elder, as do *CClR, 1385–9*, pp. 79, 82. As the only records explicitly referring to Baldwin the elder are small local land transactions, I believe the active royal knight was Baldwin the younger. The indenture in Bean (above, n. 9) specifically refers to the younger Baldwin.

[13] *CPR, 1391–6*, pp. 493, 494, 499. On 29 April 1394 Bereford received letters of protection the same day as John Golafre, probably another juror.

[14] *Rot. Parl.*, 3, 374b, 'At the end of this petition as added: pledges de pursuer: Monsr. Symond Felbrygge, Monsr. Baudewyn Bereford, Monsr. Philyp la Vache, Monsr. Joh'n Lyttelbury'. All these were veteran courtiers, and Bereford and la Vache in particular are found together in other records. The eight men who brought this appeal were the earls of Kent, Huntingdon, Salisbury, Somerset, Rutland, and Nottingham, Lord Despenser, and William le Scrope. See my unpublished dissertation, 'Richard II and the Counter-Appellants' (Yale University Ph.D. thesis, 1979), for detailed discussion of these men. At the time of the Duketti uprising, Kent, Huntingdon, Salisbury and Despenser were the leaders of the revolt. Nottingham and Scrope had already died, Somerset (Henry IV's half-brother) was loyal to Henry, and Rutland allegedly joined the plot and then betrayed it. See n. 2.

[15] *CPR, 1399–1401*, pp. 16, 22, 75.

[16] *CPR, 1399–1401*, p. 211.

[17] Exemptions: *CPR, 1399–1401*, p. 223; *1401–5*, p. 25; only the second specifies his 'great age'. Commissions of array: *CPR, 1401–5*, pp. 285, 287. Note that Philip de la Vache also served on this commission in another county; for his death, *CFR, 13 (1405–13)*, 2.

[18] *CPR, 1377–81*, p. 563.

[19] *Rot. Parl.*, 3, 152b, 156b–7b.

[20] *CPR, 1385–9*, pp. 93, 444.

[21] Ibid., pp. 416, 427; J.J.N. Palmer, *England, France and Christendom* (Chapel Hill, NC, 1972), p. 119.

[22] *CClR, 1385–9*, p. 414.

[23] Ibid., p. 504.

[24] Ibid., pp. 537, 570.

[25] *CPR, 1388–92*, p. 175.

[26] Ibid., p. 214.

[27] *CClR, 1392–6*, pp. 158, 163.

[28] *Rot. Parl.*, 3, 326b.

29 *CPR, 1391–6*, pp. 487, 554.

30 *CClR, 1396–9*, p. 128.

31 *CPR, 1396–9*, pp. 536, 545, 551.

32 *CPR, 1399–1401*, p. 214.

33 *CClR, 1399–1402*, p. 397 (2 June 1401). This is definitely 'John Drayton of Oxfordshire, knight'. He is suing Henry Ilcombe of Cornwall, another well-known knight. It is possible that John Drayton collecting a tax in Northants. on 14 March 1401 is also this Drayton, but as the Northants. man is not described as 'knight' I doubt it. *CFR, 1399–1405*, p. 116. There were at least two other John Draytons active at this time: *CPR, 1401–5*, p. 100. One served as the king's pavilioner, *CPR, 1399–1401*, pp. 9, 147; *1401–5*, p. 285.

34 *CFR, 1399–1405*, pp. 261, 263; *CClR, 1402–5*, p. 520.

35 *CClR, 1405–9*, p. 400; *CFR, 1405–13*, p. 92.

36 *CPR, 1409–13*, p. 222.

37 *CPR, 1413–16*, pp. 221, 262.

38 *CFR, 1413–22*, p. 93.

39 *Victoria County History of Oxfordshire, 7 (Dorchester and Thame Hundreds)*, ed. Mary Lobel (London, 1962) (hereafter *VCH, Oxford*), p. 27; A.E. Preston, *The Church and Parish of St. Nicholas, Abingdon* (Oxford, 1935), pp. 59–60. 'He caused a great number of armed men and archers to be placed in a wood of his at Nuneham who shot with bows, crossbows and cannons at a wood of the Abbot's . . . saying this oak is the Abbot of Abingdon and this oak is the Vicar of Culham, so that the Vicar and parishioners dared not make their customary procession around the precinct of the manor, and the herons, egrets and other birds nesting there left the wood for the horrible sound of the cannons.'

40 *CFR, 1413–22*, pp. 195, 246, 255, 258; *1422–30*, p. 32; *VCH, Oxford*, 7, 60; *CIM, 7 (1399–1422)*, pp. 306–7.

41 *CPR, 1422–9*, p. 97.

42 In 1388, a William Lisle was to serve at Roxburgh and did not, and William the elder was to serve at Calais and did not, *CPR, 1385–9*, pp. 377, 477. Retained as king's knights: *CPR, 1391–6*, pp. 198, 385, both William son of Robert (William the younger); *CClR, 1396–9)*, pp. 43, 80 (William the younger), 292 (William the elder). Going to Ireland: *CPR, 1396–9*, pp. 494 (younger), 522 (elder). Confirmation by Henry IV: *CPR, 1399–1401*, pp. 11 (younger), 255 (elder). The relationship between the two William Lisles – William the elder and his nephew, William son of Robert, brother of the elder William – is set forth in a parliamentary petition from John de Windsor. *Rot. Parl.*, 3, 310a–b.

43 *CPR, 1396–9*, p. 494.

44 *CClR, 1396–9*, p. 469.

45 *CClR, 1399–1402*, p. 243; *CPR, 1399–1401*, p. 533 (wine); *CClR, 1399–1402*, pp. 452, 493 (commissions); *CPR, 1401–5*, pp. 138 (against Glyndŵr), 46; *CPR, 1409–13*, p. 112; *CClR, 1409–13*, pp. 5–6; *CFR, 1405–13*, p. 221; *CIM, 7 (1399–1422)*, 285–6; *CFR, 1413–22*, pp. 209, 262–3, 358; *1422–30*, pp. 12, 52.

47 *CPR, 1413–16*, pp. 285–6; *1422–9*, p. 487.

48 *CClR, 1381–5*, pp. 427, 449. Witnesses to the second include Bereford and Barantyne. The next year Abberbury and Paynell both witnessed a grant by John Wroth. *CClR, 1385–9*, p. 97.

49 *CPR, 1385–9*, p. 272; *1388–92*, p. 133.

50 *CClR, 1389–92*, p. 304.

51 *CPR, 1391–6*, p. 575.

52 *CPR, 1401–5*, pp. 1, 190; *1416–22*, pp. 172, 216.

53 *CPR, 1381–5*, p. 404; *CClR, 1381–5*, p. 477.

54 *CPR, 1391–6*, p. 498. A reference to Mabel, widow of a Peter Besiles, appears in 1397, but this was apparently a different man. *CClR, 1396–9*, p. 90.

55 *CPR, 1399–1401*, pp. 209–11.

56 *CPR, 1399–1401*, p. 556; *1401–5*, p. 515; *1405–9*, p. 489; *1416–22*, p. 457.

57 *CPR, 1401–5*, pp. 128, 287.

58 *CClR, 1402–5*, p. 367; *CFR, 1405–13*, pp. 19, 167; *CPR, 1405–9*, p. 197; *CClR, 1405–9*, pp. 55, 203; *CFR, 1413–22*, p. 81.

59 *The Boarstall Cartulary*, eds H.E. Salter and A.E. Cooke (Oxford Historical Society, 88, 1930), pp. 266, 300. This cartulary contains many documents relating to the jurors, especially Robert James, whose family compiled it. Cited hereafter as *Boarstall*.

60 *CPR, 1416–22*, pp. 198, 212, 251, 457; *CFR, 1413–22*, p. 316; H.E. Salter, *Medieval Archives of the University of Oxford*, vol. 1 (Oxford Historical Society, 70), p. 27; W.H. Stevenson and H.E. Salter, *The Early History of St. John's College* (Oxford Historical Society, New Series, 1, 1939), p. 13; *CFR, 1422–30*, pp. 83, 204; *CPR, 1422–9*, p. 409; *CClR, 1429–35*, p. 63.

61 Preston, p. 462.

62 *VCH, Oxford, 6: Ploughley Hundred*, ed. M.D. Lobel (London, 1959), p. 161.

63 *CClR, 1405–9*, p. 459.

64 *CClR, 1381–5*, pp. 624–5; *1385–9*, p. 297; *CIM, 7 (1399–1422)*, pp. 306–7.

65 *CClR, 1385–9*, p. 657; *CFR, 1383–91*, p. 249.

66 *CClR, 1389–92*, pp. 305–6; *CPR, 1388–92*, p. 520; *1391–6*, p. 483. This last protection for Ireland was issued to Thomas 'Pole' who may or may not be Poyle.

67 *VCH, Oxford, 8: Lewknor and Pyrton Hundreds*, ed. M.D. Lobel (London, 1964), p. 9 for the marriage; J.S. Roskell, *The Impeachment of Michael de la Pole Earl of Suffolk, in 1386* (Manchester, 1984), for the first attack on Earl Michael. Edmund appears on pp. 119, 205, 207.

68 For the behaviour of Edmund de la Pole and Robert James in 1387, see A. Goodman, *The Loyal Conspiracy* (London, 1971), p. 25; *CFR, 1383–91*, p. 3; *1388–92*, p. 334; *CClR, 1389–92*, pp. 501, 503; *1392–6*, pp. 111, 130, 150, 221–2, 243–4, 357. James twice served as attorney for Walter de la Pole while the latter went to Ireland. *CPR, 1391–6*, p. 471; *1396–9*, p. 552.

69 *CClR, 1389–92*, p. 499.

70 *CPR, 1396–9*, pp. 369, 371.

71 *CFR, 1399–1405*, p. 93.

72 *CPR, 1401–5*, p. 128; *CClR, 1402–5*, p. 125; *CFR, 1399–1405*, p. 181.

73 *VCH, Oxford, 8*, 152.

74 *CClR, 1402–5*, p. 520; *CPR, 1405–9*, p. 496; *CFR, 1405–13*, p. 96.

75 *CClR, 1405–9*, p. 400; *CFR, 1413–22*, pp. 41–2, 135–6, 177.

76 *CPR, 1416–22*, pp. 251, 283; *CFR, 1413–22*, p. 317; *CClR, 1419–22*, pp. 126–7; *Boarstall*, pp. 63, 146; *CPR, 1422–9*, p. 458; *CFR, 1422–30*, p. 245; *CPR, 1429–36*, p. 39.

[77] *CClR, 1429–35*, p. 144.

[78] *Boarstall*, p. 259 (Charter 759).

[79] *CPR, 1377–81*, p. 513; *CIM, 4 (1377–88)*, 130, 133.

[80] *CClR, 1385–9*, pp. 93–4.

[81] *CFR, 1383–91*, p. 152.

[82] *CClR, 1385–9*, p. 443.

[83] *CFR, 1383–91*, pp. 209–10; *CClR, 1385–9*, p. 391.

[84] *CClR, 1385–9*, pp. 495, 558, 567, 580; *1389–92*, pp. 5, 18, 20, 177–8, 305–6; *CFR, 1383–91*, pp. 274, 298; *1391–9*, p. 8; *CPR, 1388–92*, pp. 136, 342, 520; *CIM, 5 (1387–93)*, 164.

[85] *CClR, 1392–6*, p. 87.

[86] *CClR, 1392–6*, p. 115; *CPR, 1391–6*, pp. 434, 437, 476, 477, 499.

[87] *CFR, 1391–9*, pp. 123, 131–2; *CPR, 1391–6*, p. 565.

[88] *Boarstall*, p. 261 (Charter 769).

[89] *CClR, 1396–9*, pp. 134–5.

[90] *CPR, 1396–9*, p. 236. Many of the same men are on the weirs commission: ibid., p. 372.

[91] *CPR, 1399–1401*, p. 563.

[92] *CClR, 1399–1402*, p. 180.

[93] *CClR, 1399–1402*, p. 167. The *VCH, Oxford*, 8, 62, seems slightly in error in dating Thomas's death to 1399.

[94] *CClR, 1405–9*, p. 76; *CFR, 1413–22*, p. 177; Caroline Barron, 'The Deposition of Richard II', in John Taylor and Wendy Childs (eds), *Politics and Crisis in Fourteenth Century England* (Gloucester, 1990), p. 143; M.V. Clarke, *Fourteenth Century Studies* (Oxford, 1937; repr. Freeport, NY, 1967), p. 111.

[95] *CClR, 1385–9*, pp. 583–4.

[96] *CFR, 1391–9*, p. 166.

[97] Chris Given-Wilson, *The Royal Household and the King's Affinity* (New Haven, 1986), p. 182. A brief account of the abbot's later life is given by W.G. Boswell-Stone, *Shakespeare's Holinshed* (London, 1896; repr. New York, 1966), p. 127 n. 2. See also the sources in n. 2 above.

[98] *CPR, 1399–1401*, pp. 319–20. For Walden, see Wylie, 1, 20–1, 109, and also Hutchison, p. 233.

[99] *CIM, 7 (1399–1422)*, 14; *CPR, 1399–1401*, p. 348; *CClR, 1399–1402*, p. 168.

[100] *CPR, 1401–5*, p. 290.

[101] *CFR, 1405–13*, pp. 86–7.

[102] *CClR, 1392–6*, p. 78.

[103] Palmer, pp. 108, 119, 200, based on Henry Knighton's *Chronicon*, ed. J.R. Lumby (Rolls Series, 92, 1895), 2, 296.

[104] *CClR, 1385–9*, pp. 394–5. If it were not for the Venetian evidence, I would be inclined to reject Knighton's belief that Golafre escaped abroad, as this order sounds very much as if he were in Appellant hands.

[105] *CClR, 1385–9*, p. 577.

[106] *CPR, 1388–92*, pp. 23, 130, 154, 180, 249, 297, 316, 359, 362, 374, 392, 395; *CClR, 1389–92*, pp. 29, 174, 247.

[107] *CPR, 1391–6*, p. 658.

[108] *CFR, 1391–9*, p. 197; *CPR, 1396–9*, p. 40; *CClR, 1396–9*, p. 57.

[109] *CClR, 1396–9*, p. 303.

[110] *Rot. Parl.*, 3, 360b.

[111] *CFR, 1391–9*, p. 240; *CPR, 1396–99*, p. 327.

[112] *CFR, 1399–1405*, p. 2; *CPR, 1399–1401*, pp. 42, 82, 159.

[113] *CPR, 1399–1401*, p. 369.

[114] *CClR, 1399–1402*, pp. 329–30.

[115] *CPR, 1401–5*, p. 232.

[116] *CFR, 1399–1405*, p. 256.

[117] *CFR, 1399–1405*, pp. 263, 271.

[118] *CClR, 1405–9*, pp. 397–8 (MP); for mainpernors, see note 101.

[119] *CPR, 1409–13*, p. 479.

[120] *CPR, 1413–16*, pp. 31, 92, 416.

[121] Ibid., p. 169.

[122] *CFR, 1413–22*, pp. 70, 83.

[123] Ibid., p. 338.

[124] M.J. Bennett, 'The Court of Richard II' in *Chaucer's England*, ed. Barbara Hanawalt (Minneapolis, 1992), p. 12, 'Though he [Chaucer] remained close to many courtiers, including John of Gaunt . . . and Philip de la Vache, steward of the new queen's household, he seems not to have frequented the court' (in the 1390s); Derek Brewer, *Chaucer and His World* (London, 1978), p. 188, sees Chaucer's poem to Vache as advice to be careful during the Appellant crisis.

[125] *CPR, 1422–9*, p. 73.

[126] Bean, p. 262; *CPR, 1396–9*, p. 539.

[127] *CClR, 1399–1402*, p. 14; *CPR, 1399–1401*, p. 114.

[128] Ibid., p. 188.

[129] It seems possible that Symeon was already very old at this time, as there are references to a Robert Symeon in parliament in 1377–9. *CClR, 1377–81*, pp. 105, 220, 253. This may, however, be the Sir Robert Symeon mentioned by *VCH, Oxford*, 8, 102, as dead by 1386. A Robert Symeon also appears in 1434: *CPR, 1429–36*, pp. 392–5, and in 1438 and 1449: *Boarstall*, pp. 144 (Charter 491) and 197 (Charter 606).

[130] T.A. Green, *Verdict According to Conscience* (Chicago, 1985), p. 379, 'I have given considerable attention to the idea of the jury as a bulwark against tyranny, an idea that, from the seventeenth century until recently, has loomed large in historical scholarship. But I have attempted to demonstrate that this traditional view does not capture what was behaviourally the most significant aspect of the jury's place in medieval and early modern English culture . . . as a mitigator of capital sanctions in felony trials.' Whether the 1400 jury was more a bulwark against tyranny rather than a mitigator of sanctions might be debated, but it certainly could be understood as contributing to both rôles.

9

THE LANCASTRIAN COLLAR OF ESSES: ITS ORIGINS AND TRANSFORMATIONS DOWN THE CENTURIES

Doris Fletcher

The collar of esses can be traced to John of Gaunt, duke of Lancaster. It was worn by him and his retainers at a time when collars were unknown as liveries. As far back as 1371, the collar of esses was already in use. Proof of this may be deduced from the effigy at Spratton church, Northants., of Sir John Swynford, who died in 1371. The wearer of the SS collar was the retainer of one of the most powerful lords in England, which meant that he was well protected from all odds. Moreover, he had access to all his lord's castles, including the Savoy in London which was renowned for its opulence and refinement. Very often an SS collar meant advancement both up the financial and social ladders, ending with a place at the king's court. However, at certain times it had its disadvantages. In 1377 Gaunt angered the London crowds for befriending Wycliff and as a result Gaunt's followers had to go about their business without the SS collar, for safety's sake. During the reigns of Edward IV and Richard III the collar of esses was frowned upon, to say the least. It disappeared from court and was replaced by the Yorkist collar which consisted of the white rose of York and the sun.

On his return from Spain in 1389, Gaunt was met by his nephew, Richard II. At the time Gaunt was wearing a collar of esses; Richard took it from his uncle's neck and placed it on his own. In 1394 Richard, fourth earl of Arundel, complained in parliament that the king was in the habit of wearing the livery collar of the duke of Lancaster and that persons of the king's retinue did the same. The king answered that he wore the livery of his uncle Gaunt as a sign of love, as he did the liveries of his other uncles.[1] In 1392 Richard ordered and paid for a gold collar of seventeen esses and had another made with esses and the flowers of '*souvenez vous de moi*'.[2] The wardrobe accounts for the year 14 May 1391 to 14 May 1392 of the earl of Derby, the future Henry IV, show that he paid the sum of £23 10*s* 10*d* for a collar of seventeen esses after the manner of feathers with scrolls and a swan in the tiret.[3] It is evident from his accounts that Henry, while still earl of Derby, was in the habit of giving his friends collars of esses. In the year 1387–8 he presented collars to Sir William Bagot, the steward of his household, to Philip Darcy, a Yorkshire baron, and to Sir John Stanley, a promising young nobleman in the royal household.[4] Moreover, he distributed SS collars among those who joined him on his return to England from exile, to dethrone his cousin Richard. The earl's accounts for 1393–4 mention the purchase of a silver collar of rolled esses to be given to Robert Waterton esquire, since Henry had given Robert's collar to another gentleman. The accounts for 1396–7 show that the earl bought another collar of esses, this time adorned with enamelled flowers of forget-me-nots. It weighed eight ounces. The accounts do not state to whom Henry gave it, so very probably he kept it for himself.[5]

The initial letter of the charter granted to the city of Gloucester in 1399, the year Henry was crowned king as Henry IV, contains a crown encircled by a collar of esses ending in two lockets from which hangs a swan pendant.[6] Henry treated the collar of esses as though it were an order of chivalry. In 1400 he granted 10 marks annually to one of his squires the better to maintain the dignity of the Order of the Collar.[7] In the following year, 1401, the collar became a royal livery, when a statute was passed which gave permission to all the king's sons, dukes, earls, barons and lesser barons of the realm to wear the collar both in the presence and in the absence of the king, while knights and squires were to wear it only in the royal presence.[8]

Although the statute mentions no women, their effigies in churches throughout the breadth and length of England testify that ladies from different backgrounds were allowed to wear the collar of esses. In the Waterton chapel, in Methley church outside Leeds, the effigy of Cecily Fleming wears an SS collar. She was the daughter of landed gentry and the wife of Robert Waterton.[9] At St Mary's church, Staindrop, Co. Durham, there is an alabaster monument to Ralph Neville, first earl of Westmorland, and his two wives. All three wear the collar of esses. Ralph Neville's first wife was Margaret, eldest daughter of Hugh, earl of Stafford and his wife Philippa, daughter of Thomas Beauchamp, earl of Warwick. Ralph's second wife was Joan Beaufort, only daughter of John of Gaunt by his mistress Katherine Swynford whom he married in 1396.[10] On the day of his wedding, 7 February 1402, Henry IV gave his bride, Joan of Navarre, widow of the duke of Brittany, a collar with the motto *soveignez* and with esses all set in gold with pearls, sapphires, rubies and diamonds, one of which weighed eight ounces. The cost of the collar came to £385 6s 8d, an enormous sum in those days.[11] However, the collar of esses on Queen Joan's effigy over the tomb which she shares with her husband in Canterbury cathedral is not a replica in alabaster of her wedding gift. The effigy wears a collar very similar to that worn by the fifteenth-century brass effigy of Joan Perient in Digswell church, Hertfordshire. Joan Perient was the queen's chief lady-in-waiting until her untimely death in 1415. She, like her husband John, was born in Brittany. The Perients were aristocrats originally from Gascony and the first John Perient had arrived in England in 1385 with the Black Prince, whose sergeant-at-arms he was. Soon after the death of Richard II the family joined the Lancastrian cause.[12] On the left lapel of her mantel Joan wears a swan badge which is very similar to the brooch in the British Museum, London, known as the 'Dunstable Swan Jewel'.[13]

In the Lancastrian period the collar of esses and the swan badge usually went together, the swan being the emblem of the family of Mary de Bohun, Henry's first wife who died in 1394 when he was still earl of Derby. Again in the British Museum, London, there is a fifteenth-century bronze pendant showing a swan holding in its beak a leather collar of esses with a buckle at one end.[14] In a manuscript entitled *Catalogus Benefactorum Monasteri S. Albani* in the Cotton bequest in the British Library, London, there is an illumination showing Thomas of Woodstock, duke of Gloucester, holding in his right hand a swan with open wings encircled by a chain, while his left hand points towards the swan. Next to the illumination a Latin inscription states that Thomas, duke of Gloucester, in 1388 donated to the monastery cloth of gold and a circular collar with a white swan with open wings as though about to fly.[15] Thomas of Woodstock was John of Gaunt's brother and was married to Eleanor de Bohun, who was Mary de Bohun's sister. The de Bohuns' ancestor was supposed to have been

Loherangrin, the swan knight, son of Lady Blanchefleur and Sir Percivale, one of the knights of King Arthur's round table, hence the swan emblem. Thomas of Woodstock's descendants, the dukes of Buckingham and the earls of Stafford, kept the swan with open wings as one of their heraldic devices.[16]

During the Lancastrian period the esses were usually made either of silver-gilt, silver or gold and were either linked together with small rings or fastened to bands of gold, silk, velvet or leather. Some collars had their esses fastened backwards. Esses of bronze, lead and pewter have been found. These for the most part were originally brooches worn by the retinues of great lords who favoured the house of Lancaster. Some leather collars had a buckle at one end and could be buckled like a garter. The garter-type collars were usually worn over armour in the battlefield. A good example of such a collar is the one on the effigy of Sir William Ryther at Harewood church, Harewood. Examples of fifteenth-century and earlier collars, where the esses alternate either with the Garter knot or with the Lancastrian rose, are very rare. Only one example of each has been located. In Harewood church, the recumbent figure of Sir Richard Redmayne, who died in 1442, wears a collar of esses and Garter knots, while the effigy of his grandson, of the same name, in the same church, bears a collar of esses and roses. No intricate collars of this period have survived. The three that are known to exist are very simple. The Victoria and Albert Museum, London, has two. One is silver, the other is silver-gilt.[17] The third is at the Museum of London. It is twenty-four inches long and made up of forty-one silver filigree esses linked together with small rings. The twenty-first S has a hook so that the wearer could fasten the collar at the back. It is a simple but a very fine piece of workmanship.[18] The collar which Henry IV ordered in 1407 from the London goldsmith Christopher Tyldesley was anything but simple. It was a gold collar with enamelled letters of S and X. It also had a large number of jewels, the motto *soveignez* and a triangular clasp hanging from it adorned with a big ruby and four large pearls. At an unknown date the same goldsmith made Henry another collar with twenty-four esses pounced with the word *Soverain* and fastened by a clasp set with a balas ruby and six pearls.[19] Perhaps these collars were made for special occasions, while for day-to-day use Henry wore less expensive ones, like the one of black silk dotted with silver esses which was reported missing from his wardrobe in 1406.[20]

The collars of silk, velvet and leather could be of different colours. In the manuscript entitled *The Lovell Lectionary*, there is an illumination of a blue and red silk SS collar encircling the Lovell-Holland coat-of-arms, red being the colour of the Lovells and blue that of the Hollands.[21] In old St Paul's, completely destroyed by fire in 1666, there was a stained glass window depicting a black collar with gold esses. It encircled John of Gaunt's arms and those of his first wife, Blanche of Lancaster.[22] A window of Wells cathedral chapter house shows an azure and argent SS collar with the arms of the Mortimers, azure and argent being royal colours. In Elford church, Staffordshire, lie the effigies of Sir Thomas Arderne and his wife Matilda, daughter and heiress of Sir Richard Stafford of Pipe and Clifton Campville. Both effigies wear the Lancastrian collar. In each case the ground of the collar was originally green and the letters gilt.[23] The collar on the effigy of Robert, Lord Hungerford in Salisbury cathedral was originally green with gilt esses. He died in 1455. In Ashwelthorpe church, Norfolk, lie the effigies of Sir Edmund de Thorpe and his wife Joan. Both wear the Lancastrian collar, his originally had a blue ground and gilt esses while hers was all gilt. A very fine example of the Lancastrian collar where the band was originally black and the esses gilt is found on the effigy of John FitzAlan, seventh earl of Arundel and duke of Touraine in the FitzAlan chapel, Arundel castle, Arundel. John FitzAlan died of wounds sustained at the siege of Gerberoi in 1435.[24] In the illuminated manuscript of *The Bedford Hours*, John, duke of Bedford, Henry IV's second son, is depicted kneeling in prayer and wearing a brown leather collar with gold esses alternating with roots, roots being the duke's personal device. The collar has a tiret pendant with a ring from which hangs an eagle.[25]

Most Lancastrian collars had a pendant which consisted of a trefoil-shaped tiret with a ring hanging from it. The tiret was attached to the collar by means of a buckle at either end. The effigy of Queen Joan in Canterbury cathedral has this type of pendant hanging from its collar. A like pendant is found on the collars of Henry IV's and Henry V's statues in the niches of the choir at York minster. The collar of John Gower's effigy in Southwark cathedral, London, has a swan attached to the ring.[26] The three collars painted on the ceiling of the canopy over Henry IV's and his wife's tomb at Canterbury have golden eagles hanging from the rings, the eagle being a device of Plantagenet kings. The owner of an SS collar could attach to the ring a royal or family emblem, a fashionable pendant or a religious image. The collars on the effigies of Sir Thomas Arderne and his wife Matilda in Elford church, Staffordshire, have a jewel attached to the ring. Both jewels are of the same size and design. In the portrait which hangs in the National Portrait Gallery, London, Henry VI wears a gold Lancastrian collar of esses with a cross pendant which does not hang from a ring. In fact, his collar lacks buckles and a trefoil-shaped tiret pendant and some of the esses on the collar are backwards.[27]

There is no evidence that the already mentioned silver collar of esses in the Victoria and Albert Museum, London, ever had a pendant. On the other hand, there is ample proof that the silver-gilt collar in the same museum once had a pendant of some sort. The already referred to SS silver collar in the Museum of London has a trefoil-shaped tiret pendant with a ring hanging from it. The pendant is attached on either side to a simulated silver buckle which in turn is attached to the collar. In his portrait of 1446 by Petrus Christus, Edward Grimston, who was then Henry VI's ambassador to Bruges, holds in his right hand a silver collar as though to show his diplomatic rank.[28] The collar is very similar to both collars in the Victoria and Albert Museum and to the one in the Museum of London. Since all these three existing collars date back to the first reign of Henry VI it would be interesting to find out who were the ambassadors who owned them, assuming that such a type of SS collar in Henry VI's reign was always given to ambassadors.

When Henry Tudor married Elizabeth of York, the Lancastrian collar was altered to fit the new dynasty. The swan disappeared and the trefoil-shaped tiret appeared infrequently. The red rose of Lancaster and the white rose of York appeared side by side along with Garter knots which represented the marriage of Elizabeth and Henry. The portcullis began to figure prominently both on the collar and the pendant. It was the emblem of John of Gaunt, the founder of the Beaufort family from whom Margaret Beaufort was descended, she being the great granddaughter of John of Gaunt by Katherine Swynford and the only legitimate survivor of the Beaufort family. In giving prominence to the portcullis, Henry wanted to show that his claim to the throne, through his mother, went back beyond the Lancastrian House of Henry IV right to John of Gaunt in the direct male line. By so doing, Henry tried to legitimize his right to the English throne.

Ralph Neville, first earl of Westmorland, and his two wives. All three figures wear the SS collar. Reproduced from A.E.S. Bray, *The Monumental Effigies of Great Britain*, by permission of the British Library.

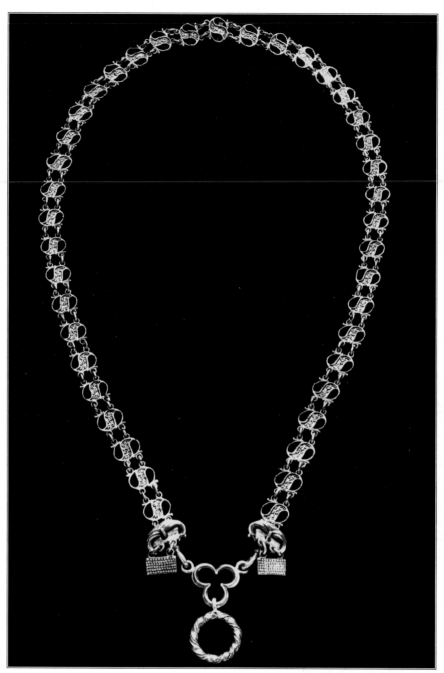

Silver collar of esses, *c.* 1440. It was found virtually intact in the River Thames near Kennet Wharf, London, and is now the property of the Museum of London.

The effigy of John FitzAlan, seventh earl of Arundel and duke of Touraine, in the FitzAlan Chapel, Arundel Castle, Sussex. The earl died in 1435.

The effigy of Queen Joan, Henry IV's second wife, wearing a collar of esses, on the north side of the Trinity Chapel in Canterbury Cathedral. Reproduced by permission of the Dean and Chapter of Canterbury Cathedral.

A replica in marble of Count Baldassar Castiglione's collar of esses in the Castiglione Chapel, Church of Santa Maria delle Grazie (Our Lady of Graces), near Mantua. Reproduced by permission of the Ministry of Culture, Department for the preservation of historic and artistic works, Mantua.

In actual fact, Henry was a usurper. He had no right to the throne through his mother, for although the Beauforts were legitimized by an act of parliament in 1397, they were subsequently excluded from succession to the throne. On the other hand, whatever the ambitious Gaunt had assumed, the fact remained that Richard II had nominated as his successor the son of his cousin Phillippa, Roger Mortimer, fourth earl of March, since Phillippa was the daughter of Lionel, duke of Clarence, Edward III's second son who died in 1368. Roger Mortimer had a daughter Anne who was the great-grandmother of Elizabeth of York. Elizabeth was the only surviving child of Edward IV, whose father was Richard, duke of York, Anne Mortimer's son. Thus, according to Richard II's will, Elizabeth of York was the rightful heir to the English Crown. Henry needed all the props he could think of to steady his position on the throne. In his wisdom, he married Elizabeth of York. Claiming to be the rightful Lancastrian claimant to the throne and having married Elizabeth of York, Henry made the collar a symbol of the unification of the Yorkist and the Lancastrian lines of Plantagenet kings, and on this unification he was determined to build a strong dynasty.

With Henry VII the SS collar of leather bands, silk and velvet disappeared. The Tudor collar was, for the most part, a solid gold chain. The collars of gold bands became wider, longer and a rarity. At Elford church, Staffordshire, the effigy of Sir William Smythe, who died on 10 January 1525/26, wears a collar with esses fastened to it and a cross pendant. The collar, esses and the cross pendant were originally gilt. This means that very probably the real collar was made of cloth of gold with gold esses and a gold cross pendant.[29] In the same church the supposed effigy of William Staunton esquire, who died c. 1500, wears a collar of esses. In his case, the esses are linked together to form a heavy chain typical of the Tudor period.[30] The effigy of Sir Richard Knightley (d. 1534) in Fawsley church, Northamptonshire, wears an SS collar with a Tudor rose pendant. The esses which are fastened to a band are larger and the band is wider and longer than in the previous century. His wife also wears an SS collar.[31] Their son, another Sir Richard Knightley who died in 1537, three years after his father, is buried with his wife at Upton church, Northamptonshire. His effigy wears a Tudor collar of esses with a tiret pendant. His wife's SS collar is light, feminine and very long; it goes twice around her neck and has a cross pendant. The monument had been badly damaged, but carefully put together again; however, it has been removed from its original place and some pieces are missing.[32] William Parr, lord of Horton, who died after 1545, was the uncle of Katherine Parr, Henry VIII's sixth and last wife. He is buried at Horton church, Northamptonshire. His effigy above his tomb wears a collar of esses which goes over the shoulders and has a Tudor rose pendant. In this case the esses are fastened to the collar.[33] At Thruxton church, Hampshire, there is an effigy of a Lesle who died *c.* 1550. It wears a collar of esses alternating with knots and roses; it has a cross pendant.[34] The effigy of Sir Thomas Andrew (d. 1564) in Charwelton church, Northamptonshire, wears a heavy chain of esses with a Tudor rose pendant.[35] It is similar to the collar given to Sir Thomas More by Henry VIII.[36] The effigy of Sir George Forster (d. 1526) over his tomb at Aldermaston church in Berkshire has esses laid sideways alternating with Garter knots. It has a portcullis and rose pendant.[37]

In Henry VIII's Book of Payments for 1519 an entry is found: 'to Sir Richard Wingfield for a collar of esses 55¾ ozs. at 40*s* and £6 for the fashion'.[38] At the marriage of Prince Arthur to Catherine of Aragon in 1501, Sir Nicholas Vaux wore a collar of esses weighing eight hundred pounds of nobles.[39] In 1499 a gold collar weighing 7 oz was donated to the cathedral of Norwich to adorn the image of the Blessed Trinity. The collar consisted of twenty-five esses, two tirets, two portcullises and a double R with an enamelled red rose. The effigy of Sir John Cheyney KG, who died in 1489, wears a collar of esses with a large portcullis pendant.[40]

Judging from the date and description of the last mentioned collar, it seems that once Henry had won the day at Bosworth, on 22 August 1485, and having been crowned king on 30 October of the same year, he wasted no time in redesigning the collar of esses to satisfy his needs, although there is a brass at Muggington, Derbyshire, depicting a collar of esses with a portcullis pendant which probably dates back to 1479.[41] The collar worn by Robert Waterton's effigy also has portcullises. He died in Henry IV's reign. The collar donated in 1499 to the image of the Trinity was probably a gift from Henry VII for graces received, namely for his victory at Bosworth, his coronation soon afterwards and his wedding on 18 January 1486. The double R stand for *rex* and *regina* while the red rose signifies his victory over the white rose of York, thus asserting his Lancastrian lineage.

Such symbols are easily interpreted, but the significance of the mysterious S is another matter. As early as 1348, Gaunt's mother, Queen Philippa, had a set of wall hangings of red Sindon stamped with the letter S. Moreover, in Edward III's accounts for the years 1350–2 there is an entry for a cloak for the queen, 'powdered with gold roses of eight petals and bordered with white pearls, in the middle of each rose an S of large pearls'.[42] This proves that Gaunt did not invent the S sign, but that it was already some sort of royal emblem when he was still a boy. Probably he borrowed it from his mother, hoping that he would be universally loved and respected as she was. However, we are none the wiser as to its meaning. In the past many guesses have been made. Originally the S may have had a religious meaning; it may have stood for *Sanctus* or for *Simplicus*, who was a Roman lawyer and a senator martyred in AD 287. Later the S may have stood for the motto *souvenez vous de moy* which was popular in the fourteenth and fifteenth centuries. Once Gaunt borrowed it and made it his own, it may have stood for *seneschal*, which means steward. John of Gaunt was High Steward of England, and the actual collar of esses has been traced to him. Then again the S may have stood for *Souveragne*, sovereign, the chief, superior to all. The word also conveys the idea of defender. Henry IV used this device when he was still earl of Derby and retained it when he became king. It is found written around the cornice of the canopy of his and his wife's tomb in Canterbury cathedral, as well as on the great Dublin civic sword which he probably gave to that city in 1403 when he granted the mayor of Dublin and his successors the right to have a sword borne before them.[43]

Whatever the S stood for, once the collar of esses became a royal livery it was much favoured by English kings, with the exception of Edward IV and Richard III. Besides being worn by royalty and the English nobility, monarchs bestowed it with discretion on noblemen, ambassadors and rulers abroad for favours received or as tangible proof of their admiration. It was also given to commoners at home for valour on the battlefield or high achievement in civil life. Very probably Henry IV bestowed the collar of esses on John Gower because he was a highly esteemed poet who greatly influenced the poets of his day, as well as being a staunch supporter of the Lancastrian cause.[44] In his speech before the battle of Agincourt, Henry V declared that all those not of noble birth who were willing to fight bravely would be given the SS collar.[45]

Henry VI bestowed the collar of esses on Conrad von Scharnachtal, a nobleman from the northern shores of Lake Thun, Switzerland, because he was a great soldier and a traveller honoured and respected throughout Christendom.[46] In 1436 Henry bestowed the SS collar on Gianfranco Gonzaga, first marquis of Mantua, in return for the hospitality received by his counsellor, John Le Scrope. Moreover, as a gesture of good will, Henry gave the marquis permission to distribute fifty SS collars to individuals of noble birth.[47] In 1506 Henry VII honoured the Urbino ambassador, Count Baldassar Castiglione, with an SS collar because of his personal qualities as well as to please Guidobaldo da Montefeltro, lord of Urbino, who was brother-in-law to Pope Julius II from whom Henry obtained the dispensation to marry his son Henry to Catherine of Aragon, widow of his eldest son, Arthur.[48] Sometime before or during 1527 Sir Thomas More received the collar of esses from Henry VIII. It is not known why it was given to him. No doubt Henry saw in More a great statesman as well as one of the leading humanists of his day and perhaps wanted to show him his appreciation by giving him an SS collar. Certainly the collar of esses was not bestowed on More because of his high office in the law courts, as is sometimes stated, since it was only in the latter part of the Tudor period that the collar of esses began to be worn by members of the legal profession.

Sir William Yelverton, justice of the King's Bench who died *c.* 1472, is depicted wearing an SS collar in his brass effigy at Rougham, Norfolk. However, in his case the collar was bestowed on him in virtue of his military valour and not because of his legal capacity.[49] The only other effigy of a man of law which has been found wearing the SS collar even before the beginning of the Tudor period is that of Chief Justice Sir Richard Newton in Wyke church. He died in 1449.[50] After a gap of more than a century, we come across the stone effigy of Lord Chief Justice Sir Richard Lyster at Southampton. His effigy wears the collar of esses. He died in 1554 but his monument was not erected until 1567.[51] At St Stephen's church, Hackington, near Canterbury, there is a wall monument erected to Sir Roger Meanwood. His bust wears an SS collar. He was chief justice in the reign of Elizabeth I. He supported the 1571 Treason Bill and was one of the joint commission of the two Houses which advised the execution of Mary, Queen of Scots.[52] It seems that by the end of Elizabeth I's reign the SS collar was well established among men of law because at Easter 1594, at the time of the call of serjeants, the chief justices and the chief barons were asked to wear the SS collar.[53] In Salisbury cathedral there is a mural monument to Lord Chief Justice Robert Hyde. His bust wears the collar of esses. He belonged to the famous Hyde family; his cousin Edward was created earl of Clarendon and Clarendon's daughter Ann married the duke of York, the future James II. Robert Hyde represented Salisbury in the Long Parliament and voted against the bill for the attainder of Strafford. In 1651 he harboured in his home the future Charles II who was then on the run. After the Restoration, he was knighted and in 1663 was appointed lord justice of the King's Bench. He died two years later.[54] A document dated 23 February 1684/5, of articles to be provided for important officers of state at the coronation of James II, mentions nine collars of esses plus their price. These were probably intended for high-ranking members of the legal profession.[55] By this time, it seems, the collar of esses had become restricted to judges and other officials. Today it is worn by the lord chief justice, the serjeants, the kings-of-arms and heralds.[56]

The SS collar is still worn by some mayors. In 1850 the Corporation of Derby bought the SS collar of Lord Chief Justice Denmon for £100 and it has since been worn by the mayor of that town. In 1571 Elizabeth I gave an SS collar to Maurice Roche, lord mayor of Cork, and it is preserved at Ganet-Stow House. In 1755 a collar of esses and gold chains were bought for the mayor and sheriffs of Cork to be worn by them for the honour and dignity of the city. The SS collar, which is a replica of the collar worn by the lord mayor of Dublin, has since been worn by each successive lord mayor of Cork.[57] The Dublin collar of esses was given to that city by William of Orange. It is a large and heavy gold chain. The esses alternate with Garter knots and Tudor roses, and it has one portcullis from which hangs a gold pendant. Each year, in a special ceremony, this historic chain is presented by the outgoing lord mayor to the new lord mayor. In his will Sir John Aleyn left his SS collar to the city of London and ever since it has been worn by each successive lord mayor of that city. It is not known when or why Henry VIII gave Sir John Aleyn the collar. Except for the pendant which is modern, the collar is authentic. It is great in size. It has twenty-eight esses, fourteen roses, thirteen Garter knots and one portcullis. It is perhaps the finest Tudor collar in existence.[58]

All through its long history of transformations, English kings, with the help of first-class goldsmiths, have done their best to honour the SS collar and its meaning by transforming it into an exquisite work of art. But perhaps the best definition of the SS collar was given in its early days by John Gower; in his metrical chronicle appended to his poem *Vox Clamantis*, he compared it to a gift from heaven: a mark of faithfulness and true nobility.[59]

Notes

[1] E.J. Smith, 'The Livery Collar', in *The Coat of Arms* (an heraldic quarterly magazine published by the Heraldry Society), NS, vol. III, no. 151 (Autumn 1990), pp. 239–53 (p. 242). Richard seems to have been so keen in promoting his uncle Gaunt's livery that his cook used to make jumbles in the form of an S. As a rule, jumbles were then served at the banquet which followed the main feast. See Elizabeth Ayrton, *The Cookery of England* (London, 1974), p. 525.

[2] A.P. Purey-Cust, *The Collar of SS. A History and a Conjecture* (Leeds, 1910), p. 18.

[3] J.H. Wylie, *History of England under Henry IV* (4 vols, London, 1884), vol. IV, p. 161. See also Purey-Cust, op. cit., p. 17.

[4] Simon Walker, *The Lancastrian Affinity, 1361–1399* (Oxford, 1990), p. 95.

[5] W.H. St John Hope, *Heraldry for Craftsmen and Designers* (London, 1913), pp. 298–9.

[6] Ibid., p. 298.

[7] Walker, *Lancastrian Affinity*, p. 95.

[8] Purey-Cust, op. cit., pp. 17–18.

[9] Robert Waterton's effigy lies next to that of his wife. It wears an SS collar but not the one of rolled esses already mentioned. The collar which the effigy wears is made of gold esses alternating with crowns and portcullises. This means that throughout his life Robert was presented with more than one collar.

[10] Joan Beaufort is not buried at Staindrop, but lies next to her mother in Lincoln cathedral.

[11] Wylie, *History of England under Henry IV*, vol. II, p. 288.

[12] Dora Ward, *Digswell From Domesday to Garden City* (Welwyn, 1953), pp. 54–5.

[13] 'The Dunstable Swan Jewel' (Room 42, Case 9), so-called because it was found on the site of the Dominican priory at Dunstable, Bedfordshire, in 1965. It is a gold brooch covered with white enamel and was probably made in the early fifteenth century either in England or in France. It is the only one of its kind in existence. The technique of decorating gold with opaque white enamel in the round was developed in Paris in the last half of the fourteenth century.

[14] The bronze pendant (Room 42, Case 17) was presented to the British Museum by Sir Augustus Franks in 1882. Like 'The Dunstable Swan', this swan wears a crown around its neck. The esses on the collar are gothic. The pendant was badly damaged during the Second World War, but traces of black, blue, red and turquoise enamel are still faintly visible.

[15] 'Catalogus Benefactorum Monasteri S. Albani', BL, Cotton. MS. Nero D. V. II, f. 110.

[16] 'Pedigree and Extracts', BL, Add. MS. 27983, f. 52ᵛ.

[17] They are on show in Room 92, Case 12, Victoria and Albert Museum, London.

[18] The collar was found virtually intact in 1983 in the Thames near Kennet Wharf, London. It belongs to the first part of Henry VI's reign. For further information, see Brian Spencer, 'Fifteenth-century collar of SS and hoard of false dice with their container from the Museum of London', *The Antiquaries Journal* (1985), vol. LXV, part II, pp. 449–53.

[19] Joan Evans, *A History of Jewellery 1100–1870* (2nd edn, London, 1970), p. 65.

[20] St John Hope, *Heraldry for Craftsmen and Designers*, p. 302.

[21] BL, Harl. MS. 7026, f. 13. For more information concerning this manuscript, see Margaret Reckert, *Painting in Britain. The Middle Ages* (London, 1954), pp. 178–9.

[22] W.S. Simpson, *Gleamings from Old St Paul's* (London, 1889), p. 67.

[23] Edward Richardson, *The Monumental Effigies and Tombs, Elford Church Staffordshire, with A Memoir and Pedigree of The Lords of Elford* (London, 1852), pp. 11–14. The tomb of Sir Thomas Arderne and his wife bears no inscription, but according to tradition the effigies on the tomb are of Sir Thomas and Lady Arderne. The author was not sure whether tradition is right. According to the author, Sir Thomas, who died in 1391, died too early to have been given a collar. Modern research has proved the author to be wrong. The collar of esses was given much earlier than 1391. This fact, coupled with the way the statues are dressed on the monument, prove that tradition is right.

[24] C.A. Stothard, *The Monumental Effigies of Great Britain* (London, 1817), p. 98, plates 129, 130; p. 86, plates 112, 113; pp. 89–90, plates 119, 120.

[25] BL, Add. MS. 18850, f. 256ᵛ.

[26] John Gower (1330?–1402?). A courtier of some wealth and one of the leading poets of the fourteenth century.

[27] This portrait is a copy of an earlier portrait. It was produced at the end of Henry VIII's reign. See David Chambers and Jane Martineau (eds), *Splendours of the Gonzaga* (Exhibition, 4 November 1981–31 January 1982, Victoria and Albert Museum, London), p. 105, n. 5.

[28] Brian Spencer, 'Fifteenth-century collar of SS and hoard of false dice with their container from the Museum of London', *The Antiquaries Journal*, LXV, part 2 (1985), p. 451.

[29] Richardson, *The Monumental Effigies and Tombs, in Elford Church*, p. 25, plates x, xi, xii.

[30] Ibid., p. 24.

[31] Albert Hartshorne, *The Recumbent Monumental Effigies in Northamptonshire* (London, 1876), pp. 23–4.

[32] Ibid., pp. 98–9.

[33] Ibid., pp. 69–71.

[34] St John Hope, *Heraldry for Craftsmen and Designers*, p. 308.

[35] Hartshorne, *The Recumbent Monumental Effigies in Northamptonshire*, pp. 27–8.

[36] St John Hope, *Heraldry for Craftsmen and Designers*, p. 306.

[37] Ibid., p. 306.

[38] Hartshorne, *The Recumbent Monumental Effigies in Northamptonshire*, p. 114.

[39] Ibid., p. 114.

[40] St John Hope, *Heraldry for Craftsmen and Designers*, p. 306.

[41] Ibid., p. 304.

[42] Smith, 'The Livery Collar', in *The Coat of Arms*, NS, vol. III, no. 151 (1990), p. 245.

43 Jonathan Alexander and Paul Binski (eds), *Age of Chivalry. Art in Plantagenet England, 1200–1400* (Royal Academy of Arts, London, 1987), p. 526.

44 It is far from certain when John Gower was given the collar of esses. Henry was in the habit of presenting the SS collar to friends while still earl of Derby. Gower may have been given more than one collar during the course of his life.

45 Albert Hartshorne, 'Notes on Collars of SS', in *The Archaeological Journal*, vol. XXXIX (1882), pp. 376–83 (p. 379).

46 Albert Way, 'Proceedings at the meetings of the Archaeological Institute' (3 June, 1859), in *The Archaeological Journal*, vol. XVI (1859), pp. 353–94 (p. 359).

47 Ilaria Toesca, 'Lancaster and Gonzaga. The collar of SS in Mantua', in *Splendours of the Gonzaga*, pp. 1–2 (p. 1); see also pp. 105–6, the letter of Henry VI to Marquis Gianfrancesco Gonzaga, Westminster, 19 October 1436.

48 Doris Fletcher, 'Why Castiglione went to England', *Bulletin of the Society for Renaissance Studies*, vol. V, no. 2 (June 1988), pp. 7–13 (p. 13).

49 W.N. Hargreaves-Mawdsley, *A History of Legal Dress in Europe Until the End of the Eighteenth Century* (Oxford, 1963), p. 57.

50 Purey-Cust, op. cit., p. 84.

51 Hargreaves-Mawdsley, *A History of Legal Dress*, p. 57.

52 Purey-Cust, op. cit., p. 86.

53 Hargreaves-Mawdsley, *A History of Legal Dress*, p. 57.

54 Purey-Cust, op. cit., pp. 84–6.

55 Hartshorne, 'Notes on Collars of SS', in *The Archaeological Journal*, vol. XXIX (1882), p. 381.

56 Smith, 'The Livery Collar', in *The Coat of Arms*, NS, vol. III, no. 151 (1990), p. 251.

57 Hartshorne, 'Notes on Collars of SS', in *The Archaeological Journal*, vol. XXXIX (1882), pp. 381–2; Purey-Cust, op. cit., p. 83.

58 Hartshorne, 'Notes on Collars of SS', in *The Archaeological Journal*, vol. XXXIX (1882), pp. 380–1; Purey-Cust, op. cit., pp. 81–2.

59 Ibid., p. 20.

10

THE REGULATION OF PUBLIC HEALTH IN LATE MEDIEVAL ENGLAND

J.M. Theilmann

Good health was never far from the minds of people in medieval England, from the most powerful lord to the humblest peasant. People sought to obtain good health from a variety of sources including beseeching the saints for aid and turning to a variety of medical practitioners. Turn though they might to physicians, surgeons, and less well-educated practitioners, people were often critical of these same practitioners. In the twelfth century John of Salisbury enunciated what continued to be a common complaint thereafter:

> However, I have observed that there are two rules which they [medical students] are more especially prone to recall and put into practice. The first is from Hippocrates (whom they misinterpret): 'Where there is indigence, one ought not to labor'. The second maxim does not come, as I recollect, from Hippocrates, but has been added by enterprising doctors: 'Take [your fee] while the patient is in pain'.[1]

What role did medical practitioners and government have in safeguarding people's health in late medieval England? This paper, which focuses primarily on London, assays to answer this question by first breaking it down into two parts, concerning the rôle of the medical establishment and the rôle of government, and then combining the two again. At bottom the issue is this: who was responsible for fostering good health in late medieval England?

Dating back to the advice of Hippocrates and Galen, medical men have been concerned with providing adequate medical care to the population.[2] While ancient writers were not specifically concerned with medical ethics,

they indicated that the training of physicians was important by contending
that unskilled practitioners provided inferior care. Care was one thing, good
care at a reasonable cost was another, and, as John of Salisbury indicated,
people often considered medical men to be an avaricious lot, more
concerned with their own pocket-books than their patients' welfare. In the
late fourteenth century William Langland attacked the wealth of doctors
and went on to say, 'for these doctors are mostly murderers, God help them!
– their medicines kill thousands before their time'.[3] If the advice books
written for medical practitioners are any indication, Langland's fictitious,
greedy doctor described the reality of the situation. John Arderne, the
fourteenth-century English surgeon, who practised in London for a time,
advised that surgeons should not take hopeless cases and should always
consider where their fee was coming from.[4] If he heeded such advice, a
prudent medical man would avoid treating some patients in order to
preserve his reputation as a healer and would avoid treating others who
could not pay.

Happily, not all medical practitioners heeded such advice and treated all
comers. Unfortunately, they often treated with little skill and the patient was left
worse off than before. The medical profession included practitioners with a
variety of skills from the university trained physician to the skilled surgeon to
the unlearned and unskilful empiric. The situation was further complicated
because a village cunning man might provide quite good care in matters within
his ken while a physician could easily kill through ignorance and arrogance. In
the fourteenth century physicians and, to a lesser extent, surgeons argued that
those not of their craft, whom they labelled empirics or quacks, were incapable
of healing at best and dangerous at worst.[5]

Physicians' and surgeons' efforts at controlling medical practice had the
ostensible goal of guaranteeing better medical care, but, if accomplished, helped
to line their pockets since competitors were excluded from practice. London
physicians, who, unlike their Parisian counterparts, often stood above the fray,
finally petitioned the king in about 1421 against practice by the 'uncunning and
unapproved in the aforesaid science [physic]' as well as medical practice by
women.[6] Henry V responded to this petition by prohibiting anyone who was
not a graduate of a university medical school from practising medicine.[7]

Generally, however, the royal government did not intervene in matters of health. Local governments were both closer to the problem of public health and more susceptible to pressure from local medical groups.

Surgeons took a more formal approach to organizing and controlling medical practice than did physicians in the fourteenth century. While the London surgeons were never organized as a guild, they did form the Fellowship of Surgeons in 1368 or 1369.[8] Although the Fellowship did not have the power of a guild, it was influential and enjoyed support from the London municipal authorities. In 1369 the mayor and council appointed three surgeons as master surgeons to supervise medical practice, repeating this order twenty years later as they appointed four supervising surgeons.[9] In 1423 the Fellowship joined with London physicians to form the College of Medicine.[10] The College was charged with supervising medical practice and the education of medical practitioners. However, it never enjoyed strong support from the physicians and its authority was quickly challenged by the barber-surgeons. By 1430 the College was dead, setting physicians and surgeons on separate paths for the rest of the century. To protect their position, surgeons had the London city government reconfirm their regulations in 1435.[11] The Fellowship's regulations provided for administrative details, such as meeting dates, but also deontology. Advice was given on setting fees and members were warned against moral lapses with their female patients. The surgeons also tried to monopolize medical practice by requiring that non-London surgeons pass a competency test and pay an entry fee in order to practise.

A third major group of medical practitioners were the barber-surgeons. The London barbers organized themselves as a guild in 1376 and gained influence within the city even though they did not enjoy the power and prestige of such powerful guilds as the goldsmiths. The barber-surgeons' guild recognized two classes of members: those who practised surgery and those who combined a practice of phlebotomy, dentistry, shaving, and barbering.[12] In 1409 the barber-surgeons struck a blow at the surgeons when the London city government confirmed their surgical and barbering rights 'as is now used or in the future to be used within the craft of the said barbers'.[13] The barbers continued to gain in numbers and influence throughout the fifteenth century, and in 1462 Edward IV recognized the right of the Barber-Surgeons Company to govern all surgeons who acted as barbers in the city of London.[14] While most surgeons of the Fellowship were unaffected by this action since they generally did not barber, it further demonstrates their declining political influence. Finally, in 1493 the surgeons and the barber-surgeons formed a rough alliance to supervise the faculty of surgery in London – a move directed against interlopers from abroad and the provinces.[15]

Physicians conducted much of their practice through the prescription of drugs. The purity of these drugs, as well as the accuracy of the prescriptions, was thus important. The apothecaries, who compounded prescriptions, belonged to the Company of Grocers throughout the Middle Ages even though they appointed their own surveyors as early as 1365.[16] City authorities as well as the apothecaries were concerned with drug quality. In 1394, for example, William Witman was condemned to the pillory for having delivered 'divers false powders for good ginger, and tansy seed for good worm seed'.[17] In 1472 the mayor and aldermen ordered that two physicians and seventeen apothecaries investigate barrels of treacle (the new 'wonder drug') being imported into London. After investigation they found the treacle unwholesome and it was publicly burned at three locations in the city.[18] As was the case with other medical practitioners' efforts at quality control that were directed primarily toward protecting guild integrity, these investigations produced benefits for public health. As always, enforcement was problematic and a variety of drugs of dubious quality continued to be administered, often without the necessity of an afflicted person consulting a physician.

If we turn to the provinces, we find that, with the exception of the university towns of Oxford and Cambridge, barber-surgeons were more numerous than physicians and surgeons, often providing the only 'professional' medical care available, although unlettered folk practitioners who relied on herblore and magic were often to be found in the countryside. Provincial barber-surgeons generally organized themselves as guildsmen and followed the usual guild practices of trying to limit entry into their craft and establish quality control.[19] Physicians they perforce ignored, directing their attention to the various sorts of empirics, some of whom were no less skilled than themselves. Our knowledge of provincial medicine may be biased because of a lack of information, but it appears that provincial barber-surgeons were more concerned with protecting their craft than with the public's health.

Can the same be said for London? Did the market-place and private bodies protect the people's health or deny them medical care except at a price? John Alford reminds us that medicine, by which he means university-educated physicians, was a profession in the Middle Ages; in particular he equates medicine and law. As a profession, Alford contends, medicine was bound to render good service, but because it was a profession, physicians could justify taking a profit from its practice.[20] Theoretically, Alford may be correct, but in practice what did medical men do as a community to protect people's health?

Some authors of advice books for medical practitioners urged their readers to provide free medical care to the poor. John Mirfield, a late fourteenth-century cleric and author of an advice book for medical men, maintained that the physician 'ought to cure a Christian patient without making even the slightest charge if the man is poor; for the life of such a man ought to be of more value to the physician than his money'.[21] He went on to say that 'he who fails to preserve the sick from death, when he is able to do so, is held to have caused their death'.[22] Mirfield did not say that physicians should always practise for free, just that they should make medical care available to all. The thirteenth-century Lanfranc of Milan advocated that surgeons should make the wealthy pay for the care of the poor, a novel way of preserving the surgeons' income while providing medical care for the poor.[23] If all medical men followed this advice, their efforts at controlling access to medical care might have been better received. John Arderne is more typical in reminding his readers to put the patient's welfare first but not to neglect their fee.[24] Contemporary writers often echoed Arderne although drawing a different moral. Both Chaucer and Langland were critical of physicians' love of fine clothes and gold.[25] Even though literary sources must be treated with care, the medical establishment stands condemned by its own advocates as often caring more for gold than for their patients.

If physicians and surgeons ignored poor patients, did they devote their time to those truly ill who could at least pay? Again, sad to say, the answer gleaned from the advice books seems to be no. The standard response enunciated by John de Mirfield was that physicians or surgeons should decline to undertake any case which appeared to be hopeless for fear of damaging their reputations.[26] Mirfield may have recognized practitioners' inability to diagnose for he also advised medical men to tell their patients to look to their spiritual welfare as well as seeking medical care.[27] A more charitable interpretation would be that the advice came from the medieval conception of health as derived from God's grace; hence poor moral conduct led to health problems and moral reform could lead to a return to health.

Medical men were not always successful. While Robert Gottfried contends that all medical practitioners, save surgeons, suffered from a negative popular image in the late Middle Ages, even this may be too charitable.[28] Not all medieval commentators so nicely segregated physicians, surgeons, barber-surgeons, and empirics, as Gottfried does. While some authors may have been careless in specifying categories of practitioners, others issued a blanket indictment. One early fourteenth-century poet simply said:

> . . . these physicians
> that help men die.[29]

Later in the century, Langland echoed this indictment: 'For these doctors are mostly murderers, God help them – their medicines kill thousands before their time'.[30] In the fifteenth century Agnes Paston continued to reflect this view as she warned her son John to avoid physicians while on a visit to London.[31] This distrust of medical practitioners came partially from the popular perception of their avarice, but also from their inability to heal. The response of physicians and surgeons often was that a tighter rein needed to be kept on medical practice so that quacks would not be allowed to practise. Empirics often were purveyors of poor medical care, but the medical aristocrats, unless they avoided all but the most simple cases, could also kill or maim with their ministrations.

One source of information concerning medical failures and legal responses to them is malpractice suits. While such suits were not common in late medieval England, those reported enable us to see that the authorities tried to make distinctions between proper and improper practices and accidental error and wilful error. Although physicians and surgeons tried to control medical practice, it was the civil authorities who dealt with malpractice, often in a fashion in which a professional organization played only a tangential role.[32] In 1377 John Dunhevel, one of the appointed master surgeons of London, and two other surgeons were called to give expert testimony in the case of Walter del Hull's injured leg. They testified that Richard Cheynduit's lack of skill and poor care of his patient caused him to be in danger of losing his leg after Cheynduit's treatment. The jury found against Cheynduit, fining him 50*s* and ordering his imprisonment.[33] Unfortunately for Walter del Hull, the fine went to the city and he received nothing except the satisfaction of helping to put a quack out of business.

As one of the city's master surgeons, John Dunhevel was charged with 'presenting to the mayor and aldermen the defaults of those who undertake cures', in addition to giving 'truthful information to the affairs of the city concerning such maimed, wounded, and others if they be in peril of death'.[34] In the Walter del Hull case, Dunhevel gave expert testimony but the case was brought by the injured party, not the Fellowship of Surgeons. So it goes for other malpractice suits. Injured parties or their relatives sued the medical practitioner involved. The authorities generally called in medical men to give expert testimony, but the medical élite did not bring suit against quacks on its own. Roger Clerk was easy game for the mayor's court in 1382 when he was charged by the mayor and aldermen with deceit and falsehood for practising medicine although he was unlicensed and unlearned after being sued by Roger atte Heche for failing to cure his wife of a fever. The malpractice accusation sprang from Heche's suit, since it was evident from the testimony presented that Clerk was illiterate and 'totally ignorant of the arts of medicine and surgery'.[35] Clerk's punishment was intended to deter other empirics as he was led through the city to the tune of trumpets and pipes with a parchment he had used as a cure, a whetstone for his lies, and two urine flasks all hung fore and aft about him.[36] Even though Roger Clerk's incompetence was manifest, as attested by the examining committee, neither physicians nor surgeons nor barber-surgeons had brought suit against him. In their defence they could not know of every quack who set himself up to practise medicine and the extant evidence of malpractice suits is scant. Yet the suspicion remains that the medical establishment was content with high-sounding protestations instead of action. This perspective seems to be borne out by a London ordinance of 1376 granted at the behest of the barber-surgeons who complained of provincial medical men, uninstructed in the craft of surgery, who practised in London. While the gist of the ordinance is directed against non-resident medical practitioners, it provides for examination and accreditation before admission to practise, as well as providing a fine for malpractice.[37] Such provisions beg the question, however, for they were intended to exclude outsiders from practice as much as to protect the public.

One means of guarding against malpractice suits was to avoid treating high-risk patients, a solution strongly recommended by the authors of advice books. Others were arranging malpractice insurance and obtaining second opinions before beginning a treatment régime. By the early fifteenth century, some London medical practitioners in theory, if not in fact, had adopted these latter two options. Before attempting high-risk cases, barber-surgeons were expected to notify the wardens of their guild and post a bond with the civil authorities.[38] In doing so, the surgeon could obtain expert advice as well as, in essence, pre-paying his fine if a malpractice suit occurred. No means was provided, however, for indemnifying a patient who was harmed.

The medical profession was certainly aware of the potential problem of malpractice in late medieval England. Even though they might criticize each other, physicians, surgeons, and barber-surgeons appear to have adopted a uniform response, taken partially in conjunction with municipal authorities. The response entailed emphasis on better education and the exclusion of the uneducated from practice. By the fifteenth century, examinations and licensing of provincial and foreign practitioners were means of accomplishing this goal. Working with the city government in malpractice suits was another method. Trying to protect themselves from charges of malpractice through consultation and prepayment of malpractice fines was a third. Only in advocating improved education and prepayment of malpractice fines did the medical men admit any complicity in the poor state of medical care. Medical deontology, aside from advocating the avoidance of the appearance of immoral behaviour, seemed to flow in the direction of protecting practitioners, not the public. No wonder that, although their income might be high, their reputation was not.

Government at all levels was somewhat concerned by medical malpractice. In the cases noted above, the London city government took charge of the prosecution and the Crown does not seem to have interfered. As already noted, the London city government tried to regulate who practised medicine and to protect its people from out-and-out quacks as well as established practitioners who provided poor care. Elsewhere the evidence is scanty, but local officials also displayed a concern with medical practitioners whose ministrations proved harmful.[39] Provincial medical men were generally less well-organized than their London counterparts and people may have been willing to tolerate a higher degree of error, so prosecution for malpractice was probably less common than in London.

In at least two provincial malpractice cases the Crown took a hand. This situation may have reflected local governmental weakness in dealing with such cases or simply a special set of circumstances. The first case involved Pernell, a female practitioner from Devon, convicted of malpractice in 1350 by causing the death of a miller through her ignorance. She was sentenced to be banished from London, but upon appeal she received a royal pardon.[40] The king also intervened in 1385 in the case of John Leche. A woman sued Leche, a court surgeon who had practised in Chester, for malpractice for the death of her husband following an operation. The punishment in this case was severe indeed for Leche was fined his 'goods and tenements', but a royal pardon relieved him from the penalty.[41] In both instances we know few of the facts of the case so it may have been that royal action came to prevent an injustice of judgement or punishment, or even to protect a royal servant in the case of Leche. It seems that royal intervention occurred in provincial malpractice cases as part of appellate jurisdiction rather than as a display of concern with malpractice.

One caveat to the preceding discussion is immediately apparent: it did not concern all practitioners. Village healers, midwives, cunning folk, and the like might provide poor quality medical care and even be hauled into court occasionally, as happened to Roger Clerk, but they often provided the only available medical care. Many cunning folk or midwives were not inherently dishonest or incompetent; they did what they could within the limits of their skills. In one sense, too much regulation of their behaviour could be counterproductive since competent folk practitioners as well as the incompetent would be driven out of business by licensing requirements.

From the cases extant, a suspicion emerges that city governments – at least in London – were as much concerned with preventing fraud and protecting a recognized profession as with protecting the health of their citizens. This is not an altogether fair appraisal since driving out inept medical practitioners should have led to better medical care. Unfortunately, if the remaining practitioners did not treat the poor, they were left with no care or the ministrations of folk healers and the mercies of the saints.

London, at least, had a better record in another avenue of public health in the late Middle Ages, that of preventive medical care. Preventive care is a term that must be used loosely when applied to the late Middle Ages; it implies a concern with sanitation and the provision of foodstuffs. Such concerns could be motivated by other interests such as enforcing guild quality control regulations, but the end result was an improved public health picture. A cleaner city with better food was likely to be a healthier city. Moreover, it may have been easier to enforce standards of cleanliness than to pursue every unlicensed or incompetent medical practitioner.

Butchering, in particular, was a noisome craft for most medieval cities, often carried out on the outskirts of the city. Quality had to be maintained and the offal had to be disposed of properly lest it become a health problem. The first issue is illustrated when the masters of the butchers of St Nicholas Shambles reported on 10 December 1364 that a pig found at the shop of John Huntyndon 'was corrupt and abominable to the human race'.[42] Another member of the guild paid the 20s fine and mainprised John to appear before the mayor and aldermen. Keeping meat from turning putrid was a difficult proposition even in winter, as the cook, Thomas Sprothergh, found. On 11 November 1375 he was convicted in the recorder's court of selling a peck of eels 'unfit for human beings', and after acknowledging his guilt he was sentenced to spend an hour in the pillory and to have the eels burnt in front of him.[43] In both cases the authorities enforced quality control standards, but standards that also protected the health of the people of London. A full-scale inspection programme should not be assumed based on a few examples, but they are indicative that a combination of guild and municipal action may have protected the food supply of at least some people.

The other side of butchering, offal, leads to a broader concern for sanitation. Even though people did not understand the germ theory of disease or the danger of typhoid posed by contaminated water supplies, they understood noxious odours and made the connection that the streets were not appropriate places for offal or the overflow of privies. Aldermen were responsible for ensuring that the streets in their wards were clean.[44] At times they had to be prodded into action, as occurred in July 1368. On the petition of the bishop of London, the earls of Salisbury and Warwick, and the countess of Pembroke, Edward III ordered the city government to deal with the blood and offal being dropped on the streets as it was being transported to a dumping spot along the Thames bank.[45] Tower Hill seemed to be a favoured spot for dumping refuse. In February 1377 the king pointed out to the city government 'the accumulation of refuse, filth and other fetid matter on Tower Hill, whereby the air was foully corrupted and vitiated and the lives of those dwelling or passing there are endangered' threatening a fine of 100 marks if action to clean up the dump were not taken.[46] In the following inquest, the mayor and aldermen found several people who had deposited refuse on Tower Hill, including John Gardiner who had dumped one hundred cartloads of rubbish there.[47] In leaving sanitation to city authorities, respect for London self-government took precedence over a concern for public health and the royal nostrils.

To be fair, city authorities did act on their own to deal with the problem of filth in the streets. In 1309 the city ordered the collection and disposal of 'ordure' from houses, reminded householders not to place their rubbish in front of their neighbours' houses (threatening a fine of 40d), and warned against dumping on the king's highway.[48] Efforts seem to have been made to enforce these ordinances, even if only sporadically. On 2 February 1372 'Richard Bakere, a brewer, was fined 2s. for casting dung into the streets against the ordinances'.[49] Even when the aldermen could not find the perpetrators, they reported refuse in the streets and urged its collection.[50] The Common Council also tried to ensure that public latrines, such as those on London Bridge, were kept in repair.[51] These actions dealt with major offenders, but did not always catch the less obvious offender or the person who simply used the street as a privy. Indeed, some Londoners found inventive ways to dispose of their personal waste. In 1348 two men ran a pipe from the privy in their solar into the cellar below, filling it up with filth.[52] The city government seems to have investigated and dealt with the more obvious sewage problems and followed up on complaints from the crown or citizens. Their success was tarnished by the large number of cesspools which posed a hazard to wells and cisterns well into the nineteenth century.

If London is taken as an example, the behaviour of municipal governments made sense in the light of prevailing medical knowledge. Concentrating on preventive health care helped to make London and other cities somewhat cleaner and less noxious places in which to live.[53] Even ordinances prohibiting the using of swords, which were intended to further public order, led to fewer wounds if not cuts, broken bones, and concussions from whatever blunt instruments people found handy.

As other commentators have pointed out, the state of medical knowledge and care in late medieval England was lamentable.[54] Medical knowledge had advanced little from the days of Galen. Medical practitioners operated within a paradigm based on reference to authority, not experimentation; moreover, some works of classical practitioners were unavailable. The knowledge of empirics was even worse than that of physicians and surgeons. Licensing and prosecution served to drive out some obvious imposters, who took advantage of the woes of others, but could also drive from practice herbalists who provided a modicum of relief to their patients.

Concentrating on preventive care allowed municipal authorities to affect public health in a fashion in which their actions could bear fruit. The occasional legal case warned the more flagrant quacks to desist. Municipal government did what it could and left the rest to private relationships. The Crown did even less than local authorities in promoting public health. This situation stemmed less from a callous disdain for the health of the king's subjects, than from an awareness of late medieval monarchs that they could better turn their energies elsewhere, leaving health to local governments and private individuals.

Medical men, at whatever level of expertise, did not step into the void left by a lack of governmental action. Medical education became more formal in the late Middle Ages than before, but the texts remained largely the same. Surgeons improved their techniques, but ultimately the lack of anatomical knowledge limited their effectiveness.[55] Professional organizations and the obtainment of licensing ordinances were more in the nature of self-protection than something designed to improve medical practice.

Medical writers clearly specified a deontology, but when examined this code of ethics seems rather threadbare.[56] The compilers of advice books tended to repeat one another, and often their standards for ethical conduct dated back to

Galen, if not Hippocrates. There was nothing wrong with reiterating older standards of conduct but when standards took on a formulaic cast, something to be passed over on the way to other advice, we might question the impact on medical practice. Some writers, such as John Mirfield, urged practitioners to treat the poor at the expense of the wealthy. Such advice was lost on folk practitioners, both the village midwife who might charitably help her neighbours and the quack who bilked his patients. The translations of the advice books of Guy de Chauliac, Lanfranc of Milan and others into English widened their potential readership in the fourteenth and fifteenth centuries. At least some rural practitioners, such as John Crophill of Wix Priory, Essex, turned to these writers.[57] The popularity of these advice books indicates that some practitioners were trying to improve their knowledge, while the public sought medical knowledge from sources other than the medical profession.

Non-medical writers were less sure than were medical writers of the skills and ethics of medical men. Common depictions of physicians and surgeons were of men motivated by a desire to acquire wealth, not a desire to help their fellows. Even so, there is a grudging respect for the knowledge and abilities of some physicians and surgeons. The unanswered question is how much did writers reflect official opinion in the late fourteenth and fifteenth centuries and how much did they influence official opinion.[58]

It seems fair to argue that writers reflected the general suspicion of the medical profession in late medieval England. This suspicion is reinforced by the number of men who provided medical care with no concern for avoiding harm to their patients, such as Richard Cheynduit, or the even more obviously incompetent Roger Clerk, did. Even though Roger Clerk did not bear the trappings of a physician or surgeon, his actions helped to discredit the medical profession. In response, medical men pushed for the total exclusion of unlicensed practitioners.

We may now return to the question of who was responsible for safeguarding public health in late medieval England. The Crown, local government, and medical practitioners all had a concern for medical care and the health of the population. The people, too, were able to influence medical treatment by turning away from obvious quacks or even taking them to court on occasion. Englishmen could be their own doctors by reading popular medical tracts, although such works did not become commonplace until the late sixteenth century.[59] Outside London, most people turned to village healers of a variety of stripes, some competent, such as John Crophill, and others more deadly in their ministrations. Here the workings of the market-place seemed to be the only regulation of medical practice.

In theory, English monarchs were concerned with the health of their people. In practice, they tended to leave such issues to local government or to professional groups. Even when royal courts provided a hearing for complaints, they were complaints lodged by individuals. Henry V gave support to the attempt to combine the physicians and surgeons in 1423, but the impetus for this action came from below. As was the case with many other concerns, the Crown, perhaps wisely, left action regarding medicine to others.

The London city government was both prescriptive and reactive in matters of public health. The mayor and aldermen tried to enforce minimal standards of cleanliness in the city, though not always with success. While this goal extended beyond improving the health of the population, removing filth from the streets and waterways decreased the likelihood of the spread of some types of disease. The prevention of epidemic disease also fell within the purview of city government. Typical was an order dated 15 March 1346 that specified that lepers vacate the city within fifteen days and the appointment of a group to round them up for removal.[60] The city government was also concerned with regulating medical practice so as to drive out quacks and protect the monopoly of the medical establishment, a prescriptive goal. However, this was a reactive approach since the authorities generally did not take action unless someone brought a suit against a practitioner. Local officials had no other choice. Without an extensive governmental structure, it was impossible to intervene more obtrusively in medical practice and to have tried to do so would have done little good.

The physicians, the Fellowship of Surgeons, the barber-surgeons' guild, and even the apothecaries all established rules governing the treatment of patients and professional conduct. These rules were largely self-protective, to ensure their monopoly of their craft by keeping out interlopers, and to protect against possible lawsuits. Some good for the community at large came from these rules as a few quacks were driven out of practice. Setting up a practice of consultation in difficult cases helped to protect the attending surgeon from charges of malpractice, but it may also have saved a few patients from faulty treatment. Overall, the self-regulating aspects of medical practice did not convey a feeling of confidence in the medical profession and was non-existent in many places. Until medical science improved, practitioners' ability to treat was bounded by their knowledge-base. Their neglect of the poor may have reflected a growing callousness regarding the poor in the late Middle Ages, an attitude which the medical establishment shared with other élite guilds.[61] There were bright spots of individual charity, such as a mercer who left £25 in his will in 1467 so that the surgeon Thomas Thorneton could provide medical care for the London poor.[62] While the business of medical practitioners might be more important to society than that of other guilds, to condemn them for adopting an attitude characteristic of men of their class would be anachronistic.

The attainment of good health for society was everyone's business, yet no one's business in late medieval England. Another form of medical treatment, the supplication of the saints to intervene with God, continued to be widely used in the fourteenth and fifteenth centuries.[63] To some the healing of the saints was better than that provided by physicians and surgeons. After all, all healing ultimately emanated from God so why not deal with Him directly rather than through medical men? People also turned to other forms of magical healing, such as magical stones and thaumaturgy. God rarely intervened directly, so other forms of healing and protecting the health of the population were necessary. Government, at least in London, tried to achieve a small measure of preventive care with sanitary regulations. Otherwise, the primary governing structure for health care was the market-place. To expect more is to expect medieval society to be something it was not.

While the Ricardian era was one of rethinking the relationship of Crown and people, the situation in medical affairs was much as it had been earlier in the century and as it continued to be early in the fifteenth century. In retrospect we can see that the medical profession was becoming more organized, but, at the time, the approach seemed to be one of stasis.

Late medieval Englishmen wisely sought to obtain health care from a variety of sources. Often they took an active part in ensuring good health by preventive measures. Much remained to be done in protecting the health of society. None the less, medical care improved over time even though many medical men continued to ignore the examples of Saints Cosmas and Damian and failed to provide medical care for all.

Notes

¹ John of Salisbury, *Metalogicon*, trans. David M. McGary (Berkeley, 1955), p. 18.

² For the ancient background, see Guido Majno, *The Healing Hand: Man and Wound in the Ancient World* (Cambridge, Mass., 1975); Wesley D. Smith, *The Hippocratic Tradition* (Ithaca, 1979); Oswei Tempkin, *Galenism: Rise and Decline of a Medical Philosophy* (Ithaca, 1973). For the Middle Ages, Vern L. Bullough, *The Development of Medicine as a Profession* (New York, 1966); Nancy G. Siraisi, *Medieval and Early Renaissance Medicine* (Chicago, 1990): C.H. Talbot, *Medicine in Medieval England* (London, 1967); R.T. Beck, *The Cutting Edge: Early History of the Surgeons of London* (London, 1974); Robert S. Gottfried, *Doctors and Medicine in Medieval England, 1340–1530* (Princeton, 1986); and the references in the above. Developments in England should be compared with those in Florence: Katharine Park, *Doctors and Medicine in Early Renaissance Florence* (Princeton, 1985).

³ William Langland, *Piers the Plowman*, trans. J.F. Goodridge (Harmondsworth, 1966), p. 88. Carole Rawcliffe shows that some doctors were able to take advantage of their position to enhance their income and status. 'The Profits of Practice: the Wealth and Status of Medical Men in Later Medieval England', *Social History of Medicine*, 1 (1988), 61–78.

⁴ John Arderne, *Treatise of Fistula in Ano*, ed. D'Arcy Power (Early English Text Society, 139, 1910), pp. 5–6, 16.

⁵ The best documented physicians' condemnation of empirics occurred in Paris, although the same attitudes prevailed in England. Pearl Kibre, 'The Faculty of Medicine at Paris, Charlantanism and Unlicensed Medical Practice in the Late Middle Ages', *Bulletin of the History of Medicine*, 27 (1953), 1–20.

⁶ Printed in J.F. South, *Memorials of the Craft of Surgery in England*, ed. D'Arcy Power (London, 1886), p. 50. For an overview of medical practice in London, see Carole Rawcliffe, 'Medicine and Medical Practice in Later Medieval London', *Guildhall Studies in London History*, 5 (1981), 13–25.

⁷ J. Strachy et al. (eds), *Rotuli Parliamentorum* (6 vols, Record Commission, 1783), 4, 158.

⁸ South, *Memorials of Surgery*, p. ix; Beck, *Cutting Edge*, p. 42. Groups of surgeons had been appointed earlier to hold inquests into reputed medical malpractice, as when three surgeons were appointed in 1354 to see if John le Spicer de Corhull was guilty of negligence in treating a wound. R.R. Sharpe (ed.), *Calendar of Letter Books of the City of London* (11 vols, London, 1899–1912), 'Letter Book G', p. 21; H.T. Riley (ed. and trans.), *Memorials of London and London Life in the XIIIth, XIVth, and XVth Centuries* (London, 1868), pp. 273–4.

⁹ Riley, *Memorials of London*, pp. 337, 519; South, *Memorials of Surgery*, pp. 7, 19. One of the surgeons, Master John Hynstoke, was on both lists.

¹⁰ Sharpe, *Calendar of Letter Books*, 'Letter Book K', p. 11; South, *Memorials of Surgery*, pp. 47–55 (the regulations are printed on pp. 298–306); Beck, *Cutting Edge*, pp. 124–5.

¹¹ South, *Memorials of Surgery*, pp. 302–8; Beck, *Cutting Edge*, pp. 30–5.

[12] Sidney Young, *The Annals of the Barber-Surgeons of London* (London, 1890), pp. 30–4.

[13] South, *Memorials of Surgery*, p. 22.

[14] Ibid., pp. 326–30.

[15] Ibid., pp. 331–4.

[16] L.G. Matthews, *History of Pharmacy in Britain* (London, 1962), p. 34; Matthews, *The Royal Apothecaries* (London, 1967), p. 5. For apothecaries outside London, see T.D. Whittet, 'The Apothecaries in Provincial Guilds', *Medical History*, 8 (1964), 245–73.

[17] Sharpe, *Calendar of Letter Books*, 'Letter Book H', p. 42.

[18] Ibid., 'Letter Book L', p. 103.

[19] Gottfried, *Doctors and Medicine*, pp. 43–50; idem, 'English Medical Practitioners, 1340–1530', *Bulletin of the History of Medicine*, 58 (1984), 164–82.

[20] John Alford, 'Medicine in the Middle Ages: The Theory of a Profession', *Centennial Review*, 23 (1979), 377–96. For a different view of professional obligation, see D.W. Amundsen, 'Causitry and Professional Obligation: The Regulation of Physicians by the Court of Conscience in the Late Middle Ages', *Transactions and Studies of the College of Physicians of Philadelphia*, 3 (1981), 22–39, 93–112.

[21] John de Mirfield, *Florarium Bartholomei*, printed in P. Horton-Smith Hartley and H.R. Aldridge, *Johannes de Mirfield of St. Bartholomew's Southfield, His Life and Works* (Cambridge, 1936), pp. 132–3.

[22] Ibid.

[23] Lanfranc of Milan, *Lanfrank's Science of Cirurgie*, ed. Robert von Fleishhaker (Early English Text Society, 102, 1894), p. 9. Lanfranc's Latin treatise was translated into English by 1400.

[24] John Arderne, *Treatise of Fistula in Ano*, pp. 5–6, 16.

[25] Geoffrey Chaucer, *The Canterbury Tales*, trans. R.M. Lumiansky (New York, 1971), General Prologue, p. 9; Langland, *Piers the Plowman*, p. 88.

[26] John de Mirfield said that the surgeon 'should not choose difficult cases, nor desperate cases, nor commit himself to long courses of treatment, at least in my opinion. For all those things blacken the good reputation of a physician and give to the public material for defamation.' John de Mirfield, *Surgery*, ed. and trans. J.B. Colton (New York, 1969), p. 19.

[27] Mirfield, *Florarium Bartholomei*, pp. 126–7.

[28] Gottfried, *Doctors and Medicine*, pp. 8–9, 71.

[29] 'A Poem of the Times of Edward II', in Thomas Wright (ed.), *The Political Songs of England from the Reign of John to that of Edward II* (Camden Society, OS, 6, 1839), p. 252.

[30] Langland, *Piers the Plowman*, p. 88.

[31] Norman Davis (ed.), *Paston Letters and Papers of the Fifteenth Century* (2 vols, Oxford, 1971–6), 1: no. 77.

[32] Good discussions of English medieval malpractice are Madeline P. Cosman, 'Medieval Medical Malpractice: The Dicta and the Dockets', *Bulletin of the New York Academy of Medicine*, 2nd series, 49 (1973), 22–46; idem, 'Medieval Medical Malpractice and Chaucer's Physician', *New York State Journal of Medicine*, 72 (1972), 2439–44; M.T. Walton, 'The Advisory Jury and Malpractice: Fifteenth Century London: The Case of William Forest', *Journal of the History of Medicine*, 40 (1985), 478–82.

[33] A.H. Thomas (ed.), *Calendar of Plea and Memoranda Rolls; A.D. 1364–1381* (Cambridge, 1929), p. 236. For Dunhevel's appointment, see Riley, *Memorials of London*, p. 337.

[34] Ibid.

[35] Ibid., pp. 464–6; Sharpe, *Calendar of Letter Books*, 'Letter Book H', p. 184.

[36] Ibid.

[37] Riley, *Memorials of London*, pp. 393–4.

[38] Ibid., p. 609.

[39] Cosman, 'Medieval Medical Malpractice', pp. 43–4; G.A. Auden, 'The Gild of the Barber-Surgeons of the City of York', *Proceedings of the Royal Society of Medicine*, 21 (1927), 70–6; M.C. Barnet, 'The Barber-Surgeons of York', *Medical History*, 12 (1968), 19–30; George Parker, 'Early Bristol Medical Institutions: The Medieval Hospitals and Barber-Surgeons', *Transactions of the Bristol and Gloucestershire Archaeology Society*, 44 (1952), 155–77; R.M. Walker, 'The Barber-Surgeons of Bristol', *Bristol Medico-Chirurgical Journal*, 90 (1975), 51–3; Charles Williams, *Masters, Wardens and Assistants of the Gild of the Barber-Surgeons of Norwich* (Norwich, 1910).

[40] *CPR, 1348–50*, p. 561. Cosman, 'Medieval Medical Malpractice', p. 43. While Cosman considers banishment to be an unduly severe punishment, it was often used in London for those who preyed upon public innocence. For example, John Berkyng, a soothsayer, was banished from London in 1390 after being convicted of false magical practice. Riley, *Memorials of London*, p. 519.

[41] *CPR, 1381–5*, p. 182.

[42] Thomas, *Plea and Memoranda Rolls, A.D. 1364–1381*, p. 12. That same year, John de Roulegh was convicted of selling twenty-nine pigeons unfit for human consumption and John Russelle was convicted of selling thirty-seven tainted pigeons the following year. Sharpe, *Calendar of Letter Books*, 'Letter Book G', pp. 175, 176.

[43] Sharpe, *Calendar of Letter Books*, 'Letter Book H', p. 16.

[44] E.L. Sabine, 'City Cleaning in Mediaeval London', *Speculum*, 12 (1937), 19–43.

[45] Thomas, *Plea and Memoranda Rolls, A.D. 1364–1381*, p. 93. This seems to have been an ongoing problem, as Edward III had sent a message to the city on 30 September 1357, stating that 'when passing along the water of Thames, we have beheld dung, laystolls, and other filth accumulated in diverse places in the said city, upon the bank of the river aforesaid and have also perceived the fumes and other abominable stenches arising therefrom'. Riley, *Memorials of London*, pp. 295–6.

[46] Thomas, *Plea and Memoranda Rolls, A.D. 1364–1381*, p. 140.

[47] Ibid., pp. 140–1.

[48] Riley, *Memorials of London*, pp. 67–8.

[49] Thomas, *Plea and Memoranda Rolls, A.D 1364–1381*, p. 135.

[50] Riley, *Memorials of London*, pp. 367–8 (1372); Sharpe, *Calendar of Letter Books*, 'Letter Book H', p. 216 (1383); ibid., p. 283 (1385); A.H. Thomas (ed.), *Calendar of Plea and Memoranda Rolls, A.D. 1413–1437* (Cambridge, 1943), p. 137 (1422).

[51] Sharpe, *Calendar of Letter Books*, 'Letter Book H', p. 212.

[52] E.L. Sabine, 'Latrines and Cesspools of Mediaeval London', *Speculum*, 9 (1938), 314.

[53] Fourteenth-century Bristol also prohibited the dumping of 'ordure' in the streets, on pain of a 40d fine. F.B. Bickley (ed.), *The Little Red Book of Bristol* (2 vols, Bristol, 1900), 2, 31.

[54] Gottfried, *Doctors and Medicine*; Rawcliffe, 'Medicine and Medical Practice in Late Medieval London'.

[55] In late fifteenth-century London, the barber-surgeons guild seemed to be providing medical lectures for its members. V.L. Bullough, 'Training of the Non-university-educated Medical Practitioner in the Late Middle Ages', *Journal of the History of Medicine*, 14 (1959), 453–6.

[56] Amundsen, 'Causitry and Professional Obligation', Amundsen, 'Medical Deontology and Pestilential Disease in the Late Middle Ages', *Journal of the History of Medicine*, 23 (1977), 403–21.

[57] J.K. Mustain, 'A Rural Medical Practitioner in Fifteenth-Century England', *Bulletin of the History of Medicine*, 46 (1977), 473.

[58] Literary views of medicine are examined in I.B. Jones, 'Popular Medical Knowledge in Fourteenth Century English Literature', *Bulletin of the Institute of the History of Medicine*, 5 (1937), 405–51, 538–88.

[59] John Crophill, a literate fifteenth-century layman, was able to practise medicine based on common sense and reading vernacular medical treatises. Mustain, 'Rural Medical Practitioner', pp. 469–76; Paul Slack, 'Mirrors of Health and the Treasures of Poor Men: The Uses of the Vernacular Medical Literature of Tudor England', in Charles Webster (ed.), *Health, Medicine and Mortality in the Sixteenth Century* (Cambridge, 1979), pp. 238–73.

[60] Riley, *Memorials of London*, pp. 230–1.

[61] The ordinances of the combined College of Physicians and Surgeons of 1423 did provide for free treatment of the poor, however. South, *Memorials of Surgery*, pp. 302–3. Changing attitudes toward the poor in the late Middle Ages are detailed in Michel Mollat, *The Poor in the Middle Ages*, trans. Arthur Goldhammer (New Haven, 1986).

[62] S.L. Thrupp, *The Merchant Class of Medieval London* (Ann Arbor, 1948), pp. 178–9.

[63] J.M. Theilmann, 'English Peasants and Medieval Miracle Lists', *The Historian*, 52 (1990), 286–303.

11

ST ANTHONY'S HOSPITAL, LONDON: A PARDONER-SUPPORTED ALIEN PRIORY, 1219–1461

David K. Maxfield*

Hospitals were numerous in the Middle Ages, but not necessarily long-lived. Eleven hundred have been identified for England and Wales alone, while London possessed thirty-four in all.[1] There have been numerous articles and books dealing with individual institutions, but many are merely antiquarian. Likewise, relatively little serious history has been written about English medieval hospitals collectively.[2] Certain of these establishments, along with sundry monasteries, granges, etc., were 'limbs' of larger foreign organizations and, when the Hundred Years' War approached, received hostile treatment as 'alien priories'. Even less has appeared about them.[3] Various hospitals, including some of the alien priories, obtained financial support from distribution of indulgences, that is, from the activities of the *quaestorii* (or *quaestores*), commonly called pardoners. Chaucer and other writers have given such ecclesiastical officers a bad name, so that much of what has been written about them is biased, polemical, or merely incidental to literary criticism of the *Canterbury Tales*. In as much as hospitals and pardoners played significant parts in medieval English life, and since alien priories were important at the time of the Hundred Years' War, it should be worthwhile to investigate one or more pardoner-supported alien priory hospitals.

One such study has appeared, dealing with the Hospital of St Mary Rouncivale, Charing Cross.[4] St Anthony's Hospital, London, was a very different alien priory that depended upon pardoners.[5] Both institutions were managed by Augustinian canons who operated networks of hospitals all over Europe. St Mary's and its dozen or so sisters had their mother house in the Pyrenees pass of Roncesvalles. They existed primarily to serve ill and weary pilgrims going to and from St James's shrine at Santiago de Compostella. Their Charing Cross branch cared for seriously ill persons – whether pilgrims or not – from about 1230 until the Reformation ended its existence.

St Anthony's, London, belonged to a network that eventually numbered over 200 establishments, extending from Scotland to Sicily and from Marienburg to Seville. It began in 1095 as a lay society approved by Urban II and sponsored by the Benedictine priory at Vienne in the Dauphiné. To end increasing friction between the society and the Benedictines – including physical violence – Pope Boniface VIII reorganized the rapidly-growing body as an order of canons regular under the Rule of St Augustine. He also reorganized the priory at Vienne to serve as their mother house.[6]

From modest beginnings, the society/order cared for victims of then rampant St Anthony's Fire (ergotism), a painful, loathsome and disfiguring disease that slowly died out as people learned to recognize diseased rye. As this plague waned, the Order cared for poor travellers and pilgrims, and even gained the privilege of caring for the sick of the papal household. By the fourteenth century, for whatever reason, its London branch merely served twelve worn-out, sometimes bedridden, old men whose chief malady was indigence – rather like the pensioners of Hiram's Hospital in Trollope's Barchester. Nevertheless, its pardoners did not hesitate to seek alms for the benefit of persons 'so tortured and burned by fire as of the Inferno, that being deprived of every function of their limbs, they appear to be monsters rather than human beings'.[7] Although this establishment flourished until the Reformation, and its ghost lingered for some time longer, the present essay will particularly stress the period 1377–1414, when alien priories were especially important.

Unlike their Barchester counterparts, the inmates at St Anthony's, London, did not enjoy the privilege of individual spaces. Despite their relative health, their institution still was a typical medieval hospital, as was St Mary Rouncivale. Basically, both were chapels where religious offices were carried out at one or more altars, while the naves were filled with beds. The patients were expected – to the extent that they were able – to take part in frequent prayers and masses not only for their own souls, but for the souls of the hospitals' founders and benefactors. It was only toward the end of the Middle Ages that grouped single-occupant almshouses replaced the earlier chapel/hospitals.[8]

Why such emphasis upon religion? Sickness was believed to be brought on by sin: purification of a patient's soul improved his total condition. Souls being more important than bodies, a hospital's basic mission was to cure souls, preparing sick and frail people for good deaths. Charity being a virtue, however, much kindly care was provided so that restored patients frequently were discharged – though not at St Anthony's, London. Happily, perhaps, a double standard applied. Hospitals, where common-sense folk remedies were used, were strictly for the poor. Physicians, surgeons and apothecaries reserved their expensive services for those who could reward them well. Moreover such folk were cared for in their own well-appointed households. Ironically, the poor frequently fared better than their betters, for folk remedies often were more effective – and sometimes less painful – than academic Galenistic medicine and anaesthetic-less surgery.[9] Thus, the bedesmen at St Anthony's, London, saw no medical professionals, even when at death's door.

It is possible that victims of St Anthony's Fire once were massaged with pork fat. Whether or not this is true, pigs traditionally were associated with the Vienne network. Early on, the London branch built a pigsty and obtained a unique municipal privilege. It could take from the city's markets any young pigs considered unfit for sale. For 300 years these waifs, housed at the hospital and provided with identifying bells and slit ears, were the only porkers allowed the run of alleys and streets to become fat upon the rich heaps of dung and offal. Thus, while many hospitals fed their patients poor fare, the inmates at St Anthony's dined upon fresh pork. Their institution was located at the corner of what is now Old Broad and Threadneedle Streets. For good reason, the latter long was known as Pig Street.[10]

Hospital services were expensive, even without medical personnel, because priests and canons were indispensable. In fact, the stipends of wardens and other officiating clergy came to take up more and more of available revenues, so that such posts tended to become valuable benefices, much sought after. At the same time, the servants – almost always women – who provided the actual patient care (except for occasional confession and absolution) received relatively little. Such a situation particularly applied at St Anthony's, London, for, unlike most hospitals, it became rich. Its pardoners eventually brought in substantial sums that were quite additional to other income.

Indulgences (pardons), which merely reduced penance, were not to be sold to anybody, but given freely to truly penitent sinners in return for alms. This procedure has been discussed elsewhere,[11] so that little need be said here, except with respect to St Anthony's, London. For three centuries this alien priory had its share of corrupt/false pardoners.[12] In fact, Chaucer almost as logically could have named this hospital as sponsor of his evil Pardoner as St Mary Rouncivale! Nevertheless, St Anthony's, perhaps unlike St Mary's, distributed properly authorized indulgences.[13]

Pardoners from St Anthony's, Vienne, came to England with papally approved pardons at least as early as 1219, the year when an English king, Henry III, first granted them protection. In 1243 Henry gave them not only an annual subsidy of 20 marks (later changed to the advowson of a Hereford church with two dependent chapels), but a former synagogue (and in 1256 adjacent land) to be developed as a branch hospital.[14] This building was newly built, and has been called 'magnificent and stately'.[15] A letter of 1420 asserts that sometime later (c. 1268?) the Antonian canons received additional land and houses in the parish of St Benet Fynk that had been the property of a denizen of London named Alexander le Ferim, who had started a hospice for the 'poor and needy'.[16]

Edwards I, II and III constantly renewed protection for the 'master and brethren' of St Anthony's and 'their attorneys and proctors' to collect alms in churches, at first only in England but, from 1327, in Wales and even Ireland.[17] Even before the Hundred Years' War, however, branches of French religious houses in England were considered to be 'alien priories'. To curtail the flow of money contributions across the Channel, and to ensure that their personnel did not serve as enemy spies, many such institutions were treated as spoils of war and leased out to loyal Englishmen. A few French priories had been seized as early as 1295 by Edward I, while Edward II and Edward III followed suit, especially after 1337, the generally accepted starting date for the war.[18]

The Dauphiné, where St Anthony, Vienne, was located, was, however, part of the Holy Roman Empire, and representatives of the French royal house did not owe homage for it until 1349. Nevertheless, the properties and income of St Anthony's, London, were improperly taken into the English king's hand sometime before 1323. In that year Edward II granted it to his brother,

Edmund of Woodstock, having taken it back from a grantee who had become a rebel. In 1336 Edward III assigned its temporalities to John Savage, an English secular clerk. This king, however, recognized the mother house's Dauphiné location by granting its proctor in London full royal protection at least from 1334. It is not known how St Anthony's, London, fared in the Black Death of 1348–9, but after the treaty of Brétigny-Calais in 1360, there was full restoration to the Dauphiné abbey, which then appointed Canon Geoffrey de Lymona master (or warden) of the London hospital. He visited Vienne in 1363, 1366 and 1367, leaving Savage in charge. That both he and Savage were aggressive in pushing their pardons is suggested by the fact that they, and two of their pardoners, were prosecuted by a rector in 1361 for trespassing.[19] St Anthony's indulgences certainly were popular for, as early as 1267, English kings frequently found it necessary to order the arrest of persons fraudulently seeking alms in St Anthony's name.[20]

When warfare resumed in 1369 the London hospital's mother house had been located for twenty years in territory held by the French king. Repeatedly in the last years of Edward III the Commons petitioned that French religious be expelled from the realm, and that all alien priories – now including St Anthony's – be confiscated. It was not until 13 October 1377 – in the first year of Richard II's reign – that a royal decree was issued to this effect.[21] Unhappily, the Great Schism in 1378 caused further problems both for the mother house and for its London branch. England and the Holy Roman Empire adhered to Urban VI at Rome, while France was loyal to Clement VII at Avignon. In the confusion, both popes came to claim jurisdiction over St Anthony's, London.

An unnamed warden was assessed 10*s*, and three named 'chaplains' 2*s* each, for the poll tax in 1379. There is no record of St Anthony's being damaged in the 1381 Peasants' Revolt, although more than one hospital was hard hit at that time. The French warden, Geoffrey de Lymona, was out by then, having received none of the revenues since 1377. St Anthony's, London, was seized by the youthful Richard II, who in 1382 granted it for a mere 20 marks per year to Michael de la Pole – soon to be his chancellor – even though it was extremely lucrative property.[22] In fact, in 1386, de la Pole declared its annual income to be some 400 marks (855 marks for two years).[23] In the 1450s this income came to be at least £549 13*s* 4*d*.[24]

Lymona died before 21 August 1386. Soon thereafter Clement VII tried to appoint a London warden, but Richard Brighouse, a canon of St Anthony, Vienne, nominated by Urban VI, had received the wardenship with royal licence in 1385.[25] Chancellor de la Pole treated him harshly, and to his own profit, demanding not only the 20 marks' rent, but an annuity of £100 and a 1,000-mark penalty bond. Two privy seal clerks were each given £5 yearly out of the rent.[26] Although the rent was soon cancelled, the two clerks still had to be paid.[27]

De la Pole became unpopular with the Commons, and was impeached by the Wonderful Parliament of 1386. Among various charges were malversation of revenue belonging to the king (that is, the 400 marks per year from St Anthony's), and 'sale of law' in his dealings with Brighouse. In the end, all moneys from the hospital, as well as the yield of the annuity, were forfeit, while the latter was cancelled.[28] Unfortunately for Brighouse, the bond was considered to be an enforceable debt to the Crown, which took possession of St Anthony's. The ex-warden was able to arrange restoration to his post on 30 May 1389 for £40 in cash and an annual rent of £40. Somewhat later he died 'outside the papal *curia*', having sought the pope's support after a further ouster.[29]

On 28 October and 24 November 1389 Richard bestowed the hospital, 'in the king's gift in default of the religious' of the Order of St Anthony, upon the priest, John Macclesfield, for life. This privy seal clerk was now a valued royal secretary who would receive eventual promotion to keepership of the Great Wardrobe.[30] In 1390 the new warden was sending out the hospital's pardoners with royal protection and, on 27 March 1391 Richard relieved the hospital of the penalty bond. Sometime between June 1390 and June 1391 Macclesfield began a programme of repair and reconstruction of the hospital's fabric.[31]

Although St Anthony's *was* an alien priory, Richard perhaps had been ill-advised in appointing Macclesfield, because the hospital could not properly be managed by a secular priest. The confiscation decree of 1377 specifically exempted 'conventual' priories, and the London hospital was one of these. Unlike many foreign religious properties in England, it was supposed to be operated according to the strict monastic rule. Members of the Order of St Anthony not only had the obligation of constant celebration of divine services, but corporate responsibility to own property and to manage their own revenues.[32] In the 1380s the hospital's conventuality certainly seemed attenuated, especially when there was no papally-approved warden. Boniface IX, however, had no doubts after he was elected pope at Rome on 2 November 1389. He considered St Anthony's not only to be of his own appointment, but conventual as well. Since he did not want to offend the English king, some time after 16 December 1389 he ordered James Dardani, papal collector in England, to make Macclesfield a canon of the Order of St Anthony, and to invest him with the London wardenship, after he had worn for three months the Order's black habit with blue *tau* cross on the left breast.[33]

Although otherwise well-qualified, monastic restrictions would not have suited Macclesfield at all, for he lived an active, worldly life-style – including a concubine. A letter of credit was arranged on 14 June 1391 so that he could appeal this order at the Roman *curia*.[34] But, although Boniface issued five-year letters of conservancy for the London hospital on 22 July,[35] it is not certain that the warden-elect actually made a journey at this time. If he did so, hoping to obtain dispensation from wearing Antonian garb, he was disappointed. Collector Dardani informed the pope of his non-compliance, and of the willingness of a London priest, John Pouere, to accept the habit. Thus, on 22 August 1391 Boniface ordered the bishop of London to remove Macclesfield from the wardenship and award it to Pouere.[36]

Richard could not accept this arrangement, but he did not wish to defy the pontiff absolutely. On 21 February 1392 he temporarily assigned the hospital to a young relative of his rejected nominee, a John Macclesfield, 'chaplain', who had been parson at Denham, Buckinghamshire, since 12 August 1387.[37] Meanwhile, on 26 January, 14 and 28 February 1392, the king had granted letters of protection so that the senior Macclesfield could go (again?) to Rome.[38] This mission was quite successful, for on 15 June 1392 Boniface IX compromised regarding St Anthony's. He granted the wardenship to the elder John, 'at the petition of King Richard, whose secretary he is', not absolutely but *in commendam* for ten years.[39] Nevertheless, the hospital was to enjoy all the 'privileges, exemptions, liberties, immunities and indulgences' that had pertained to it in the past, when the Order's habit had been worn. The revenues of the parish church of All Saints and two chapels at Hereford, whose advowson only had been given by Henry III, were papally appropriated to St Anthony's, London. On top of this, an indulgence of seven years and seven periods of forty days was granted for penitents who contributed funds for the fabric and ornaments of its chapel and for support of its sick. Thus, Macclesfield returned to England not only with his appointment confirmed, but with his wallet 'Bretful of pardoun comen from Rome al hoot'.[40]

Back in England, the Benedictine abbey of Westminster, the normal holder of the advowson of Denham, had moved John Buckingham, bishop of Lincoln, to investigate the incumbency at Denham. Between 1 and 8 April 1392 the latter's inquisitors met and declared the living vacant on account of incompatibility with the wardenship which, like Denham, involved cure of souls. The abbot then presented a suitable priest to replace the younger Macclesfield. It is not known whether this man actually assumed charge *pro tem* at Denham, but Richard II did not reappoint John Sr. to the wardenship – releasing John Jr. to return to Denham – until 8 April 1393.[41]

After the elder Macclesfield returned to St Anthony's, he sought permission from various bishops for the hospital's pardoners – utilizing the new indulgence he had brought back – to solicit alms within their dioceses. Not all were cooperative, for some (or their officials) hindered the work, and some even demanded fees. Finally, on 10 July 1397 the warden procured a papal mandate ordering these prelates to give freely the local support the hospital's agents needed.[42]

Some of St Anthony's revenue, however, came from sources other than its pardoners – from leased-out tenements, and appropriated churches. In 1309 the warden and brethren had constructed a handsome new chapel especially designed for Christian worship to replace their converted synagogue. The rector of the parish church of St Benet Fynk across the street opposed this chapel, fearing fewer contributions at his own altar. After meetings of the provincial council and of a special archiepiscopal commission, the bishop of London, Ralph Baldock, threatened not only demolition of the new building, but excommunication of the canons and perpetual interdict for the hospital. The warden resisted for three months, but gave in on 2 November 1311. In accordance with canon law, he agreed to pay half of the offerings received at his new altar to St Benet Fynk.[43] In as much as oblations were generous and the canons considered this settlement unfair, there were constant disagreements thereafter between parish and hospital. These affairs became particularly acute sometime before 1389, for St Anthony's chapel became the home of a religious guild dedicated to St Katharine.[44] This body put great stress on masses for the dead, but was greatly disadvantaged by having to share its offerings with the parish church.

In an effort to end this situation, Macclesfield and several co-feoffees – presumably members of the guild – acquired the advowson of St Benet Fynk on 14 May 1395. In order to make the hospital's chapel services more acceptable to English worshippers, the warden procured a papal indult on 19 January 1397 allowing its priests to follow the English use of Sarum instead of their traditional rite of Vienne. When five years had gone by with no opportunity to appoint a new rector for St Benet Fynk, Macclesfield obtained a mandate from the pope on 13 January 1400 appropriating the church to the hospital, effective upon the death or resignation of the rector. A lifetime pension was authorized to encourage the latter's immediate retirement. The fruits of the church then were to go to St Anthony's, which would assume care of the fabric and supply a priest.[45] Supported by his congregation, however, the rector would not resign, and so the unpleasantness continued.

The revolution of 1399 ended Macclesfield's hopes of continued royal favours. Nevertheless, on 20 October the new king, Henry IV, did ratify his estate in three of his benefices, including his wardenship of St Anthony's. The acceptability of the hospital's pardoners to bishops and their clergy depended, of course, upon continuing papal favour, whereas Macclesfield's ten-year *in commendam* appointment was due to expire in 1402. Thus, on 24 August in that year he arranged to go to Rome where, eventually, he persuaded Boniface IX to renew his appointment for life. On 25 May 1403 the pope also prohibited the activities of a false pardoner ('a pretended hermit') who was collecting alms outside the city of York in the name of St Anthony.[46]

The warden's royal and ecclesiastical appointments had made him a rich man, and enabled him to acquire much property in his native Cheshire.[47] Thus, he had come to spend more and more of his time there, as well as in travelling back and forth. Necessarily, he depended heavily upon experienced deputies at the hospital. Very likely it was John Savage, an old man,[48] who was designated to manage St Anthony's while the warden was in Rome, but a Roger Straunge (pensioned in 1414) may have replaced him.[49]

Be this as it may, a coup evidently took place in Macclesfield's absence, with Adam de Olton, a disgraced Augustinian canon from Norton abbey, Cheshire, usurping the wardenship. After his return, the true warden was forced to obtain a writ against him from the King's Council on 22 March 1405,[50] as well as expensively-acquired word from Innocent VII in 1406 that the latter did not intend to remove 'a good and useful governor' from his post.[51] Four years later challenge came from another quarter. On 12 August 1409 the abbot at Vienne persuaded Alexander V to declare that the wardenship had been vacant since the death of Warden Lymona in the 1380s, and that Canon Humbert de Brione of Vienne was now the proper warden. The abbot was easily frustrated on 15 August 1410, however, with letters conservatory obtained from Alexander's successor, John XXIII.[52]

After his defeat of Olton, Macclesfield – presumably supported by the hospital's guild – threatened to use force to implement Boniface's appropriation of St Benet Fynk to St Anthony's. Thirteen of the rector's supporters, tradesmen of the city of London, made it necessary on 17 January 1406 for the warden to find four knights to give surety that he, and his servants, would keep the peace toward the rector, Henry Tranke, who had sought refuge in Essex.[53] Eventually, Macclesfield won out, for he was able to appoint David Fyvyan as rector sometime after 4 June 1410.[54]

Except for these incidents, the years of Henry IV's reign brought substantial gains to the hospital. The network of pardoners was expanded.[55] The religious services were markedly increased, so that six priests celebrated mass daily. The upgrading of fabric and facilities continued. The 1409–11 chapel was enlarged and enriched with books, chalices, ornaments. Increased space, new beds and utensils were provided for the inmates, as well as improved quarters for the warden. The whole was crowned with a new tower with a peal of four bells.[56] Many of these improvements – particularly the bells – especially benefited the hospital's guild. Adam de Olton, apparently forgiven and seemingly loyal, continued on the staff and, from about 1407, gradually became Macclesfield's most trusted lieutenant.[57]

This happy period ended in 1413 with the accession of Henry V, and the renewal of the Hundred Years' War. The king neglected to ratify the warden's estate in the wardenship. Parliament proposed a new confiscation of the alien priories. On 26 August 1413 Henry ordered most of them into his own hand, excepting only conventual priories and those authorized by Edward III, Richard II and Henry IV. On 27 January 1414 he assigned a long list of alien priories to his stepmother, Dowager Queen Joan. The Leicester Parliament (30 April–29 May 1414) ratified this action with its well-known confiscation statute.[58] Unfortunately, without a roster of disciplined Antonian canons, it would have been impossible for the hospital to demonstrate that it was properly conventual. This parliament also directed England's bishops to visit the hospitals in their respective dioceses and report their condition to the King's Chancery.[59] Although St Anthony's was flourishing, such a visitation would bring to light its lack of conventuality, as well as Henry V's failure to renew the warden's appointment. Furthermore, *in commendam* appointments recently had come under attack.[60]

Macclesfield valiantly attempted to manage the situation, but seriously misjudged Adam de Olton. In as much as the seven-year ordeal endured by hospital and warden has been detailed elsewhere,[61] it is merely summarized here. First of all, the warden sought papal confirmation of the hospital's ancient rights and privileges, as well as confirmation of his own appointment. Secondly, he desired the abbot at Vienne[62] to confirm the hospital's conventuality by certifying it a true 'limb' of the Vienne network. Aged and in poor health, Macclesfield chose, on 15 December 1414, to send Olton as his representative to the Council of Constance, where both pope and abbot were in attendance, and provided him with £40 in gold for his legal expenses.

Olton promptly betrayed his superior, and used the scarce gold coin for his own purposes. He asked the abbot to make him a habited canon of St Anthony, and to appoint him the proper warden at London. Nothing loathe, the abbot not only complied, but started ejection proceedings against Macclesfield at the papal *curia*. Olton, meanwhile, petitioned the pope for confirmation of his new appointment. Becoming alarmed, the warden sought the help of Proctor William Swan and other appropriate personages at the papal court. Sometime after the Council closed, after many difficulties – and ruinous expense – he obtained a certificate from a papal auditor that *he* was the proper warden. In the meantime, he had lost a parallel suit at the king's court, so that a temporary warden had been appointed. This officer, William Kynwolmarsh,[63] had promptly evicted him from the hospital, while Olton had been outlawed. The ex-warden eventually was able to use his papal certificate for a direct appeal to Henry V himself. Sometime after 21 March 1421, the monarch personally reinstated him. It is unlikely, however, that Macclesfield was able to resume effective management at the hospital, for his health continued to decline. 'Seeing the danger of death', he made his will on 23 March 1421,[64] and he died 7 April 1422.[65]

The ancient dispute with St Benet Fynk had broken out again sometime earlier. After one or more re-enfeoffments of the advowson, an attempt was made in 1414 – without licence of the king – to vest the right of appointing the rector solely in Macclesfield's sons, John, William and Thomas. About 1417 these men apparently tried to put Chaplain Edmund Tebbot in place of Rector David Fyvyan. The latter held on to his benefice, however, and, in an effort to pacify him, he was granted an annuity on 21 December 1417. Nevertheless, he was still vindictive in 1422, when he 'expressly refused' to be an executor of Macclesfield's will. Although his annuity was renewed in 1423, the unsatisfactory relationship of hospital to church continued for another sixteen years.[66]

Except during the ill-starred wardenship of Canon Brighouse (1385–9), the alien priory of St Anthony's, London, had not been connected to its French mother house since 1377. This break would have been definitively confirmed by parliament's act of 1414, if Macclesfield and Olton had not involved the abbot, the king and the pope in its situation. The treaty of Troyes (1420) and Henry V's death (1422) made the infant Henry VI king, not only of England, but of France as well. Thus, his English Council made Adam de Olton – the choice of the abbot at Vienne – warden of St Anthony's Hospital, London, on 28 June 1423, Adam's outlawry having been lifted while Macclesfield was still alive.[67]

After three years of ruinous exploitation by the temporary warden, the short return of the dying Macclesfield, and in the following year no warden at all, Olton found the hospital neglected, depleted and burdened with debt. Early on he attempted to blame Macclesfield for this state of affairs, but without apparent result.[68] Assisted by one or more true canons from the mother house, he soon sought to upgrade the hospital to Vienne standards. He increased to fourteen the number of priests who celebrated mass daily, something the hospital's Guild of St Katharine certainly approved. Pope Martin V not only issued him letters conservatory, but re-authorized the use of English (instead of Antonian) rituals by his clergy. The archbishop, Henry Chichele, provided support for his pardoners, while permitting only three other British hospitals to seek alms through such agents.[69] The increasing activities in the chapel, especially masses for the dead of the guild, had made it necessary to house the increasingly harassed inmates elsewhere. Accordingly, Olton arranged with the king for the abbot of St Albans next door to transfer ground for a suitable almshouse, and for the acquisition of other, nearby property.[70]

Adam de Olton's achievements as warden were notable. He died, however, before 27 October 1430. On this date the Council of the young Henry VI ordered two clerks and a layman to act as temporary 'surveyors and governors' of the hospital. Early in 1431 it appointed another canon of Vienne, John Snell, perhaps one of Olton's assistants, to be its warden. This man built the badly-needed almshouse.[71]

What happened next is not clear, but on 17 March 1433 the Council appointed one of Henry's chaplains, John Carpenter, a distinguished Oxford Doctor of Theology, to replace Snell, who died 'outside the papal court', seeking restoration of his benefice. The Council required that Carpenter join the Order of St Anthony within a year. On 16 November 1434 Pope Eugenius IV authorized him to continue his teaching at Oxford and – when he had become a proper canon – to limit his wearing of the Order's full habit to the confines of the hospital. He also granted the new warden special powers of absolution. Carpenter did not become a canon of St Anthony, however, for on 9 June 1438 the pope attempted to oust him, saying that he had used 'pretended letters' from the abbot at Vienne to gain his London preferment. The canon whom Eugenius IV nominated to replace him was already warden of St Anthony's Hospital, Rouen.[72] Carpenter continued his wardenship, however, for the English rights claimed by the Vienne abbot had steadily lost their credibility from 1435, as the Hundred Years' War turned against the English.

To enhance the prestige of the hospital's guild, Warden Carpenter obtained papal permission in 1434 to make St Anthony's chapel a minor pilgrimage site by obtaining several relics of the Eleven Thousand Virgins of Cologne. In 1442 he specified some of the institution's special needs in an open letter which supported a petition that Henry VI had sent to the pope the year before. Eugenius IV responded with several helpful bulls. One contained new letters of conservancy. Another authorized the moving of the hospital's annual founding-day celebration from the dreary days of Lent to more joyous October. A third authorized its religious to eat and sleep elsewhere than in the common dormitory and refectory mandated by the Rule of St Anthony – amenities that the London institution had never possessed. A fourth and fifth granted special powers of absolution to the priests who confessed brothers and sisters of the guild. The indulgences thereby authorized were so liberal that by 1454 many non-Londoners, even monks of St Augustine's, Canterbury, had sought to join the London organization.[73] Also, in 1445 Eugenius IV clarified a dependent relationship of St Anthony's Hospital, York, to St Anthony's Hospital, London.[74]

Henry VI had become a strong advocate of education at both university and sub-university levels. On 12 September 1440 he appointed a special commission consisting of Archbishop Chichele of Canterbury, three bishops, and eight other clerical or lay notables. He transferred to them the assets of the alien priories that had been vested in the Crown since 1414, so that schools and colleges might be fostered. In the distribution that followed, St Anthony's received several manors in 1442 with the stipulation that their income was to support five scholars from Henry VI's newly founded Eton so that they could study at Oxford. Warden Carpenter, however, also started an educational programme at the hospital itself. In 1439 he had obtained a royal settlement of the long-standing advowson/appropriation dispute with St Benet Fynk. In 1441, with the approval of the bishop of London, he used the revenue from the church to hire a schoolmaster.[75]

By this action he laid the foundation for the soon-to-be-famous St Anthony's school. In May 1446 various unqualified pedagogues were exploiting the London public. Henry VI approved an order of the archbishop of Canterbury that there should be no more than five officially-approved grammar schools in London. These were to be at St Paul's, St Martin le Grand, St Mary le Bow, St Dunstan in the east, and St Anthony's.[76] The latter has been called the 'chief school of London . . . for two hundred years'.[77] In as much as it reached its zenith long after the parent institution had ceased to be an alien priory, its history will not be presented here.

In 1443 the pope provided Carpenter to the bishopric of Worcester. The king then named another of his chaplains, Walter Lyhert, also an eminent Doctor of Theology from Oxford, to replace him as warden. Lyhert received a dispensation from the pope for his illegitimacy, as well as permission to hold St Anthony's in addition to one other benefice with cure of souls.[78] In 1446, before he could accomplish very much at the hospital, he was provided to the bishopric of Norwich. Henry VI then nominated yet another royal chaplain with Oxford credentials, Master William Say. Say also obtained a dispensation to hold the hospital in addition to other benefices, as well as papal ratification of his wardenship.[79]

Henry VI's appointment of three such distinguished men to be wardens suggests that he wished St Anthony's, London – almshouse, guild, school – to thrive and make contributions to national life. On 28 January 1447 he obtained authorization from Eugenius IV to set up a commission to formulate, and to implement, new 'statutes and ordinances' for the tri-fold institution. Among the commissioners chosen by the king were the bishops of Worcester and Norwich (former wardens, Carpenter and Lyhert), Master William Waynflete, provost of Eton, soon-to-be-founder of Magdalen College, Oxford, and future chancellor, as well as Warden Say.[80]

This body got to work at once, and their first concern was the cutting of the ties to Vienne. The new pope, Nicholas V, obliged them on 4 April 1447 by ending the jurisdiction of the mother house, assigning the hospital directly to the papal see. He also authorized the London warden to create new canons of St Anthony as staff needs required. So far, so good. But then the pontiff violated the second statute of Provisors (1390), by mandating that future wardens should be chosen by special 'guardians', and not presented by the king. Furthermore, the statute of Praemunire (1393) forbade the bringing of such papal bulls into the kingdom.[81] Warden Say, evidently the agent of the commission, thus was sued for violation of one or both of these statutes, despite the fact that the commission had been set up by the king. Say sought relief and, on 28 June 1449, he was pardoned for any violations he might have committed. Moreover, his appointment as warden was ratified. In this process Henry VI clumsily breached the statute of Provisors himself by allowing that, if he should nominate any warden unacceptable to the pope, a group composed of the abbot of

Westminster, the abbot of St Mary's, York, and the papal collector in England could expel such a person from the hospital.[82] Why he was so unwise, however, is easily explained. Between 1445 and 1450 the King's Council had 'gradually ceased to be a coherent body capable of giving considered and dispassionate advice', while Henry himself was in the process of becoming mentally ill.[83] Happily, wiser counsels soon prevailed, so that the pope's three representatives never acted.

From this period, the warden and other clergy of St Anthony's, London, were always English secular priests, while almshouse, guild and school prospered under their royally-sponsored regulations. In fact, their combined income was at least £549 about this time. In 1449 a barber-surgeon, very likely a member of the Guild of St Katharine, left to the hospital a brewery in the London parish of All Hallows. Its revenue was to be used to upgrade services in the chapel by providing for an earlier-envisioned singing master who would train six choir-boys.[84]

The displeased abbot in far away Dauphiné was heard from one more time. He was, in fact, the same Humbert de Brione whom Alexander V had wanted to be warden in London in 1409. On 28 June 1455 he moved Pope Calixtus III to reassert the ancient dependency of St Anthony's, London, upon St Anthony's, Vienne, and to order the secular arm to undo what the king's commissioners had done. The only readily-available secular arm, however, was Henry VI, more or less recovered from his illness of 1453–4. On 26 June 1456 the king (or his revived Council) defied pope and abbot by assigning the appointment of the hospital's wardens to Bishop Lyhert. On 22 June 1461 the next king, Edward IV, confirmed William Say's wardenship.[85] St Anthony's Hospital, London not having been an alien priory for some years, the present essay properly closes at this point.

The institution's further history may be quickly summarized. In 1475 Edward IV granted 'the house, hospital or free chapel' of St Anthony to the dean and chapter of St George's, Windsor.[86] Its pardoners continued to operate under lease agreements for some decades. Like those of St Mary Rouncivale, Charing Cross, they no doubt distributed pardons that had been mass-produced by Caxton or other early printers.[87] Macclesfield's chapel was enlarged in 1501. Neither guild nor almshouse survived the Reformation. The twelve old bedesmen were pensioned off, while the chapel was taken over by a refugee

Huguenot congregation. One or more of the buildings, dilapidated under negligent lessees, housed a fading school until all burned in the Great Fire of London in 1666. St George's, Windsor, still held tenements in Threadneedle Street in the nineteenth century.[88]

Although it has been widely assumed that the alien priories were all confiscated in 1414,[89] New, Morgan and McHardy have made it clear that various institutions survived for some time,[90] while the present writer has shown that St Anthony's, London, and St Mary Rouncivale, Charing Cross,[91] still had some connection with their mother houses well into the fifteenth century. Unlike other late-surviving alien priories, however, these two institutions remained fully intact until the Reformation.

To conclude: the story of a second pardoner-supported alien priory hospital has been told, although further work will be required before comprehensive conclusions may be drawn. Additional study of the alien priories is overdue, while their connections in France and elsewhere should be further scrutinized. More writings on hospitals, especially London hospitals, would be welcome.

Notes

* The writer is grateful to M.J. Bennett, C.M.D. Crowder, J.L. Gillespie, J.M. Horn and J.T. Rosenthal, who graciously criticized this essay in draft and made important suggestions.

[1] D. Knowles and R.N. Hadcock, *Medieval Religious Houses: England and Wales* (London, 1971), pp. 310–410; C. Rawcliffe, 'The Hospitals of Later Medieval London', *Medical History*, XXVIII (1984), 1–21. Only three hospitals were inside the walls, St Mary's Within Cripplegate (Elsyng's Spital), St Thomas of Acon, and St Anthony's: H.B. Honeybourne, 'A Sketch Map of London Under Richard II', *London Topographical Society Publication*, no. 93 (1960).

[2] R.M. Clay, *The Mediaeval Hospitals of England* (London, 1909), stood alone for some eight decades. Knowles and Hadcock, *Medieval Religious Houses*, pp. 310–410, provides a more up-to-date list of hospitals. E.C. Prescott, *The English Hospital c. 1050–1650* (London, 1992), is limited to institutions that have left remains above ground. The important work of N. Orme and M. Webster, *The English Hospital, 1070–1570* (New Haven, 1995), dissects a wide variety of hospitals topically. Also useful are *The Hospital in History*, eds L. Granshaw and R. Porter (London, 1989), pp. 21–59; W.H. Godfrey, *The English Almshouse With Some Account of Its Predecessor, the Medieval Hospital* (London, 1955); J.D. Thompson and G. Goldin, *The Hospital: A Social and Architectural History* (New Haven, 1975), pp. 15–53.

[3] C.W. New, *History of the Alien Priories in England to the Confiscation of Henry V* (Chicago, 1916); B. Thompson, 'The Laity, the Alien Priories, and the Redistribution of Ecclesiastical Property,' in N. Rogers, ed., *England in the Fifteenth Century: Proceedings of the 1992 Harlaxton Symposium* (Stamford,

1994), 19–41; M.M. Morgan, 'The Suppression of the Alien Priories,' History n.s. XXVI (1941–2), 204–12; A.K. McHardy, 'The Effects of War on the Church: The Case of the Alien Priories in the Fourteenth Century,' in *England and Her Neighbors, 1066–1453, Essays in Honour of Pierre Chaplais*, eds M. Jones and M. Vale (London, 1989), 277–95.

⁴ D.K. Maxfield, 'St. Mary Rouncivale, Charing Cross: The Hospital of Chaucer's Pardoner', *Chaucer Review*, XXVIII (1993), 148–63.

⁵ The standard study is R. Graham, 'The Order of St. Antoine de Viennois and its English Commandery, St. Anthony's, Threadneedle Street', *Archaeological Journal*, LXXXIV (1927), 341–406 (hereinafter cited as 'Graham'). It makes notable use of important documents. Some pertinent volumes of the Public Record Office abstracts, however, had not yet been issued in 1927. The most important English archives are abstracted in J.N. Dalton (ed.), *The Manuscripts of St. George's Chapel, Windsor* (Windsor, 1957), pp. xxvi, 1–2, 275–95 (hereinafter cited as 'Dalton'). Useful material is found in Bodleian Library, MS Arch. Selden B23 (hereinafter cited as 'Selden'). Unexamined documents may still remain in the Archives Nationales and at the Vatican.

⁶ Although Graham discusses it, the definitive history of this European-wide network is A. Mischlewski, *Grundzüge der Geschichte des Antoniterordens bis zum Ausgang des 15. Jahrhunderts* (Bonner Beiträge zur Kirchengeschichte, VIII, 1976). See also his 'Expansion et Structures de l'Ordre Hospitalier de Saint-Antoine-en-Viennois', *C.E.R.C.O.R. Travaux et Recherches, Centre Européen de Recherches sur les Congrégations et Ordres Religieux, Université Jean Monnet, Saint Etienne, Loire* I (1991), 195–209, as well as his 'Männer und Frauen in hochmittelalterlichen Hospitälern: Das Beispiel der Antoniusbruderschaft', *Berliner historische Studien*, XVIII (1992), 165–76. Unfortunately, Mischlewski's exhaustive bibliographies omit major sources relating to the London hospital. For a short bibliography, see *The Historia Occidentalis of Jacques de Vitry*, ed. J.H. Hinnebusch, *Spiciligium Friburgense*, XVII (1972), 281–2. Not received in time to be utilized by this study is Dr Mischlewski's *Un ordre hospitalier au Moyen Age: les chanoines réguliers de Saint-Antoine-en-Viennois* (Grenoble, 1995), as well as the recently launched journal, *Antoniter-Forum*, which he issues from Grossottstrasse 8½, D-85567 Grafing bei München, Germany.

⁷ *The Register of Edmund Stafford [Bishop of Exeter] 1395–1419: An Index and Abstract*, ed. F.C. Hingeston-Randolph (London, 1886), pp. 311–12.

⁸ See n. 2 above.

⁹ See also C. Rawcliffe, *Medicine & Society in Later Medieval England* (Stroud, 1995).

¹⁰ *Liber Albus: The White Book of the City of London* [1419], trans. H.T. Riley (London, 1862), pp. 235–6, 508–9; Selden, f. 96ʳ; J. Stow, *A Survey of London* [1603], ed. C.L. Kingsford, 2 vols (Oxford, 1908), I, 183–4; D. Hughson, *Walks Through London*, 2 vols (London, 1817), I, 47; Honeybourne, 'A Sketch Map'.

¹¹ Maxfield, 'St Mary Rouncivale', pp. 149–50.

¹² *CPR, 1266–72*, p. 171; *1313–17*, p. 111; *1317–21*, pp. 17, 389; *1321–4*, p. 26; *1327–30*, p. 114; *1364–7*, p. 151; *CPL, 1396–1404*, pp. 549–50.

13 References to St Anthony's pardoners appear in many bishops' registers, sometimes with texts of their licences or indulgences. Five examples: 14 March 1370 – [William of] *Wykeham's Register* [as bishop of Winchester] ed. T.F. Kirby, *Hampshire Record Society*, XIII (1899), 107–9; 30 November 1389 – *The Register of John Trefnant, Bishop of Hereford*, ed. W.W. Capes (Hereford, 1914), p. 7; 1 May

and 12 June 1399 – *The Register of Edmund Stafford*, pp. 311–12; 20 February 1410 and 16 September 1418 – *The Register of Nicholas Bubwith, Bishop of Bath and Wells, 1407–1424,* ed. T.S. Holmes (2 vols, Somerset Record Society, XXIX–XXX, I (1914), pp. 4–5; II (1914), p. 336; 2 June 1416 – *The Register of Henry Chichele, Archbishop of Canterbury, 1414–1443,* ed. E.F. Jacob (4 vols, Canterbury and York Society, IV, 1947), pp. 153–4.

[14] *CPR, 1216–25,* pp. 201, 555; *1225–32,* p. 262; *1232–47,* pp. 179, 180, 381, 412; *1247–58,* pp. 12, 624; *1266–72,* p. 206; *1292–1301,* p. 138; *CCR, 1242–7,* p. 142; *1247–51,* p. 202; *1254–6,* pp. 369–70; *CChR, 1226–57,* p. 345; Dalton, p. 275.

[15] A.M. Hyamson, *A History of the Jews in England* (2nd edn, London, 1928), p. 55. It had been confiscated in 1232 and had served as a chapel dedicated to St Mary before it was granted to St Anthony's.

[16] Selden, f. 100[r]. Selden is a letter book of William Swan, an English notary at the court of the Roman pope: A.B. Emden, *A Biographical Register of the University of Oxford to A.D. 1500* (3 vols, Oxford, 1957–9), III, 1829–30. Selden contains some transcribed letters of St Anthony's warden, John Macclesfield. Le Ferim was perhaps a Jewish convert, since such persons were required to forfeit their property: R.C. Stacy, 'The Conversion of Jews to Christianity in Thirteenth-Century England', *Speculum,* LXVII (1992), 263–83.

[17] *CPR, 1272–81–1367–70,* passim.

[18] New, *History of the Alien Priories,* pp. 45–85.

[19] *Cambridge Medieval History,* eds C.W. Previté-Orton *et al.* (8 vols, Cambridge, 1911–36), VIII, 327; *CPR, 1321–4,* p. 337; *1334–8,* pp. 6, 44, 330, 344, 500; *1358–61,* p. 513; *1361–4,* p. 394; *1364–7,* p. 336; *1367–70,* p. 26. Selden, f. 100r, contains two letters of Edward III granting St Anthony's to Savage that do not appear in any Public Record Office calendar. Savage died c. 1384: Selden, f. 100r.

[20] *CPR, 1266–72,* p. 171; *1313–17,* p. 111; *1317–21,* pp. 17, 389; *1321–4,* p. 26; *1327–30,* p. 114; *CPL, 1396–1404,* pp. 549–50.

[21] *Rot. Parl.,* III, 22–3; New, *History of the Alien Priories,* pp. 75–6; A.K. McHardy, 'The Alien Priories and the Expulsion of Aliens from England in 1378', *Studies in Church History,* XII (1975), 133–41.

[22] A.K. McHardy, 'The Church in London, 1375–1392', *London Record Society Publications,* XIII (1977), 2; *CPL, 1362–1404,* p. 240; *CFR, 1377–83,* p. 324. Michael's eight-year-old son was co-feoffee with his father.

[23] J.S. Roskell, *The Impeachment of Michael de la Pole, Earl of Suffolk, in 1386 in the Context of the Reign of Richard II* (Manchester, 1984), pp. 178–9. Note 9 on p. 183 points out that Graham (p. 358) seriously underestimated the financial status of the hospital in the 1380s.

[24] Graham (p. 380) provides this figure, but cf. J.L.C. Bruell, 'An Edition of the Cartulary of John de Macclesfield' (unpublished University of London MA thesis, 1969), pp. 127–8, which gives £557 13s 4d (plus £25 13s 4d in rents). Such enormous sums justify R.N. Swanson, *Church and Society in Late Medieval England* (Oxford, 1989), p. 228 in citing the experience of St Anthony's, London, as an example of 'the considerable scale of the indulgence trade' in England.

[25] *CPL, 1362–1404,* p. 254; Selden, f. 92[r]; *CPR, 1381–5,* p. 528.

[26] *An Exact Abridgement of the Records in the Tower of London, From the Reign of King Edward the Second unto King Richard III, of All of the Parliaments,* ed. R. Cotton, rev. W. Prynne (London, 1657), pp. 315–16; *CFR, 1383–91,* pp. 84, 289; *CPR, 1381–5,* pp. 528, 553; *1388–92,* pp. 208, 389; *CCR, 1381–5,* p. 593.

27 *CPR, 1381–5*, p. 582. One of the clerks was the future warden, John Macclesfield.

28 *Rot. Parl.*, III, 215–21; Roskell, *The Impeachment*, esp. pp. 172–84.

29 *CFR, 1383–9*, p. 289; *CPR, 1388–92*, p. 208; *CCR, 1389–92*, p. 42; Vatican archives quoted in E.F. Jacob, 'The Fifteenth Century: Some Recent Interpretations', *Bulletin of the John Rylands Library*, XIV (1930), 386–409, at p. 407, n. 5.

30 *CPR, 1388–92*, pp. 124, 129, 158, 164. On 25 August the king had made him warden of the hospital of St Giles-in-the-Fields: *CPR, 1388–92*, p. 115. For Macclesfield's life, his other benefices, etc., see D.K. Maxfield, 'Pardoners and Property: John Macclesfield, 1351–1422, Builder of Macclesfield Castle', *Journal of the Chester Archaeological Society*, LXIX (1988 for 1986), 79–95, and related articles in *Cheshire History*, nos 22, 23, 27, 28, 32, 35 (1988–96).

31 *CPR, 1388–92*, pp. 214, 389; PRO, Exchequer, Accounts, Various, E101/509/19, f. xiv/21.

32 For definitions of, and distinctions between, 'conventual' and 'dative' priories, see New, *History of the Alien Priories*, p. 37.

33 *CPL, 1362–1404*, p. 419. For the habit, see illustration in Graham, facing p. 345.

34 *CCR, 1392–6*, p. 545.

35 *CPL, 1362–1404*, p. 386. Renewed on 25 April 1397 for ten years: *CPL, 1396–1404*, p. 29. Such a bull appointed conservators who gave the warden and his staff protection against possible spoilers. For examples of such conservators, see J.E. Sayers, *Papal Judges Delegate in the Province of Canterbury, 1198–1254* (Oxford, 1971), pp. 108–9.

36 *CPL, 1362–1404*, p. 419.

37 *CPR, 1385–9*, p. 352; *1391–6*, p. 33. Actually John Sr. had been given Denham on 24 June 1387 but, by 12 August, he evidently had hopes of becoming warden of St Anthony's with its cure of souls, and wished to avoid a charge of pluralism. Denham was at the king's disposal in 1387 because the temporalities of Westminster abbey temporarily were in his hand: *CPR, 1385–9*, p. 331.

38 Édouard Perroy, *L'Angleterre et le grand Schisme d'Occident: Étude sur la Politique réligieuse de l'Angleterre sous Richard II (1378–1399)* (Paris, 1933), p. 330, citing documents in PRO, Treaty Rolls and Chancery Warrants.

39 *CPL, 1362–1404*, p. 430. Such conditional grants were then a novelty in England: R.L. Storey (ed.), 'Clergy and the Common Law in the Reign of Henry IV', in *Medieval Legal Records Edited in Memory of C.A.F. Meekings*, eds R.F. Hunnisett and J.B. Post (London, 1978), pp. 340–408, at p. 346. By 1414 they were considered quite undesirable; see D. Wilkins, *Concilia Magnae Britanniae et Hiberniae A.D. 476–1718* (4 vols, London, 1737), III, 362.

40 *CPL, 1362–1404*, p. 430; Graham, p. 359; *Canterbury Tales*, 'General Prologue', line 687. Macclesfield's indulgence still exists at Windsor, copied into the 1517 *Black Book* of Canon James Denton, *senescallus* of St George's chapel: Dalton, pp. 1–2. For medieval travel between England and Italy, see G.B. Parks, *The English Traveler to Italy: The Middle Ages* (Stanford, Calif., 1954).

41 R.H. Lathbury, *The History of Denham, Bucks.* (Uxbridge, 1904), pp. 149, 380–2, which prints a Westminster abbey document; *CPR, 1391–6*, p. 260.

42 *CPL, 1396–1404*, p. 18.

43 Muniments of St Paul's cathedral, cited by Graham, pp. 351–3, 402–3.

44 H.F. Westlake, *The Parish Guilds of Mediaeval England* (London, 1919), p. 183; J.J. Scarisbrick, *The Reformation and the English People* (Oxford, 1984), pp. 19–39. St Mary Rouncivale, which also had such a guild, experienced similar difficulties with its parish church: *CPL, 1417–31*, pp. 238, 282–3.

45 *CCR, 1392–6*, p. 417; British Library, MS. Cotton, Cleopatra D vi, ff. 92v–93r; *CPL, 1396–1404*, pp. 4, 311. Cleopatra D vi is John Macclesfield's personal cartulary.

46 *CPR, 1399–1401*, p. 4; *Annual Report of the Deputy Keeper of the Public Records* (hereinafter cited as *DKR*), nos 1–120 (London, 1840–1958), XXXVI (1875), app. 2, 313; *CPL, 1396–1404*, pp. 549–50, 558. In 1419 Macclesfield indicated that his 1403 reappointment had been for life: Selden, f. 98v.

47 BL, Cleopatra D vi; Maxfield, 'Pardoners and Property', pp. 84–8. In 1992 some ancient stones – all that remains of John's large and richly-furnished 'castle' at Macclesfield – were dedicated as a memorial in the courtyard of a new town hall addition (personal communication, 11 October 1995).

48 *Calendar of Wills Proved and Enrolled at the Court of Hustings, London, A.D. 1258–A.D. 1688*, ed. R.R. Sharpe (2 vols, London, 1889–90), II, 390–1. Mentioned as of St Anthony's, London, 1380 (*CPR, 1377–81*, p. 429); attorney for Macclesfield when the latter accompanied King Richard II to Ireland in 1394 (*CPR, 1391–6*, p. 498); co-feoffee with Macclesfield for advowson of St Benet Fynk (*CCR, 1392–6*, p. 417); assisted Macclesfield with construction activity (Selden, f. 97v); 'living at Hospital of St. Anthony' 1407, and mainpernor with Macclesfield in a provision case, 1407 (Storey, *Clergy and the Common Law*, pp. 400–1). Very likely he was the son, or other relative, of the John Savage who received the hospital's property from Edward III in 1336, and who died some forty-eight years later (Selden, f. 100r).

49 *CPR, 1422–9*, p. 109.

50 BL, MS. Cotton, Cleopatra F iii, f. 52/76. Unfortunately, the text of this writ has not been found. Olton had been ejected in disgrace from the abbey of Norton in Cheshire: Selden, ff. 91r, 95r; *CPR, 1416–22*, p. 340. For Norton see *Victoria History of the County of Chester*, ed. B.E. Harris (Oxford, 1980), III, 165–71.

51 Selden, ff. 28r–v.

52 *CPL, 1401–15*, p. 162; *Reg. Chichele* (Jacob), IV, 44–7.

53 *CCR, 1405–9*, pp. 86–7; Selden, f 32r–v.

54 *CPR, 1436–41*, pp. 279–80. For Fyvyan, see G.L. Hennessy, *Novum Repertorium Ecclesiasticum Parochiale Londoninese* (London, 1898), pp. clii, 377, which wrongly dates his first appointment as 1420.

55 The bishop of Hereford authorized indulgences for repair (1406) and support (1407) of St Anthony's: *The Register of Robert Mascall, Bishop of Hereford (A.D. 1404–1416)*, ed. J.H. Parry (Hereford, 1916), p. 190. Likewise, the ordinary of Salisbury in 1408: *The Register of Robert Hallum, Bishop of Salisbury, 1407–17*, ed. J.M. Horn (Canterbury and York Society, LXXII, 1982), p. 135; and the diocesan of Bath and Wells in 1409, 1410, 1411, *Reg. Bubwith* (Holmes), I, 4–5, 20, 58. In 1409 Macclesfield leased out distribution of indulgences in the archdeaconries of Chester and Lancaster for seven years at 16 marks per year: *DKR*, XXXVI (1875), app. 2, 232.

56 Selden, ff. 92r, 95r, 96v. For the buildings as they were in the next century, see R. Graham, 'A Plan of the Site and Buildings of St. Anthony's, Threadneedle Street c. 1530', *London Topographical Record*, XVI (1932), 1–8.

⁵⁷ In 1417 Macclesfield stated (Selden, f. 94ᵛ) that Olton was 'in my service and continually in my presence for seven years' (that is, before 1414). In 1414 the warden proposed that Olton 'rule and govern' in his 'name' and 'place' (Selden, f. 95ᵛ).

⁵⁸ *Rot. Parl.*, IV, 13, 22; *CCR, 1413–19*, pp. 31–2; *CPR, 1413–16*, pp. 164–7. An English version of the 1414 confiscation statute appears in *English Historical Documents 1327–1485*, ed. A.R. Myers (London, 1969), p. 670.

⁵⁹ *SR*, II, 175; *Rot. Parl.*, IV, 19–20, 80–1. Evidence that laxity and corruption were rife in many medieval English hospitals will be found in M.A. Seymour, 'The Organization, Personnel and Functions of the hospital in the Later Middle Ages' (unpublished MA thesis, University of London, 1947). Agitation for reform may have been encouraged by the Lollard movement: Orme and Watson, *The English Hospital*, pp. 131–6.

⁶⁰ Wilkins, *Concilia*, III, 362.

⁶¹ D.K. Maxfield, 'A Fifteenth Century Lawsuit: The Case of St. Anthony's Hospital', *Journal of Ecclesiastical History*, XLIV (1993), 199–223.

⁶² The abbots in this period were Hugues de Chateaunerf (1410–18), Falques de Montchenu (May–October, 1418), and Artaud de Grandval (1418–27): Mischlewski, *Grundzüge*, pp. 353–4.

⁶³ *Reg. Chichele* (Jacob), II, 235–7, 660.

⁶⁴ D.K. Maxfield, 'The Will of John Macclesfield, 1351–1422', *Cheshire History*, no. 22 (1988), 11–14. Page 11 prints an English version of PRO, PROB11/2b, P.C.C. 53 Marche.

⁶⁵ PRO, CHES, Inquisitions Post Mortem, 3/37/10, inquisition at Macclesfield.

⁶⁶ BL, Cleopatra D vi, 92ᵛ–3ʳ, 97ᵛ, 121ᵛ–2ʳ; Selden, f. 96ʳ; *CPR, 1422–9*, p. 156; *1436–41*, pp. 238, 279–80; Maxfield, 'The Will', p. 11. For Tebbot, see Hennessy, *Novum Repertorium*, pp. xxxix, 37; D.H. Jones, *The Church in Chester, 1300–1540* (Chetham Society Remains, 3rd series VII, 1957), p. 150.

⁶⁷ *CPR, 1416–22*, p. 340; *1422–9*, p. 108.

⁶⁸ *CPL, 1417–31*, p. 374; D.K. Maxfield, 'Was John Macclesfield a Scoundrel?', *Cheshire History*, no. 28 (1991), 19–20. Nevertheless, the affair of the St Benet Fynk advowson in 1414–17 suggests that Olton may not have been wholly wrong.

⁶⁹ *CPR, 1422–9*, p. 517; *CPL, 1417–31*, pp. 21, 373; *Reg. Chichele* (Jacob), IV, 256–62. Unsurprisingly, the hospital of St Mary Rouncivale, Charing Cross, was not given such permission.

⁷⁰ *CPR, 1422–9*, pp. 517–18; Dalton, p. 275.

⁷¹ *CPR, 1429–36*, pp. 100, 103–4, 118; Dalton, p. 275.

⁷² *CPR, 1429–36*, p. 262; Emden, *Oxford*, I, 360-1; *CPL, 1427–47*, pp. 504, 524; *1431–47*, pp. 3–4.

⁷³ Denton's *Black Book* cited in Graham, pp. 363–4; *Official Correspondence of Thomas Bekynton, Secretary to King Henry VI and Bishop of Bath and Wells*, ed. G. Williams (2 vols, Rolls Series, LVI, 1872), I, 234–5; II, 357–8; *CPL, 1427–47*, p. 296; *1431–47*, pp. 44, 214–15, 217, 219; *1447–55*, p. 163.

⁷⁴ Even though the York hospital intended to move inside the walls, and to set up a guild of its own, none of the rights (including an annual pension) of the London hospital were to be prejudiced thereby: *CPR, 1441–6*, p. 442; *CPL, 1431–47*, p. 527. Although at various times there were hospitals all over England dedicated to St Anthony, almost all were leper hospitals, and/or jointly dedicated to other saints, as no Vienne-related hospital would be: Knowles and Hadcock, *Medieval Religious*

Houses, pp. 310–410. Only the St Anthony's Hospital at York is certainly known to have had a relationship with St Anthony's, London. A St Anthony's Inn at Portsmouth was part of the property of the London hospital in 1560, suggesting that the earlier St Anthony's hospital there might have been of Vienne origin (Dalton, p. 57). Knowles and Hadcock (p. 404), and *VCH, Sussex*, eds L.F. Salzman et al. (9 vols, London, 1904–87), IX, 70, hint of an establishment at Winchelsea. Dalton (p. xxvii) calls St Anthony's, York, a 'constituent property' of St Anthony's, London, but his volume contains no pertinent documents. Very little is known about the hospital at York: *VCH, Yorks.*, eds W. Page et al. (4 vols, London, 1907–25), III, 351; A. Raine, *Medieval York* (London, 1955), 273–4. The St Anthony's Hospital with four Antonian canons founded at Leith about 1429 was, of course, entirely unrelated to any English hospital: *CPL, 1431–47*, pp. 405–6.

75 *Foedera*, X, 802–3; *CPR, 1436–41*, pp. 238, 279–80; *1441–6*, p. 43; Dalton, p. 275; A.P. Leach, *The Schools of Medieval England* (London, 1916; New York, 1968), p. 261.

76 *CPR, 1441–6*, p. 432; A.P. Leach, *Educational Charters and Documents 598 to 1909* (Cambridge, 1911), pp. 416–18.

77 Leach, *The Schools of Medieval England*, p. 260. For an unsatisfactory history, see his 'St. Anthony's Hospital and School' in W. Besant, *London: City* (London, 1910), esp. pp. 409–29. Relevant documents are in Dalton.

78 *CPR, 1441–6*, p. 266; Emden, *Oxford*, II, 1187–8; *CPL, 1431–47*, pp. 484, 497.

79 *CPL, 1431–47*, pp. 572–4; Emden, *Oxford*, III, 1649–50.

80 *CPL, 1431–47*, p. 563; Emden, *Oxford*, III, 2001–3.

81 *CPR, 1446–52*, pp. 279–80; *English Historical Documents 1327–1485*, pp. 659–61 (Provisors), 661–2 (Praemunire).

82 *CPR, 1446–52*, pp. 279–80.

83 R.A. Griffiths, *The Reign of King Henry VI* (London, 1981), pp. 284, 714–16.

84 Graham, p. 380; Bruell, thesis cited, pp. 127–8; Sharpe, *Calendar of Wills*, II, 524–5; Dalton, pp. 25, 59–60.

85 *CPL, 1455–64*, pp. 13–14; *CPR, 1452–61*, p. 283; *1461–7*, p. 11. For Brione, see Mischlewski, *Grundzüge*, pp. 184–94 and passim.

86 *CPR, 1467–77*, p. 484. Stow, *Survey of London*, pp. 184–5, and Graham, pp. 376–93, tell much of the later story, while many documents appear in Dalton.

87 P. Needham, *The Printer and the Pardoner* (Washington, DC, 1986). For these pardoners, see Dalton, pp. 275–7.

88 Dalton, p. 491.

89 For example, 'They were all dissolved by act of Parliament 2 Henry V, and all their estates vested in the crown, except for some lands granted to the college of Fotheringhay', J. Nichols, *Some Account of the Alien Priories and of Such Lands as They are Known to Have Possessed in England and Wales* (2 vols, London, 1779–86), I, x.

90 New, *History of the Alien Priories*, pp. 87–96; Morgan, 'Suppression of the Alien Priories', pp. 211–12; McHardy, 'Effects of War on the Church', pp. 287–8.

91 Maxfield, 'St. Mary Rouncivale', p. 156, esp. n. 59.

INDEX